D0206213

Wilkie Collins

Twayne's English Authors Series

Herbert Sussman, Editor

TEAS 544

PORTRAIT OF WILKIE COLLINS.
Frontispiece, The Works of Wilkie Collins, *Vol. 1 (New York: Peter Fenelon Collier {1900}).*

Wilkie Collins

Lillian Nayder

Bates College

Twayne Publishers
An Imprint of Simon & Schuster Macmillan
New York

Prentice Hall International
London • Mexico City • New Delhi • Singapore • Sydney • Toronto

Twayne's English Authors Series No. 544

Wilkie Collins
Lillian Nayder

Twayne Publishers
An Imprint of Simon & Schuster Macmillan
1633 Broadway
New York, NY 10019

Library of Congress Cataloging-in-Publication Data

Nayder, Lillian.
    Wilkie Collins / Lillian Nayder.
        p.   cm. — (Twayne's English authors series ; TEAS 544)
    Includes bibliographical references and index.
    ISBN 0-8057-7059-3 (alk. paper)
    1. Collins, Wilkie, 1824–1889—Criticism and interpretation.
    2. Literature and society—Great Britain—History—19th century.
    I. Title. II. Series
    PR4497.N39   1997
    823'.8—dc21   97-21447
                                                                CIP

The paper used in this publication meets the minimum requirements of American National Standard for Information Sciences—Permanence of Paper for Printed Library Materials. ANSI Z39.48-1984. ∞ ™

10 9 8 7 6 5 4 3 2

Printed in the United States of America

For Matt, Nate, and George

Contents

Preface

At the Reverend Henry Cole's boarding school in Highbury, a suburb north of London, the young Wilkie Collins studied Homer's *Iliad*, among other classical works. Writing home in September 1839, the 15-year-old sent his mother a sample of the schoolwork he had been assigned. Asked to argue that "the government of many is not good," a lesson drawn from the unruly behavior of the common people in Book II of Homer's epic, Collins proceeds through the stages of his rhetorical exercise, measuring the benefits of a benevolent monarchy against the evils of democratic rule. Noting that "many kingdoms, after having prospered under the government of one, have been exposed to the horrors of anarchy and revolution, through the government of many," he arrives at his conclusion: "Diverse nations require different forms of government; but the most perfect and most happy form of government has generally been found to be, a wise and good monarchy."[1]

Like most English schoolboys in the 1830s, Collins was taught to question the wisdom of democracy, the threatening "government of many" adopted by rebellious British subjects on the other side of the Atlantic 50 years before. Yet even as Collins constructed his rhetorical proof that "a wise and good monarchy" is the best form of rule, he was learning, through painful and personal experience, that undemocratic forms of authority often prove to be despotic rather than benevolent. Scapegoated by his schoolmaster, who held him up as a bad example to his peers and punished him for trifling misdemeanors, and whipped with a cat-o'-nine-tails by the school bully whom he later compared to the "oriental Despot" in *The Arabian Nights*,[2] the young Collins clearly perceived that "governments of one" had their dangers and were more often tyrannical than happy, wise, or good.

The fiction, melodramas, and essays that Collins wrote as an adult are peopled with corrupt figures of authority, whom he represents in profoundly critical ways. Focusing on race, class, and gender relations, his works are deeply political in their orientation and repeatedly dramatize the abuses of power—imperial, social, as well as domestic. His stories often acknowledge and frequently justify the resentment and resistance of characters victimized by British imperialists in the colonies, by members of the upper classes in England, and by tyrannical husbands and fathers in the privacy of their homes. Typically, Collins juxtaposes and interconnects the exploitation of the "subject races," of domestic servants, and of wives and daughters, and develops analogies between sexual and imperial domination. *The Moonstone* (1868), for example, opens with the Siege of Seringapatam in India (1799), during which a host of crimes are committed against Hindus and Muslims by English officers and their men, and then stages the symbolic rape of an Englishwoman, endowed with Eastern traits, by the gentleman she loves and eventually marries. Repeatedly comparing the rape of British colonies to the lawful violation of wives by their husbands, Collins questions widely accepted views of patriarchal and imperial privilege and extends sympathy toward rebellious and outcast figures.

Thus it is not surprising that his works were received with considerable hostility by many Victorian reviewers. Critics of *Armadale* (1864–1866) complained that Collins chose "vermin as his subjects," and described his heroine, who murders her first husband after he whips her, as a character from whom "every rightly constituted mind turns with loathing."[3] Reviewers of *No Name* (1862–1863) found Collins's sympathetic treatment of illegitimate, disinherited, and vengeful women "unwholesome," "perverse," and "polluting."[4] And Charles Dickens, who serialized many of Collins's works in his weekly journals, often felt the need to censor Collins's writing, complaining of his "tendency" to be "unnecessarily offensive to the middle class."[5]

Collins has retained his reputation as a subversive writer throughout much of the twentieth century, although modern critics tend to praise rather than condemn his unconventional views. In what has become a classic essay on the subject, U. C. Knoepflmacher valorizes the "counter-world" of Collins's fiction, treating it as a welcome antidote to the conventionalities of many Victorian novels. In his view, *The Woman in White* (1859–1860) provides "a unique instance of a mid-Victorian novel in which the author openly acknowledges an anarchic and asocial counter-world as a powerfully attractive alternative to the ordered, civilized world of conventional beliefs."[6] Drawing on Knoepflmacher, Winifred Hughes expresses her appreciation of the "subversive ironies" and likable villains of Collins's fiction, which "explores forbidden territories and releases hidden sources of energy."[7] Jerome Meckier values Collins as a "dissident moralist" who undermines Victorian social proprieties, and Philip O'Neill promotes him as a writer who "deliberately subvert[s]" oppressive gender norms.[8]

Most recently, however, literary critics have contested this view of Collins the "dissident," arguing instead that his literary works are not subversive enough. Since the publication of *Corrupt Relations* in 1982—the collaborative work of Richard Barickman, Susan MacDonald, and Myra Stark—most studies of Collins have emphasized his political ambivalence and called attention to the circuitous methods and the "strategies of indirection" he uses to convey and qualify his social criticism.[9] Rather than promoting Collins's image as a Victorian rebel, scholars now tend to argue that his novels serve a "policing" function and reveal his middle-class ambition, his complicity with empire building, and his suspicion of social and feminist revolt.

The chapters that D. A. Miller devotes to Collins in *The Novel and the Police* are perhaps the most striking examples of this revisionist criticism. Drawing on the theories of French historian Michel Foucault, Miller approaches Collins's fiction with the concept of "disciplinary power" in mind. He argues that the various and diffuse modes of social control that Foucault sees at work in the modern state operate in Collins's novels as well. In Miller's view, *The Moonstone* appears to be "dialogic" and democratic, a story narrated from socially diverse points of view, but it is actually "monologic" and reinforces rather than questions the social status quo.[10] Similarly, Miller argues, *The Woman in White* seems to call Victorian gender norms into question by representing and extending sympathy to masculine women and effeminate men, and by using the genre of sensation fiction to give male readers a case of female "nerves." Yet the novel's net effect is homophobic, and it ultimately reinforces rigid conceptions of gender difference and restores male and female characters to their "proper place."[11]

The revisionary impulse that informs Miller's readings also characterizes Tamar Heller's *Dead Secrets*, among the most important studies of Collins in recent years. Heller recognizes the subversive elements of Collins's fiction but argues that they are ultimately "contained." In her view, Collins sacrifices his radical vision to his desire to succeed as a professional writer, evading the full implications of his social critique. In choosing to write for Dickens's journal *Household Words*, Heller argues, Collins made a "political choice," allying himself with the middle class and compromising his "sympathy with socialism."[12] For Heller, the recurring motif of "buried writing" in Collins's novels becomes a fit emblem for his own literary works, in which feminist and socialist ideas become mere traces, radical messages that are "subsumed" within conventional plotlines, "toned down" and "tamed" (Heller, 8).

Such redefinitions of Collins usefully complicate what has long been the standard critical view of him as a lone rebel, a writer more openly critical of Victorian social conventions and gender norms than most of his contemporaries. Rather than defining Collins against the more conservative Dickens, Thackeray, and Trollope, as critics often have, Heller and Miller point to the similarities among them. In so doing, they remind us of the difficulties that confront social critics such as Collins, who inevitably participate in, and are shaped by, the culture they scrutinize.

But in answering the scholars who precede them, and highlighting the conservative strains in Collins's fiction, the new generation of Collins critics overstate their case. Miller's Foucauldian reading of Collins is deterministic and denies the possibility of subversion or resistance on the author's part. In Miller's eyes, as in Foucault's, rebellion is merely a political ruse. "Whenever the novel censures policing power," Miller argues, "it has already reinvented it" (20). Heller's approach to Collins is less one-sided than Miller's and astutely acknowledges the "ideological doubleness" of his fiction (163). According to Heller, Collins simultaneously subverts prevailing ideologies of race, class, and gender and reinscribes them. Yet her readings tend to emphasize the process of "containment" at the expense of the transgressive. For Heller, the many examples of "buried writing" in Collins's fiction mark his desire to bury or erase his own subversive material. But it seems equally true that this image reflects his own subversive strategy; that it is not simply a sign of his self-censorship but also a self-conscious commentary on the means he must employ to evade the censorship of Dickens and others. Like the transgressive characters who hide their views in his novels, and only express them obliquely, Collins conveys, on a subtextual level, the ideas that he is prohibited or discouraged from openly expressing.

In what has quickly become the standard biography of Collins, *The King of Inventors* (1991), Catherine Peters aptly describes him as a writer "haunted by a second self."[13] In her view, Collins is simultaneously drawn to and troubled by rebellious female figures, and their acts of "self-assertion" are inevitably followed by "retreat" in his literary works.[14] Do these shifts represent "an artistic loss of nerve," Peters asks, "or a measured assessment of the true options available to women?" (" 'Invite,' " 296). Rather than answering such questions in a definitive way, this book redresses the imbalance that has characterized Collins criticism to date by giving fair play to the "ideological doubleness" of his writing: by examining both its subversive and its conventional sides and by declining to privilege one at the cost of the other. Instead of choosing between Collins the radical and Collins the reactionary, this study considers how and why his decisions point readers in opposing directions and leave them mediating uneasily between conflicting explanations of his intentions.

Acknowledgments

I would like to thank Faith Clarke, the great-granddaughter of Wilkie Collins and Martha Rudd, for her kind permission to quote from unpublished sources in this book. I am also indebted to the following libraries and universities for allowing me to quote from the material in their collections: Harry Ransom Humanities Research Center, The University of Texas at Austin; Mitchell Library, Glasgow; New York Public Library; The Pierpont Morgan Library, New York; and Princeton University Library.

Brooke Belcher, Kara Peters, and Susan Thompson, three of my former students, have each spent a summer transcribing Collins's autograph letters from microfilm for the purposes of this volume and have done their work with intelligence and care. Graham Law, Professor of Law at Waseda University, Japan, has generously shared his research on the syndication of Collins's fiction, about which little is known, and Tamar Heller has offered welcome suggestions and advice over the years. So, too, have Herbert Sussman, my Series Editor, and my colleagues in the English Department at Bates College, particularly Cristina Malcolmson and Steve Dillon, while Tom Hayward of Ladd Library has worked wonders in the way of interlibrary loans, and Dolores O'Higgins of Classics has helped me with Collins's schoolboy Greek. I am indebted, finally, to my husband, Matt Johnson, who has made it possible for me to work on this book, and to Aileen and Leonard Grumbach, whose disagreements about Marx and Freud have helped to shape its methods.

Chronology

ton's *Not So Bad As We Seem*. Begins contributing stories to *Bentley's Miscellany,* and writing for the *Leader.*

1852   *Mr. Wray's Cash Box* published by Bentley. "A Terribly Strange Bed," first contribution to *Household Words,* appears on 24 April. *Basil: A Story of Modern Life* published by Bentley.

1853   Tours Switzerland and Italy with Dickens and Augustus Egg.

1854   *Hide and Seek* published by Bentley.

1855   *The Lighthouse* produced as amateur theatrical at Dickens's Tavistock House.

1856   *After Dark* published by Smith, Elder, and *A Rogue's Life* in *Household Words.* Joins the staff of Dickens's journal. Collaborates with Dickens on "The Wreck of the Golden Mary" and *The Frozen Deep.* Suffers from attacks of rheumatism.

1857   *The Dead Secret* serialized in *Household Words* (3 January to 13 June) and published by Bradbury and Evans. *The Frozen Deep* produced at Tavistock House, the Gallery of Illustration (London), and Free Trade Hall (Manchester). *The Lighthouse* opens at the Olympic Theatre (London) in August. Collaborates with Dickens on "The Lazy Tour of Two Idle Apprentices" and "The Perils of Certain English Prisoners."

1858   *The Red Vial* opens at the Olympic Theatre in October. "A Sermon for Sepoys" published in *Household Words* on 27 February.

1859   Moves in with Caroline Graves and her daughter Harriet. *The Queen of Hearts* published by Hurst and Blackett. *The Woman in White* serialized in *All the Year Round* (26 November to 25 August 1860).

1860   *The Woman in White* published by Sampson Low. Charles Collins marries Kate Dickens on 17 July. Collaborates with Dickens on "A Message from the Sea."

1862   Resigns from Dickens's staff in January. *No Name* serialized in *All the Year Round* (15 March to 17 January

1863) and published by Sampson Low. Begins taking laudanum regularly as painkiller.

1863   *My Miscellanies* published by Sampson Low. Travels to the continent with Caroline Graves from October to March 1864.

1864   *Armadale* serialized in the *Cornhill* (November to June 1866). Meets Martha Rudd.

1866   *Armadale* published by Smith, Elder. *The Frozen Deep* opens at the Olympic Theatre in October.

1867   Collaborates with Dickens on *No Thoroughfare*. Dramatic adaptation opens at the Adelphi Theatre (London) in December.

1868   *The Moonstone* serialized in *All the Year Round* (4 January to 8 August) and published by William Tinsley. Harriet Collins dies on 19 March. Caroline Graves marries Joseph Clow on 4 October.

1869   Collaborates with Charles Fechter on *Black and White,* which opens at the Adelphi Theatre in March. Birth of Marian "Dawson," the first of Collins's illegitimate children by Martha Rudd, on 4 July. *Man and Wife* serialized in *Cassell's Magazine* (December to September 1870) and *Harper's Weekly* (20 November to 6 August 1870).

1870   Death of Dickens on 9 June. *Man and Wife* published by F. S. Ellis.

1871   Birth of Harriet Constance "Dawson" on 14 May. *No Name* produced at the Fifth Avenue Theatre (New York) in June, and *The Woman in White* at the Olympic Theatre in October. *Poor Miss Finch* serialized in *Cassell's Magazine* (October to March 1872). "Miss or Mrs?" published in the *Graphic*. Caroline Graves returns to Collins.

1872   *Poor Miss Finch* published by Bentley. *The New Magdalen* serialized in *Temple Bar* (October to July 1873).

1873   *The New Magdalen* published by Bentley, as well as *Miss or Mrs? and Other Stories in Outline. Man and Wife* produced at the Prince of Wales's Theatre (London) in February, and *The New Magdalen* at the Olympic in May. Death of Charles Collins on 9 April. North American reading tour from September to March 1874.

1874   *The Frozen Deep and Other Tales* published by Bentley. Birth of William Charles Collins "Dawson" on 25 December. *The Law and the Lady* serialized in the *Graphic* (26 September to 13 March 1875).

1876   *The Two Destinies* serialized in *Temple Bar* (January to September) and published by Chatto & Windus. *Miss Gwilt* opens at the Globe Theatre (London) in April.

1877   *The Dead Secret* produced at the Lyceum Theatre (London), and *The Moonstone* at the Olympic.

1878   *The Haunted Hotel* serialized in *Belgravia* (June to November). *My Lady's Money* published in the *Illustrated London News*.

1879   *The Haunted Hotel* and *My Lady's Money* published by Chatto & Windus. *The Fallen Leaves* serialized in the *World* (1 January to 23 July), in the *Canadian Monthly* (February to March 1880), and published by Chatto & Windus. *Jezebel's Daughter* syndicated by Tillotson and Son for publication in provincial newspapers.

1880   *Jezebel's Daughter* published by Chatto & Windus. *The Black Robe* syndicated by Leader and Sons for publication in provincial newspapers and serialized in the *Canadian Monthly* (November to June 1881).

1881   *The Black Robe* published by Chatto & Windus.

1882   *Heart and Science* syndicated by A. P. Watt for publication in weekly newspapers and serialized in *Belgravia* (August to June 1883).

1883   *Heart and Science* published by Chatto & Windus. *"I Say No"* syndicated by A. P. Watt for publication in weekly newspapers. *Rank and Riches* opens at the Adelphi Theatre in June.

1884   *"I Say No"* serialized in *London Society* (January to December) and published by Chatto & Windus.

1885   *The Evil Genius* syndicated by Tillotson and Son for publication in provincial newspapers.

1886   *The Evil Genius* published by Chatto & Windus. *The Guilty River* published in *Arrowsmith's Christmas Annual*.

1887   *Little Novels* published by Chatto & Windus.

1888   *The Legacy of Cain* syndicated by Tillotson and Son for publication in provincial newspapers.

1889   *The Legacy of Cain* published by Chatto & Windus. Dies on 23 September. *Blind Love,* completed by Walter Besant, serialized in the *Illustrated London News* (6 July to 28 December), and in the *Penny Illustrated Magazine* (12 December to 5 April 1890).

1890   *Blind Love* published by Chatto & Windus.

1895   Death of Caroline Graves.

1919   Death of Martha Rudd.

Chapter One
Biographical Sketch

William Wilkie Collins, later known simply as "Wilkie," was born in London on 8 January 1824 to William Collins and Harriet Geddes Collins. His father, 35 at the time, was a well-established painter of landscapes and rural life and a member of the Royal Academy, and his mother, a housewife for less than 18 months, came from a family of artists herself. Like Wilkie, William Collins Sr. had been born in London, in the year 1788. He was the son of a picture dealer and man of letters who had come to England from Wicklow, Ireland, but whose ancestors were originally from Chichester, England. Wilkie traced his literary talents back to his paternal grandfather, whose published works included a novel entitled *Memoirs of a Picture,* a biography of the painter George Morland, and an abolitionist poem, "The Slave Trade."

Wilkie Collins's interest in the fringes of English society was derived, in part, from a family history of poverty and marginalization. Although his paternal grandfather was a talented and industrious man, who supplemented his income with "picture-cleaning tours" of the English countryside, he was unable to comfortably support his family and was sometimes treated rudely by the wealthy squires who hired him to clean or restore the artwork in their collections.[1] In Wilkie's first published book, the *Memoirs* of his father's life (1848), he speaks of the "petty calamities" and embarrassments that "his [grandfather's] increasing poverty inevitably inflicted" on his wife and two sons (1:37). He explains that when his grandfather died in 1812, leaving his family destitute, their furniture and household possessions were sold off to pay creditors, and they were forced to eat their "scanty meals" off an old box rather than a table (1:48). Only by attending the sale of their belongings did Wilkie's uncle Francis manage to keep the snuffbox, ring, and eyeglasses of Wilkie's grandfather as mementos (1:47).

In response to these humiliations, Wilkie's father adopted a pragmatic, if obsequious, social strategy—he took pains to cultivate the favor of wealthy and aristocratic patrons, who commissioned portraits of their castles, their parks, and their families and purchased coastal landscapes and scenes of English rural life. "As it is impossible to rise in the world, without connection," William wrote in his journal in 1816, "connection I must have" (*Memoirs*, 1:83). After receiving an advance from Sir Thomas Heathcote for a commissioned painting and later accepting a series of loans, William Collins went on to repair his family fortunes. Over the course of his career, he exhibited nearly 200 paintings at the Royal Academy and the British Institution. His patrons included Sir David Wilkie, for whom his first son was named; Sir John Leicester; Sir George Beaumont; the Duke of Newcastle; the Marquis of Stafford; the Earl of Liverpool; the Marquis of Lansdowne; and Sir Robert Peel, prime minister of England from 1834 to 1835 and 1841 to 1846. The Prince Regent, later George IV, purchased a Norfolk coastal scene from William Collins in 1815 and a Hastings coastal scene in 1825.

Anxious for his two sons to maintain the social status and the economic security for which he had labored, William Collins sent them to public (i.e., private) schools, encouraged them to draw and paint, and introduced them to European culture. Wilkie attended the Maida Hill Academy from 1835 to 1836, toured the continent with his family from 1836 to 1838, and enrolled at the Reverend Henry Cole's boarding school from 1838 to 1840. With the help of his father's friend Charles Ward, Wilkie began working for the tea-importing firm of Antrobus and Sons, the Strand, in 1841. The following year his father wrote to his patron Sir Robert Peel in the hopes that his son might be able to enter the civil service (*King*, 56). Peel's discouraging reply may have ruffled William, but it did not bother Wilkie, who was primarily interested in artistic pursuits. He exhibited a landscape painting at the Royal Academy in 1849 but spent much of the 1840s writing fiction.

For our purposes, what is most significant about William Collins's career and its influence on his son is the way in which his paintings both register and obscure the political turmoil that characterized his age. Wilkie's father produced his paintings during a period of extreme social unrest in England, a period that witnessed the Luddite riots, the Peterloo massacre of peaceful demonstrators by soldiers, the passage of the First Reform Bill, and the Chartist movement. He became a student at the Royal Academy in 1807 while the Peninsular War was being waged and anti-Jacobin feeling was rife, and he died in 1847, shortly before social revolutions took place throughout Europe. Choosing to depict contemporary scenes rather than historical subjects, he peopled his works with lower-class figures and with members of the social residuum—drunken chimney sweepers, beggars, bird and rat catchers, fishermen, private soldiers, and agricultural laborers. Many of his depictions of working-class life include images of poverty and suffering, and Wilkie Collins speaks admiringly of their treatment of "the stern and real woes of humanity" in the *Memoirs* (1:51). *The Sale of the Pet Lamb* (1813), for example, the painting that established William Collins's reputation, depicts an impoverished family and a mother forced by want to sell her daughter's beloved pet in order to survive.

But while Collins's paintings acknowledge the suffering of the English poor, they also soften that suffering to evoke a sentimental response, thus defusing its political force; they replace anger, anguish, and resentment with pathos. Indeed, it is William Collins's ability to gloss over potentially menacing political subjects that accounts for his popularity among aristocratic patrons of art. As Wilkie himself explains in his account of his father's life, William Collins's paintings are perhaps best characterized by what they exclude from consideration. Although William was willing to portray "all in Nature that was pure, tranquil, tender, harmonious," his son observes, he was unwilling to depict what he found "coarse, violent, revolting, fearful": "No representations of the fierce miseries, or the coarse contentions which form the darker tragedy of humble life, occur among [his rustic scenes]. When his pencil was not occupied with light-hearted little cottagers, swinging on an old gate—as in 'Happy as a King'—or shyly hospitable to the wayfarer at the house door—as in 'Rustic Hospitality'—it reverted only to scenes of quiet pathos" (*Memoirs,* 2:311–12).

William's desire to avoid the "fierce miseries" of working-class life is perhaps most obvious in *Happy as a King,* the painting to which Wilkie refers. In this popular work, a country boy—his arms raised in triumph—exults over his ability to remain seated on a swinging gate while some of his playmates have fallen. Composed and exhibited in 1836, at what many perceived to be the height of working-class unrest in England, it conveyed a reassuring message to upper-class viewers at the Royal Academy: that the rural poor feel contentment rather than class injury, since the simple pleasures of their rustic lives enable them to be "happy as kings." More directly than most of his works, this painting reveals the effect at which William Collins aims, an effect his son aptly describes in the *Memoirs*—it effaces the threat of class resentment and encourages spectators to forget their sense of class difference in the name of their common Englishness. As Wilkie recognizes, his father's paintings assuaged the social anxieties of the 1830s by allowing members of "all classes" to identify with "English people and English scenery" and to focus their attention on "its bright places and happy objects" (*Memoirs,* 2:327–28).

Although Wilkie speaks admiringly of his father's character and art in the *Memoirs,* he indicates that he has not accepted the social practices and the artistic strategies bequeathed to him uncritically. Wilkie argues, for example, that his father and grandfather were both "enslaved" by the system of aristocratic patronage, under which they were paid by and obligated to please particular members of the upper class, and he considers himself fortunate to have escaped such dependence. Unlike the work of the painter in the mid–nineteenth century, and the man of letters in the eighteenth, that of the Victorian novelist was serialized in inexpensive periodicals and mass-produced, a commodity available to a wide range of readers with varied political views. Thus while the "genius" of his father and his grandfather "was yet unemancipated from the fetters of patronage," Wilkie explains, his own is freed from these constraints (*Memoirs,* 1:6).

Furthermore, Wilkie suggests that his own political beliefs are free from the Tory prejudices and the class deference that characterized his father's thinking. In the *Memoirs* and elsewhere, he delineates the political differences between himself and his father. As the private journal kept by William Collins reveals, Wilkie's father felt it was necessary to cultivate aristocratic favor in order to rise in the world. But it did not offend his sensibilities to do so. He certainly did not consider himself "enslaved" in Wilkie's sense. A pious and conventional man, William Collins respected the established social order and willingly served his superiors. He encouraged his son to form the aristocratic connections that would serve him well in life.

Instead of accepting such paternal advice, however, Wilkie parodies it when describing the father and son who figure in his novella *A Rogue's Life* (1856). Uninterested in forming "aristocratic connections that will be of the greatest use," and unwilling to cater to the tastes of the English upper class, Collins characterizes the views of the father in the story as the "arrant nonsense" of an older generation.[2] Despite the tone of filial respect that pervades the *Memoirs,* Wilkie typically defines himself against William Collins, playing the part of radical to his father's "high Tory" in his various accounts of the turbulent 1830s. Whereas William decried the class unrest of his age, and the democratic reforms to which it gave rise, his son willingly embraced them. When Wilkie describes to his American friend William Winter, in 1887, the political events of 1832, he contrasts his own childhood enthusiasm for "the sovereign people" with the solemn moral judgments that his father passed on the "rebels." Noting that London residents who lived near Hyde Park were warned to place candles in their windows to show support for the Reform Bill, or else have them broken, Wilkie recounts his father's reluctant compliance, and his own "mad . . . delight":

> In the year 1832 when I was eight years old, my poor father was informed that he would have his windows broken if he failed to illuminate in honour of the passing of the First Reform Bill. He was a "high Tory" and a sincerely religious man—he looked on the Reform Bill and the cholera (then prevalent) as similar judgements of an offended Deity punishing social and political "backsliding." And he had to illuminate— and, worse still, had to see his two boys mad with delight at being allowed to set up the illumination. Before we were sent to bed, the tramp of the people was heard in the street. They were marching six abreast (the people were in earnest in those days) provided with stones . . . They broke every pane of glass in an unilluminated house, nearly opposite our house, in less than a minute. I ran out to see the fun, and when the sovereign people cheered for the Reform Bill, I cheered too.[3]

Although a witness to scenes of political violence, Wilkie treats his father's fears of social revolution as exaggerated and misplaced. He facetiously describes the anxiety that "popular revolution . . . was to sink the rights of property in a general deluge of republican equality" when he recounts the Reform Bill agitation in the *Memoirs,* and he ridicules the belief that political reform is equivalent to "the end of the aristocracy, and even the end of the world" (1:345).

Wilkie's political views and his conceptions of class and gender relations are much more radical than his father's, and he is attracted to figures of rebellion while William Collins is not. Nonetheless, Wilkie's relationship to his father is not quite as oppositional as he might have us believe. Rather than wholly rejecting his father's artistic and political legacy, he learned from it, reworking the artistic strategies and values of William Collins to suit his own ends. Wilkie's mixed feelings about his father and the importance of "aristocratic connections" are apparent, for example, in his portrait of Walter Hartwright, the protagonist of *The Woman in White.* A struggling drawing master modeled on the young William Collins, Hartwright is dehumanized and humiliated by his aristocratic patrons. Yet Wilkie rewards the artist in a way that qualifies the novel's social critique and endorses his father's desire for upper-class connections—by making Hartwright the master of a landed estate, to which his son is heir. Unlike his father, Wilkie is willing to represent class conflict and acknowledge feelings of class injury. His novels are

hardly social idylls in the manner of William's *Happy as a King*. Yet those
characters who call for social revolution in his fiction are relegated to its
margins, and the class conflicts he represents are often displaced and
resolved outside of the class system. Thus, in *The Woman in White*,
Collins establishes Hartwright's claims to gentility by sending him to
the jungles of Central America, where he is pitted against primitive
tribesmen instead of English aristocrats, and his civilized supremacy is
made clear. In their own way, such strategies are as reactionary as any
used in William's paintings, and they suggest the connection between
father and son.

Whereas Collins defined himself against his traditional and pious
father, he more fully identified with his unconventional mother, an
ambitious and self-supporting woman to whom he attributed his "poetic"
bent. In an 1887 interview, he described Harriet Geddes Collins as "a
woman of remarkable mental culture": "from her I inherit whatever of
poetry and imagination there may be in my composition."[4] Yet here,
too, we must be wary of accepting Wilkie's self-representations uncritically, for his allegiance to his mother proves to be as complex as his
opposition to his father.

The eldest child of an army officer of Scottish descent, Alexander
Geddes, and Harriet Easton Geddes, the daughter of a Salisbury Alder-
man, Harriet Geddes was born in Worcestershire in 1790. Much of her
childhood, like that of her husband, was centered around the arts. She
was the cousin of Andrew Geddes, a well-known Scottish painter, and
she and her five siblings knew him as children, when they lived near Salisbury, on a farm leased from Lord Radnor of Longford Castle. The children were allowed to copy the masterpieces by Holbein, Velazquez,
Brueghel, Reynolds, and Gainsborough that belonged to Lord Radnor,
and they may have received informal instruction from their cousin
Andrew as well. Two of Harriet's sisters, Margaret and Catherine,
became well-known portrait painters. Margaret Geddes Carpenter, the
most professionally successful of the six Geddes children, began exhibiting her work at the Royal Academy in 1816 and helped to support her
parents after her father lost virtually all his money through an impru-
dent financial investment.

Harriet, too, worked as a teacher and governess to support herself and
her family. Although she wanted to become an actress, and had been
invited to perform at the Theatre Royal in Bath, she was dissuaded from
doing so by an evangelical clergyman and his wife, who were concerned
that she would lose her middle-class respectability. With their help, Har-

riet was trained to become a teacher; she accepted her first position in 1814, working at a school in London for an annual salary of 20 pounds. When the school went bankrupt later that year, Harriet began working as a governess, a position she was to occupy, in England and in Scotland, until shortly before her marriage to William Collins in 1822.

Wilkie's parents first met in 1814, at an artists' ball in London, and saw each other again in 1816 and 1818, while the young painter was still struggling to make a living and did not feel he was in a position to marry. Not until William and Harriet met at her sister's home in 1822 did he begin to court his future wife. Knowing that his mother disapproved of Harriet—an aging governess with little money—William arranged for their wedding to take place quietly, in Edinburgh. Harriet's parents knew of the couple's plans beforehand, but Mrs. Collins apparently did not. They were married on 16 September 1822, in the English Episcopal Chapel. After a brief honeymoon, Harriet moved into the Collinses' home on New Cavendish Street, where the couple lived with William's mother and brother. Their first child was born in January 1824 and their second in January 1828.

Although William Collins was often away from home for weeks at a time, staying at the estates of wealthy patrons, and Harriet was frequently left alone with their two young sons, their marriage was generally happy. In her diary, Harriet speaks of her "joyful meetings" with her husband, and William describes his "longing for home" in his letters to his wife.[5] Nonetheless, their relationship was based on the gender inequities that characterized most Victorian marriages, but that were criticized and evaded by certain women in Harriet's immediate family. Margaret Geddes Carpenter, with whom Harriet spent much of her time both before and after her marriage, was the principal breadwinner in her own family. A feminist of sorts, she questioned the gender norms of her day in such paintings as *The Sisters* (1839), which emphasizes the importance of female community outside the circuit of courtship and marriage.[6] Like her sister Margaret, Harriet was talented, ambitious, and self-supporting. As a teacher and governess, she had earned as much as 80 pounds a year. Unlike her sister Margaret, however, who married and raised a family while also exhibiting her paintings at the Royal Academy, Harriet left the public sphere when she married because her husband did not believe that middle-class women "should be working for their bread in any way."[7] As a 32-year-old woman who had supported herself for nearly a decade, and whose married sisters were pursuing successful artistic careers, Harriet was well aware that William's wifely ideal was unnecessarily limiting. Nevertheless, she complied with his wishes, devoting herself exclusively to her family duties after her marriage to him.

With the death of William Collins in 1847, the concessions required of Harriet as a wife came to an end. As Wilkie's biographer William M. Clarke puts it, she finally "came into her own" at middle age. Although she sincerely mourned the loss of her husband, "Harriet's independence and energy were suddenly given free rein," and her opinions, long subordinated to those of William, were now expressed, particularly in regard to her eldest son (Clarke, 52). For years, William Collins had discouraged Wilkie from becoming a writer. When Wilkie refused to continue working for Antrobus and Sons in 1846, William pressured him to study the law. By that time, Wilkie had written one novel and was beginning to work on a second, but he became a student at Lincoln's Inn in May to please his ailing father. After William's death, however, Harriet encouraged Wilkie to write for a living, helped finance the publication of the *Memoirs,* and eventually began writing herself. In 1853 she started work on an autobiographical manuscript that she hoped to publish, possibly under her son's name.

Wilkie Collins was grateful for his mother's support and impressed by her capacity for independence, and he draws on her character and experiences in representing the intelligent and ambitious women who figure in his novels and melodramas. As Peters observes, Harriet's ability to "ma[k]e her way in the world as a young woman, alone and unprotected" seems to have fueled Collins's interest in such characters (" 'Invite,' " 303). His concern with the inequities of Victorian marriage was also based, in part, on what he saw of Harriet's experiences as a wife and the contrast between her married life and the lives of her professional sisters.

Yet Wilkie's treatment of his widowed mother and his handling of the autobiographical manuscript she entrusted to him suggest that she was freed from her husband's control only to become subject to that of her eldest son. The extant letters of Wilkie Collins to his mother provide a portrait of a loving but overly protective man who attempts to play a role in virtually all of his mother's decisions and is wary of letting her spend too much time in independent pursuits, outside the company of respectable friends and relations. His apparent reticence to submit her narrative for consideration—a narrative on which he drew freely in his own literary works—suggests that he was more comfortable appropriating her story for his own purposes than seeing it published in its own right.[8] In September 1855 Collins told his mother that he was working on her manuscript: editing it and providing it with more "story" in order to please potential readers. But though he read portions of it to Dickens, it never appeared in print. Instead, its contents were gradually incorporated into Wilkie's own novels—"using all the best of [her] materials," as he put it to her.[9] In Heller's view, such behavior reveals Wilkie's anxieties about his female literary precursors and rivals as well as his desire to keep daughters, wives, and mothers in their "proper place." As Heller astutely notes, *After Dark* (1856) is one of several works for which Harriet's manuscript is an important source, and it dramatizes the emasculation of a husband by a wife who takes his place as the family provider by becoming a writer and selling her books (Heller, 97, 99).

The mixture of feminist sympathy and patriarchal presumption that characterizes Wilkie's relation to his mother is apparent in his romantic relationships as well—in the love triangle he established and maintained with two women for nearly two decades, and in his decision to have his children out of wedlock. By the mid-1850s Wilkie had established himself in his own lodgings on Howland Street in London, and by 1859 he was living with a woman named Caroline Graves and her seven-year-old daughter, Harriet, first on Albany Street, then on New Cavendish Street, and later on Harley Street and Gloucester Place. According to the sensational account provided by John Guille Millais, the son of the painter John Everett Millais, Wilkie first met Caroline by coming to her aid when she escaped from a villa in St. John's Woods, where she had been imprisoned by an unnamed villain, and used her as a model for his "woman in white."[10] Although Millais's account of this meeting has been called into question by critics and biographers, much is known about the unconventional relationship of Caroline Graves and Wilkie Collins, which lasted for more than 30 years, until his death in 1889.

When Collins met Caroline Graves, a carpenter's daughter, she was a widow who supported herself by keeping a "marine store" (i.e., a junk shop) in Fitzroy Square. In 1850 Caroline had married an accountant's clerk and shorthand writer, George Graves, but her husband died of tuberculosis in 1852, leaving her the single parent of their one-year-old. Collins informally adopted Harriet Graves, affectionately known as "Carrie," and paid for her education. But although he was free to marry her mother, he chose not to do so. Instead, he and Caroline lived together as sexual partners and companions, with Caroline cast in the role of housekeeper, and financially supported by Collins. Caroline often accompanied him on his travels in England and Europe, and knew his closest friends well, but she was excluded from the formal dinner parties hosted by respectable middle-class women because of her sexual status as a "kept woman." Dickens refers to her in one of his letters as "the (female) skeleton" in Collins's closet (Clarke, 97). Less pleased with their arrangement than her partner was, Caroline left Collins in 1868, when she abruptly married Joseph Clow, a young man who apparently worked in the wine and spirit trade. But she returned to Collins two years later and remained his companion until his death.

Caroline's dissatisfaction with Collins was caused, in large part, by a liaison he had formed in the mid-1860s with another woman, Martha Rudd. The daughter of a Norfolk shepherd, Martha Rudd worked as a servant at an inn outside of Great Yarmouth, where Wilkie met her in 1864. Attracted to the young working-class woman, he developed a relationship with her over the next few years. She moved to London in 1868 and became pregnant by him, triggering the crisis in his relationship with Caroline. The eldest child of Wilkie Collins and Martha Rudd, a daughter named Marian, was born on 4 July 1869. Their second daughter, Harriet Constance, was born on 14 May 1871, and their son, William Charles, on 25 December 1874. Adopting the last name of "Dawson" for himself and his family, Collins established them in lodgings on Bolsover Street, and later on Marylebone Road and Taunton Place, while he remained in his home in Gloucester Place. Although he did not marry Martha, he provided her with a monthly allowance of 25 pounds, considerably more money than she could expect to earn as an uneducated working-class woman. When Caroline returned to Collins, he divided his time between his two families. Caroline appeared with him publicly, as his "unofficial" wife, but he spent some evenings and holidays with Martha, and their children often visited the home that their father and Caroline shared. His modest estate was evenly divided between his two families by his will, in which he openly acknowledged Martha's children as his own and stipulated that the money he left to each of his female relations was to be placed in trust "for her sole and separate use free and independently of any husband to whom she may be married."[11]

Wilkie Collins's relationships with Caroline Graves and Martha Rudd, and the birth of his three illegitimate children, are the most unconventional aspects of his life, and critics and biographers often account for these ties by attributing them to his "bohemianism," his disregard for social proprieties and his desire to publicly flaunt them. "If the arrangement closed some 'Society' doors to him," Catherine Peters argues, "so much the better" (*King,* 196). Whereas William Collins had struggled to achieve social respectability, and had spoken proudly of his aristocratic connections, Wilkie chose to father his children out of wedlock by an uneducated, working-class woman while he lived with a second lover. William had been dead for two decades by the time Wilkie and Caroline began living together. But Harriet Collins, less pious and conventional than her husband, refused to socialize with her son's mistress, and Dickens, an intimate friend, also disapproved. More circumspect about his own illicit affair with the young actress Ellen Ternan, and more wary of public opinion, Dickens registered irritation at Collins's unorthodox behavior, complaining to his sister-in-law in October 1868 that "Wilkie's affairs defy all prediction" (*Letters,* 3:676). For Dickens, as for many twentieth-century scholars, Collins's sexual behavior typified his irreverence for Victorian social conventions and marked his rejection of the values cherished by his traditional father.

More specifically, Collins's relationships with Caroline and Martha, and his refusal to marry either one, are taken as the most personal expression of what is perhaps his primary social concern—the flaws and injustices of marriage as an institution. At the very time that Collins met Caroline in 1858, he was witnessing the disastrous separation of Charles and Catherine Dickens, and had already observed the painful struggles of his friend Frances Dickinson to free herself from her abusive and adulterous husband, John Edward Geils. From his study of British law as well as his personal friendships, Collins came to see English marriage as inevitably unjust and confining. He refers to the "merciless" laws governing marriage and divorce in England in his essay "A New Mind," laws that deprived married women of their property and their parental rights, and authorized their victimization and "unutterable wrongs,"[12] and he devotes his sensation fiction to the issues raised by marriage law reform in the 1850s and 1860s.

In many of Collins's works, the wrongs of English wives are only circumvented by parents who carefully consider their daughters' vulnerability when making their bequests. Thus in *The Moonstone,* Lady Verinder grants her daughter, Rachel, only a life interest in the family property, protecting the young woman against the mercenary advances of the villainous Godfrey Ablewhite. In his own will, Collins stipulates that the money he leaves to his female relations is to remain their own, safeguarded from the men they may eventually marry. Connecting marriage with exploitation in this final written form, he casts husbands in the role of victimizers and provides an implicit rationale for his own personal behavior: that in choosing to remain unmarried, he has refused to participate in a corrupt social system, has declined to claim his children as his own private property, and has protected the women he loves against legal inequities.

Yet the social realities confronting "kept women" and illegitimate children in Victorian England make such a position paradoxical at best. As Collins himself knew, children born out of wedlock did not simply belong to their mothers instead of their fathers by default; rather, they had "no name" at all. Thus it is not surprising that the children for whom Wilkie had to invent the surname "Dawson" desired the respectability of which they felt deprived by their father. As Clarke notes, Collins's daughters Marian and Harriet felt ashamed of their origins and avoided intimacy with friends, and their brother blamed his failure to obtain a military commission on his scandalous parentage (187–89). The experiences and behavior of Caroline, Martha, and their children suggest that they felt imperiled rather than protected by Collins's decision to remain unmarried, and cast doubt on the presumption that feminist principles inform it. Although Martha Rudd was apparently content to remain both faithful and unmarried to Collins, and claimed that he had offered to legalize their union if she wished, Caroline Graves was clearly unhappy with her disreputable status as his mistress and with the existence of a rival, and she may have pursued Joseph Clow in a failed attempt to force Collins to marry her. Despite the gender inequities built into Victorian marriages, and of which Collins persistently writes, Caroline clearly desired the legal and social status she believed she would gain as his wife.

Viewed solely from Collins's perspective, his personal relations seem to tally with his impassioned critiques of Victorian marriage. But when Caroline's viewpoint is considered, they also reveal his complicity with the patriarchal system he so often condemns. In effect, Collins practiced an informal type of bigamy, using the sexual double standard to his own personal advantage. He retained the social and sexual freedom of a bachelor while Martha and Caroline remained monogamous, raised the children, and kept house.

Regardless of their feelings of satisfaction or their sense of injury, both women quietly contributed to Collins's professional success and helped to make possible his remarkably productive literary career. In a period known for its prolific writers, Collins was among the most prolific. During a career that spanned nearly five decades, he wrote more than 25 novels and novellas, published 5 collections of stories and essays, and scores of journal articles, and adapted, wrote, or produced more than a dozen plays. His works of nonfiction include a travel book to Cornwall, *Rambles Beyond Railways* (1851), as well as his biography of his father.

Since Collins's death in 1889, critics and biographers have divided his adult life and literary career into a number of distinct stages, beginning with the publication of his first novels, his early experimentation with various genres, and his apprenticeship to Dickens, whom he met in 1851. During the 1850s, Collins produced melodramas, short stories, travel narratives, and journalism, joining Dickens's staff at *Household Words* in 1856; and he decided on novel writing as his particular vocation. Amid trips to the continent with Dickens and other friends, and the onset of his rheumatic illness, he published four novels in this early period, including *Antonina* (1850), *Basil* (1852), *Hide and Seek* (1854), and *The Dead Secret* (1857). While Richard Bentley had published many of his early works, *The Dead Secret* was serialized in Dickens's weekly journal and established Collins's practice of publishing his fiction in weekly or monthly parts.

With the success of *The Woman in White* in 1859–1860, the first of his "sensation novels," Collins produced a national best-seller and entered what many consider his literary maturity. He went on to write three other novels in the 1860s: *No Name* (1862–1863), *Armadale* (1864–1866), and *The Moonstone* (1868). Although Dickens published two of these works in *All the Year Round,* Collins gradually distanced himself from his friend and mentor, resigning from Dickens's staff in 1862 and forming working relationships with other writers and publishers. His close circle of friends included Charles Ward, his financial adviser; his physician, Frank Beard; Frederick Lehmann; the novelist Charles Reade; and the actor Charles Fechter, with whom Collins wrote the melodrama *Black and White* (1869).

In 1870, the year of Dickens's death, Collins published *Man and Wife,* the first of his novels with an explicitly stated social purpose—to expose the injustices of the marriage laws of Great Britain. Between 1870 and 1889, he devoted many of his works to specific social and political causes, ranging from the reform of prostitutes to the antivivisection movement. Complaining that Collins sacrifices his art to propaganda in these novels, critics have long associated them with his extended literary decline, a process compounded by his physical sufferings from "rheumatic gout" and his growing addiction to laudanum, which he had begun to take regularly in 1862, and which reputedly caused him to hallucinate when taken in large doses. In recent years, a handful of scholars have defended the novels of the 1870s and 1880s, and critics and teachers have shown interest in some of them, particularly those reissued by Oxford University Press as "World's Classics." But most remain largely neglected and unknown, relegated to the dustheap of didactic fiction.

Although these established divisions of Collins's career usefully underscore the differences among his novels, and encourage readers to consider his artistic development, they cast his achievement and decline into too neat a pattern and downplay the underlying connections among his works. For this reason, the discussions in this book are organized thematically rather than chronologically, with the exception of the chapter on Collins's literary apprenticeship. They pair his best-known novels with those that are less so and give Collins's didactic fiction serious critical consideration. Rather than distinguishing Collins's artistic successes from his failures, the chapters that follow call attention to the shared ideological aims of Collins's works, and the ways in which his fiction proves double-edged, offering the radical social criticism for which he is best remembered, but from which he consistently retreats.

Chapter Two
Literary Apprenticeship

Although Collins wrote dozens of novels, stories, and melodramas during his remarkably productive career, only two of his works are well known to general readers: *The Woman in White* and *The Moonstone*. Despite growing interest in Collins, and the publication of new editions of individual works almost every year, one of these two novels usually represents him in college courses on Victorian fiction, and most of the attention paid to him by literary critics has focused on them.

Yet many of the central preoccupations of Collins's most famous novels are anticipated in his earliest and little-known works. Like *The Moonstone*, for example, both *Iolani* (1844–1845) and *Antonina* (1850) address questions of race and imperialism and consider the justifications commonly offered for empire building by Victorians. While *The Moonstone* dramatizes the consequences of imperial conflict in British India between the years 1799 and 1848, *Iolani* represents the non-Western culture of Tahiti before the arrival of Europeans in 1767, and *Antonina* the fall of the Roman Empire in the fifth century. Like *The Woman in White* and *The Moonstone,* Collins's early novels focus on gender relations as well as race relations and depict the victimization of women by tyrannical men who physically assault them, incarcerate them, and threaten their well-being. At the same time, Collins qualifies his social criticism in these early works, as he does in his later fiction, by highlighting the dangers of female nature and the barbarism of the subject races, reinscribing the social norms and stereotypes that he sets out to critique.

Although Collins emerged from his literary apprenticeship as a writer best known for his novels, he experimented with a host of literary forms at the outset of his career. Between the publication of his first signed work in 1843 and that of his fourth novel, *Hide and Seek* (1854), Collins wrote a travel book, a memoir, and dozens of journal articles in addition to novels, a novella, and short stories. Whether writing fiction or nonfiction, he sought to establish his professional and political position in an increasingly democratic and contentious culture.

He did so, in part, by defining himself against his Tory father, a strategy apparent in the two major works of nonfiction he wrote in the first decade of his literary career. *Memoirs of the Life of William Collins,* his first published book, is generally taken as a work of "filial piety"—a respectful account of his father's life and career, intended to compensate for the disagreements that so often divided father from son.[1] But Collins subtly criticizes his father's political beliefs and artistic practices in the *Memoirs,* suggesting that William Collins's depictions of working-class life fail to acknowledge its harsh realities. The "fierce miseries" and "coarse contentions" of the poor, Wilkie argues, are omitted from his father's idyllic or sentimental representations of them (*Memoirs* 2:311). In Wilkie's view, William Collins catered to his aristocratic patrons by eliding class conflict and working-class suffering, political subjects that wealthy and titled clients found distasteful and alarming.

When Collins turns his attention to coastal England—so often the subject of William Collins's paintings—in *Rambles Beyond Railways,* he makes up for his father's artistic omissions and misrepresentations by subordinating picturesque description to a political analysis of working conditions and wages among the poor. In such paintings as *Scene on the Coast of Norfolk* (1818) and *Prawn Fishers at Hastings* (1824), both purchased by George IV, William Collins portrays the work of English fishermen as if it were a leisure activity—a form of play enjoyed by children instead of the labor of grown men. Although *Fishermen on the Look-Out* (1819) includes an adult figure, Wilkie points out that his father represents this figure in a "contemplative attitude," as the sky overhead sheds "an influence of Elysian repose over the rest of the scene" (*Memoirs,* 1:154).

Rejecting such "Elysian" representations of working-class life, Collins focuses his attention on "the condition of the poor" in *Rambles Beyond Railways* and approaches fishing and mining as "means of subsistence" in Cornwall.[2] Certain chapters in Collins's travel book describe scenic walks and locations, but the fishermen who figure in them are waged workers instead of picturesque figures, and fishing itself a commercial industry run by merchants whose profits are "immediate and large" (90). Whether describing the hard labor of seiners, or the dangerous, eight-hour shifts of the miners at Botallack, Collins reminds us that these men are engaged in a difficult struggle to earn their bread and are subject to injury, death, and exploitation. Despite its beauty, Collins's Cornwall is a region of waged labor, with its fair share of poverty and workhouses—a place from which the poor are sometimes forced to emigrate by unemployment and possible starvation (38).

While Collins reworks the tradition of the picturesque to include socioeconomic analysis in *Rambles Beyond Railways,* he declared his sympathy with English workers in the articles he wrote for the *Leader,* a weekly newspaper founded by the middle-class radicals Thornton Hunt and George Henry Lewes in 1850. Labeled "socialist" by the *Edinburgh Review,* the *Leader* advocated " 'the rights of labour' and the duty of the state to provide work to every member of the community."[3] Collins began writing for the *Leader* in 1851, the same year in which *Rambles Beyond Railways* appeared, when his boyhood friend Edward Pigott purchased the newspaper. Over the next few years, he offered Pigott advice about the organization and content of the paper. Collins's first article for the *Leader* was entitled "A Plea for Sunday Reform." In it, he argues that the members of the working class are entitled to enjoy their weekly holiday in educational and recreational pursuits rather than in prolonged church services. Those who preach to the working man about his spiritual condition, Collins asserts, have little understanding of his circumstances, needs, and desires: "You set the church doors open and tell him to go in. If he turns away, you abandon him to the gin palaces at once; if he won't go to heaven in your way, he may go to the devil in his own. You don't take into any account his circumstances, his weaknesses, his natural human longings for one day's enjoyment, after six days' toil. You establish a code of religious exercises and restraints which suits *your* condition of life; and, no matter what the difference in your stations, that code must be *his* code too."[4] Setting the dire realities of working-class experience against the leisure and privilege of "lords and gentlemen," Collins suggests that the English worker is dehumanized and denied his fair share of life's luxuries (925). Believing that English workers are entitled to "comforts and amenities," Collins envisions them crossing class boundaries, visiting "National Picture-galleries" and "National Museums," and hearing Handel, Haydn, and Mozart on Sunday evenings (925–26).

His interest in dissolving class barriers is also revealed in his curious series of articles on animal magnetism. Entitled "Magnetic Evenings at Home," this series was published in the *Leader* in 1852 and lends credence to the powers of the clairvoyant, a figure who seemed particularly subversive to upper-class Victorians because of his or her ability to cross class and gender boundaries when "possessed" by departed spirits. In such later works as *The Frozen Deep* and *Armadale,* Collins returns to the subject of clairvoyance, again using it to a politically subversive end.[5]

In writing for the *Leader,* a paper known for its " 'Red Republicanism,' " Collins allied himself with the political and social reformers of his day.[6] His association with radical men of letters had begun eight years earlier, when Douglas Jerrold accepted "The Last Stage Coachman," the very first work of fiction to appear under Collins's name. A radical writer and magazine proprietor, Jerrold was nicknamed "savage little Robespierre" by his contemporaries and addressed his journals to the "masses of England."[7] He published Collins's story in the *Illuminated Magazine* in August 1843, no doubt interested by its critique of industrialization, so often touted as a sign of economic and social "progress" among Victorians, and by the connection it draws between industrialization and unemployment. In his story, Collins expresses regret at the advent of steam and the construction of the railways, celebrated as one of "the wonders of science" by his contemporaries. In a "vision," the emaciated figure of England's last coachman appears to him and curses the boilers and engines that have put him out of work. At the conclusion of the story, Collins describes the coachman's apotheosis, as he is taken up by a visionary stagecoach "with a railway director strapped fast to each wheel." He disappears "amidst the shrieks of the railway directors" and "the groans of James Watt," the inventor of the steam engine.[8]

In "The Last Stage Coachman," Collins expresses nostalgia for preindustrial England, a time before the "engines of destruction" "desecrated" the countryside and put coachmen, guards, hostlers, and innkeepers out of work (209). But in *Iolani,* the novel that he began writing the following year, Collins makes a case for Victorian progress by representing the dangers of the uncivilized state. Setting his novel in Tahiti before the arrival of Europeans, he represents the primitive condition in an unappealing light and implicitly defends modern European civilization. His treatment of the natives in *Iolani* serves as a reminder that Victorian radicals who respected the ways of the English working class did not necessarily extend their sympathy and tolerance to non-Western peoples.

Iolani; or, Tahiti as it was. A Romance (1844–1845)

Collins began work on *Iolani* in September 1844 and completed it the following January, when it was submitted to Chapman and Hall, among other publishers, and soon rejected. Because *Iolani* never appeared in print, and because the manuscript has remained in the hands of private collectors since the 1870s, very little is known about it. What we *do* know has been conveyed to Catherine Peters by the antiquarian bookseller who acquired the manuscript in 1991 and subsequently sold it, and gleaned from Collins's scattered references to his first written novel.[9]

Describing *Iolani* in an autobiographical article of 1870, Collins explains that its scene "was laid in the Island of Tahiti, before the period of its discovery by European navigation": "My youthful imagination ran riot among the noble savages, in scenes which caused the respectable British publisher to declare that it was impossible to put his name on the title-page of such a novel."[10] What "respectable" readers and publishers were likely to find objectionable in Collins's first novel were references to sexual license among the Tahitians, and scenes of ritualistic violence and human sacrifice. As the plotline of *Iolani* suggests, Collins's reference to "noble savages" is facetious. His story centers on the violence and cruelty of Iolani, a high priest who has fathered a child by the heroine, Idea, and who wishes to sacrifice their infant to the gods. Idea is forced to flee from Iolani to save their child and goes into hiding accompanied by her friend Aimata.

In constructing his plotline, Collins drew from the work of the missionary William Ellis, whose *Polynesian Researches* (1831) was among the volumes in Collins's personal library. Dedicating his *Researches* to the London Missionary Society, Ellis looks ahead to the time when "the barbarous, cruel, indolent, and idolatrous inhabitants of Tahiti" will be transformed into "a comparatively civilized, humane, industrious, and Christian people."[11] Representing the lives of the Tahitians in such a way that the Christian mission in the South Seas is amply justified, Ellis places particular emphasis on the practice of infanticide, a consequence of the "delusive and sanguinary idolatries" of the natives (1:v). According to Ellis, the practice of infanticide in Tahiti originated among the Areoi, a religious society whose members—"monsters of iniquity"— were required to destroy their children to satisfy the gods (1:239). From the Areoi, the practice spread among the population at large. "I do not recollect having met with a female in the islands, during the whole period of my residence there, who had been a mother while idolatry prevailed, who had not imbrued her hands in the blood of her offspring," he asserts. "Few, if any, became mothers, . . . who did not also commit infanticide" (1:252–53).

As these passages suggest, Collins not only draws from Ellis in writing *Iolani* but also departs from him, altering his source material to serve his own ends. In Ellis's accounts of infanticide in Tahiti, both parents commonly agree to kill their children, but the crime is characterized by a striking division of labor; while the mother strangles, stabs, or tramples her infant to death, the father prepares its grave (1:254). In Collins's novel, however, the murderous savagery that Ellis describes devolves on the father alone. Idea flees from Iolani to protect their child from him. Reworking Ellis's account of native life, Collins emphasizes its patriarchal violence, distinguishing the cruelty of the father from the victimization of both mother and child. Placing his emphasis on the tyranny of Iolani as a father and husband, and not simply on his violence as a native, Collins expresses what would become the dominant theme of his later works: the injustices committed by patriarchal figures of authority. For the mainspring of his plot, Collins uses what remains a noteworthy yet relatively minor point in Ellis's *Researches*—the oppression and humiliation of women in Polynesian society. Describing the "invidious distinction . . . between the sexes" in Tahiti, Ellis explains that whereas the men are considered "*ra,* or sacred," the women are considered "*noa,* or common" and denied the various social privileges enjoyed by their brothers, fathers, husbands, and sons (1:128–29). Qualifying his representation of Tahitian primitivism in *Iolani,* Collins reserves his criticism for the patriarchal abuses that, in his mature fiction, connect the savage practices of non-Western cultures to those of civilized England.

Collins's growing sense of the savagery of the civilized West becomes clear when *Iolani* is compared with his second and much later account of Polynesian life, the short story "The Captain's Last Love," published in the *Spirit of the Times* on 23 December 1876. Reworking *Iolani,* Collins constructs a narrative of European discovery and exploration. He represents the arrival of Englishmen on two uncharted islands in the Pacific, and in so doing undermines rather than justifies the imperial mission. Sent from Liverpool to the Pacific on a quest for sandalwood, the captain, officers, and crew of the *Fortuna* accidentally come upon these islands. Befriending the natives, they exchange "toys and trinkets" for a cargo of sandalwood. At first, the colonial enterprise appears harmless enough; while Mr. Duncan, the first mate, believes that annoying natives should be shot on sight, the captain is considered a kindhearted man skilled at "conciliat[ing] the islanders."[12] Nonetheless, he knowingly violates native law, and destroys the native people in the process. Catching sight of Aimata, the beautiful daughter of the native priest, he violates a taboo by traveling to the Holy Island where she and her father live. "Bewitching" the young woman, he attempts to lure her away from her father and her people. Unintentionally fulfilling the role of "the lying demon of [native] prophecy," "the predestined destroyer of [the] island" (345), the captain triggers the eruption of a seemingly extinct volcano, which destroys the natives, Aimata included. Reconceiving the hostilities of

Iolani, Collins pits Europeans against natives rather than native men against native women, and casts the native priest as well as his daughter in the role of victims. Instead of ridiculing native "superstitions" and defining them against the Christian's "true religion," as Ellis does (1:vi), Collins lends credence to native prophecy and insists on the "innocence" of the native people (336). As Aimata and her father fear, the islands are indeed destroyed by the arrival of the European "demons."

After writing *Iolani,* Collins never again represented a native culture in isolation. Instead, he complicated his analysis of civilization and savagery by turning his attention to imperial relations, representing the victimization of subject races as well as their barbarism, and dramatizing the crimes committed in the name of empire.

Antonina, or the Fall of Rome (1850)

This shift is apparent in the second novel that Collins wrote, and the first that he succeeded in publishing—*Antonina, or the Fall of Rome.* Although Collins had begun the novel in April 1846, he suspended his work on it in February 1847, when his father died, in order to write the *Memoirs.* This project occupied him exclusively until July, when he again turned to *Antonina.* He completed the novel in November 1849. It was rejected by the publishing firm of Smith, Elder but accepted by Richard Bentley and appeared in February 1850.

Antonina is a historical novel, and Collins researched his subject in the British Library, drawing from a number of historical sources, including Gibbon's account of the Fall of Rome at the hands of Alaric, king of the Goths, in A.D. 410. *Antonina* opens in the year 408, as the Goths make their way through the Italian Alps, march past Ravenna, and arrive at the gates of Rome, blockading the capital city of the empire. Constructing an elaborate series of subplots, Collins divides his attention among a number of characters in the Gothic and the Roman camps. Among the Goths, Goisvintha and her warrior brother Hermanric figure most prominently. Goisvintha, a powerful and commanding woman, is driven by feelings of revenge against the Romans, who have treacherously slaughtered her children during the massacre of Aquileia. Infuriated by Alaric's decision to blockade rather than sack Rome, she exacts a promise from Hermanric to kill the first Roman they encounter in retribution.

This Roman proves to be Antonina, an innocent young woman who wanders into the Gothic camp, seeking refuge from her male persecutors. Betrayed by the pagan fanatic Ulpius, physically assaulted by the

Roman senator Vetranio, and mistaken for a "harlot" by her tyrannical father, who banishes her from their home, Antonina looks to Hermanric for protection. Obligated by Goisvintha to kill Antonina, the Gothic warrior oscillates between his duty to his own people and his love for the young woman, but ultimately he chooses to protect her. Recovering from an illness, Goisvintha attacks the two lovers. She cuts the tendons of Hermanric's hands, the Gothic punishment for treason, and is about to murder Antonina when she is interrupted by the arrival of a party of Huns, who kill Hermanric. Left for dead, Antonina revives and searches for her father, now ridden with guilt for his unjust treatment of her. Saving her father from starvation, Antonina is again attacked by Goisvintha, who is herself murdered by Ulpius as a sacrifice to his gods. At the conclusion of the novel, Antonina's male persecutors have been reformed. Instead of assaulting Antonina, the remorseful Vetranio nurses her back to health with the aid of his physician and finds her and her father a new home, as Rome establishes a tenuous and temporary peace with its enemies.

As a novel in which an imperial power is invaded and conquered by a barbarian people, *Antonina* belongs to the subgenre of "reverse colonization narratives," a type of fiction that came to prominence later in the century and that includes such works as Bram Stoker's *Dracula* (1897) and H. G. Wells's *War of the Worlds* (1898). Whether directly or obliquely, these narratives envision a decline and fall in Britain's imperial power. They suggest that imperial decline is a just punishment for the crimes that have been committed against the subject races. But they also assuage the imperial guilt of the British by distancing them from the crimes that are portrayed. Stories of reverse colonization are complex "responses to cultural guilt," Stephen D. Arata explains, and "contain the potential for powerful critiques of imperialist ideologies": "In the marauding, invasive Other, British culture sees its own imperial practices mirrored back in monstrous forms."[13] Yet the political potential of these narratives often goes unrealized. Since the invaders remain "other" and "barbarian," the crimes they commit are displaced from the civilized power, whose guilt is simultaneously acknowledged and disavowed.

In the case of Collins's *Antonina,* these disavowals are all the more striking because the imperialists as well as the barbarians are "other"— ancient Romans rather than modern Britons. Whereas the English defend themselves against invasion in both *Dracula* and *War of the Worlds,* they are virtually absent from Collins's novel. The sole exception is a "stolid Briton begrimed with dirt," who appears in a Roman mob and reminds readers that England was itself a colony of Rome before its own rise to global power.[14]

Nonetheless, Collins clearly intends his historical novel to provide a critical commentary on British imperialism: "in Ancient Rome, as in Modern London," is Collins's persistent refrain (481). Collins repeatedly distinguishes the Roman Empire from the British, asserting that the first was based on brute strength, "incessant bloodshed," and "superhuman daring," and the second on lofty conceptions of justice and peace (40–41). Yet he also collapses the distinction between "then and now" and suggests that the expansion of the British Empire cannot be defined against that of the Roman as clearly or neatly as many of his contemporaries would have us believe.

Antonina was written before the Indian Mutiny (1857) and the Jamaica Insurrection (1865) stirred debate over the colonial policies and practices of the British and revealed the lawlessness and guilt of the imperialists to the minds of many Victorians. Even before these events, however, the British had amply demonstrated their ruthless determination to conquer the subcontinent. Collins wrote *Antonina* in 1848–1849, the years in which the British forcefully annexed the Punjab, and in this novel, as in *The Moonstone* and the melodrama *Black and White,* he criticizes such acts of imperial appropriation. With his exotic Indian singing-birds caged and exhibited in his palace, along with other oriental treasures, Vetranio becomes a mirror image of the wealthy and decadent British "nobs" who made their fortunes by looting the eastern colony. Like the British officers and men of the East India Company, who were harshly criticized in Parliament during Warren Hastings's administration for their "policy" of raping Indian women, Vetranio compounds his imperial crimes with sexual ones when he assaults Antonina, who is herself described as "Oriental" (191). [15]

Conscious of Britain's imperial crimes, yet tempted to mitigate them, Collins offers his readers a displaced critique of imperial ideology in *Antonina*—a catalog of abuses from the distant past. Collins criticizes the ancient Romans, most obviously, for their treatment of the foreign peoples they have conquered, and the atrocities they have committed in the process of colonizing portions of Africa, Europe, and the Middle East (47). Continually noting the presence of dark-skinned slaves in his Roman scenes, Collins reminds us that Rome's imperial economy—like Britain's until 1834—was based on the horrors of slavery. Vetranio refers to the "slave merchants" in his employment, who buy and sell members of the subject races throughout the empire (53); and the sinister bailiff Gordian describes his cruel methods of punishing the foreign slaves who work on the estates of the nobleman Saturniuus, exposing the brutality through which the Roman Empire was built and maintained (77–79). In particular, Collins emphasizes Roman injustice toward the Goths, who were treated like "hunted beasts" in the time of the Caesars (205) and massacred by the orders of Emperor Honorius in the years in which *Antonina* is set. Collins describes the "outrages" committed against the Goths and their "liberties" (22), and Alaric, their king, declares his intention "to overthrow by oppression the oppressors of the world," "remembering the wrongs of the Goths in their settlements in Thrace, the murder of the Gothic youths in the towns of Asia, [and] the massacre of the Gothic hostages in Aquileia" (374–75).

But as Collins notes, the tyranny of Rome is directed against her own people as well as the enslaved and conquered "barbarians" for whom Alaric speaks. In *Antonina,* the resentment of those exploited or dispossessed by their own aristocrats is "one of the most important of the internal causes of the downfall of Rome" (76), the counterpart within the empire of the vengeful rage of the invading Goths. Among the many Roman citizens portrayed by Collins, several identify the Goths as their allies rather than their enemies, since they, too, are among those victimized by the Roman elite.

For example, Probus, though born a free man, is deprived of the lands he inherited from his father by greedy noblemen, who wish "to swell their own territorial grandeur," and "whose rank . . . triumph[s] over [his] industry" (82–83). As he tells his comrades on the steps of the public baths, he welcomes the Goths to the gates of Rome, since he finds himself "the exile of [his] country's privileges" (80): "I say to the Goths—with thousands who suffer the same tribulation that I now undergo—'Enter our gates! Level our palaces to the ground! Confound, if you will, in one common slaughter, we that are victims with those that are tyrants! Your invasion will bring new lords to the land. They cannot crush it more—they may oppress it less' " (83). Developing an alliance of sorts between Probus and the Goths, Collins compares the relations among social classes in an aristocracy to race relations in the empire, and he exposes what imperial ideology obscures: the ties between members of the lower classes in the imperial homeland and those of the conquered races, despite the ostensive racial mastery of the former. In so doing, he looks ahead to *The Moonstone,* and its representation of English servants and Hindu priests; despite their racial differences, the members of both groups identify upper-class Englishmen as their enemies.

While Collins allies the oppressed members of the Roman lower classes with the Goths, he also allies the women of Rome with the subject races, developing the analogy between imperial and sexual domination. If imperialism serves the interests of corrupt Roman aristocrats, it also serves the ends of tyrannical fathers and husbands, who treat their daughters and wives in much the same way that Rome treats the Goths. Conflating the abuses of patriarchy with those of imperial dominion, Vetranio orders his slave merchants to send him the most beautiful women from the ends of the world so that he can convincingly represent Venus in his sculpture and painting. "The personification of Venus," he explains to his friends, "demands an investigation of the women of every nation": "To forward the execution of this arduous project, . . . my slave-merchants abroad have orders to send to my villa in Sicily all women who are born most beautiful in the empire, or can be brought most beautiful from the nations around. I will have them displayed before me, of every shade in complexion and of every peculiarity in form!" (53). Combining an imperial will-to-power with sexual lust, Vetranio wishes to "conquer" Antonina, with whom he is enamored. When Vetranio "treacherously . . . invades" her bedroom, Collins highlights the olive complexion and the "Oriental loveliness" of his victim, tying her violation as a woman to the conquest of racial others by the Romans (191). Similarly, Antonina's father, Numerian, acts as both patriarch and imperialist to the women in his household, marrying a dark-skinned Spaniard, whom he subsequently banishes from their home.

Like her mother, Antonina is an "exotic" woman cast out by Numerian; like Probus, she looks to the barbarian invaders of Rome for support. Denounced by her father, who blames her for Vetranio's assault, Antonina seeks refuge in the Gothic camp. The reception she receives among the Goths reveals the complexities and contradictions of Collins's views in the novel.

In certain respects, Collins's portrait of Hermanric and the culture of the Goths lends support to the critique of imperialism he develops elsewhere in *Antonina*. Although Hermanric is a "barbarian," for example, the Gothic warrior treats the vulnerable young heroine much more humanely than do either her father or her admirer back in Rome: "She was safe under the protection of the enemy and the barbarian, after having been lost through the interference of the Roman and the senator" (240). Calling into question the distinction between the civilized Romans and the savage Goths, Collins notes that Gothic culture, for all its "ruggedness," grants women the status and importance they are denied in Rome. "Courtesy to women," Collins asserts, distinguishes civilized from uncivilized peoples, and the Goths "committed the study of medicine, the interpretation of dreams, and, in many instances, the mysteries of communication with the invisible world, to the care of their women. The gentler sex became their counselors in difficulty and their physicians in sickness—their companions, rather than their mistresses—the objects of their veneration, rather than the purveyors of their pleasures" (213–15).

Identified as a forefather of modern European civilization (215), Hermanric offers Antonina protection and respect, recognizes her virtues, and learns from her, subordinating his physical strength to her moral and intellectual power. Predisposed to civilized behavior, the Gothic warrior allows himself to be "converted" by Antonina, abandoning "the warlike instincts of his sex and nation": "She had gifted him with new emotions, and awakened him to new thoughts . . . She had wound her way into his mind, brightening its dark places, enlarging its narrow recesses, beautifying its unpolished treasures" (318). Hermanric's conversion at the hands of Antonina extends Collins's critique of imperialism by suggesting that women are more civilized than men, despite their subjection. Equating barbarism with "the warlike instincts" of the male sex, and civilization with the beauty and sensibility of the female, Collins casts Antonina in the role of colonizer and missionary. While imperial literature generally associates women with the "natural" and "primitive," Collins speaks of the "dark places" in Hermanric's mind, which Antonina will enlighten.

At the same time, however, Collins reinscribes the patriarchal values that his critique of empire questions. As Hermanric becomes more civilized, he also becomes more domineering and assumes what Collins suggests is his rightful role in his relationship with Antonina—that of master. "Gradually, as they discoursed, the voice of the girl was less frequently audible. A change was passing over her spirit: from the teacher, she was now becoming the pupil" (341). In this way, Antonina is herself "converted" at Hermanric's hands. Although *Antonina* is full of sinister father figures—men who dominate, oppress, and silence the women in their lives—Collins ultimately seeks to reform and reinstate patriarchy rather than overthrow it. Instead of granting Antonina political power and social rights, he returns his heroine to a subordinate position, providing her with the good patriarch she was unable to find in Rome: " 'Yes,' continued Hermanric, rising and drawing her toward him again, 'you shall never mourn, never fear, never weep more! Though you have lost your father, and the people of your nation are as strangers to you—though you have been threatened and forsaken, you shall still be beautiful, still be happy; for I will watch you, and you shall never be harmed; I will labor for you, and you shall never want!' " (328).

One might expect Antonina, victimized by men, to seek and establish her independence after the death of Hermanric. But instead she searches for her father, who has been morally transformed in her absence. Collins ultimately praises Numerian for his benevolent control of his daughter and idealizes Antonina for her desire to serve him—the "pure purpose" that sustains her through the famine (445): "A strange, secret satisfaction at the idea of devoting to her father every moment of the time and every particle of the strength that might yet be reserved for her—a ready resignation to death, in dying for *him*—overspread her heart, and took the place of all other aspirations and all other thoughts" (474).

Collins justifies Antonina's embrace of patriarchy by reforming Numerian but also by highlighting the dangers posed to the social order by Goisvintha, who embodies the threat of matriarchal rule and female rage in the novel. Her domineering and "unwomanly" behavior blunts the effect produced by the many examples of women's victimization in *Antonina*. In representing Rome's decline and fall, Collins repeatedly dramatizes the abuse inflicted on mothers—by their husbands and sons as well as their national foes. While Goisvintha witnesses the brutal murder of her beloved infants by Roman soldiers, the mothers of Antonina and Ulpius are both forced from their children by their own husbands, who "jealously watch" their maternal expressions of love, and "ruthlessly suppress" them (133). Having protected her hunchbacked child from ridicule and oppression, similarly, the aged mother of Reburrus is spurned and deserted by her son, who flings money at her in the street, treating her as a beggar (507). In divine retribution, he is confronted by the accusatory figure of her corpse, her arms "stretched out as if in denunciation" (501), "the dead mother [set] in judgment on the degraded son" (505).

While acknowledging the victimization of these mothers, however, Collins reconciles us to the harsh treatment they receive. He does so by insisting that mother nature is inherently destructive and threatens every civilization from within. Focusing on the murderous Goisvintha, whose maternal instincts, when thwarted, reduce her to the level of a "wild beast" (225), Collins displaces the barbarism of the "primitive" or "rugged" races onto the figure of the mother, transforming the victims of patriarchal oppression into bloodthirsty victimizers of men. Significantly, the Gothic mother is "descended from a race of women who slew their wounded husbands, brothers and sons with their own hands, when they sought them after battle, dishonored by a defeat" (389). Although her children are killed by Roman soldiers, her aggression is directed against the men of her own culture and suggests that she is hostile toward the male sex as a whole, Goths and Romans alike. Goisvintha's anger, channeled against her brother, seems oddly independent of the injuries she has suffered, and reveals that the real threat to which the Gothic warrior is exposed comes from a woman who wishes to usurp man's place.

Collins first alerts us to this danger when Goisvintha and Hermanric contemplate the figure of her last dying child, and he develops the contrast between them: "The ferocity that gleamed from her dilated, glaring eyes; the sinister markings that appeared round her pale and parted lips; the swelling of the large veins, drawn to their extremest point of tension on her lofty forehead, so distorted her countenance that the brother and sister, as they stood together, seemed in expression to have changed sexes for the moment. From the warrior, came pity for the sufferer—from the mother, indignation for the offense" (20). More masculine and warlike than her male relation, the "unfeminine" and "unwomanly" Goisvintha is identified as Hermanric's *real* enemy. Killed by the Huns, he is first emasculated by the "ferocious" Goisvintha, who prevents the warrior from defending himself by mutilating his hands (403).

As the portrait of Goisvintha suggests, Collins criticizes imperial and patriarchal systems of belief in his novel, yet proves unwilling to fully acknowledge or develop his critique. If the Fall of Rome marks the guilt of the imperialists in his novel, it also registers their emasculation at the hands of primitive mothers. In *Antonina,* Rome falls, in part, because men and women forget their proper places. Representing the decline of the Roman Empire in sexual terms, as a crisis manifested in physical degeneration and male impotence, Collins underscores the "unmanly" character of its men, plebeians and patricians alike (40). While Rome's "effeminate soldiery have laid aside the armor of their ancestors because their puny bodies are too feeble to bear its weight" (372), Collins tells us, "nothing could be more pitiably effeminate than the appearance of . . . Honorius, Emperor of Rome" (38–39). In their decline, the "effeminate" men of Rome come to resemble those whom Collins identifies as the most barbarous of peoples—the Huns, a "bestial" race whose primitivism is reflected in their grotesquely "dwarfed" masculinity as well as their "swarthy" skin and "flat nose[s]" (385). Defined against the Hun, a "deformed Hercules" with the "body of a dwarf" (385), and against the feeble and effeminate Roman emperor, the "manly" Alaric proves to be the rightful inheritor of Rome's imperial might. Describing the "grand, muscular formation" of the Gothic king, and his air of command (367), Collins represents Alaric as a man among men, a leader capable of subduing and conquering "wild" and "masculine" women as well as "puny" Romans and "stunted" Huns (367).

In *Antonina,* the subversive implications of Collins's story are belied by the restoration of "manly" rule in the empire and the home, a process made possible by the scapegoating of Goisvintha. A similar reversal occurs in Collins's next novel. Collins begins *Basil* by exposing the injustice of primogeniture, an exclusive system of inheritance that privileges eldest sons at the expense of their brothers and sisters and safeguards patriarchal authority by consolidating it, placing a family's power and wealth in the hands of one man. Yet Collins ends the novel by reconciling its tyrannical father with his resentful and disinherited second son. As in *Antonina,* this reversal is accomplished through the scapegoating of certain characters. Displacing the ambition and resentment of his hero onto his two most villainous figures, Collins defends Basil's father and the political system he represents.

Basil; A Story of Modern Life (1852)

Collins began writing *Basil* in January 1852, soon after completing *Mr. Wray's Cash Box,* a novella that centers on the question of reproducing a bust of Shakespeare in Stratford-upon-Avon. He delivered the manuscript of his new novel to Richard Bentley on 1 October, and it was published in November, after Collins made a number of changes in its most sexually explicit scene, at Bentley's request.[16] More provocative than any of Collins's preceding works, *Basil* is subtitled "A Story of Modern Life" and brings Collins's vision of class resentment and domestic strife to bear on contemporary England rather than ancient Rome. Partly based on his own political differences with his father, and their disagreements over his choice of career, it describes the experience of a young gentleman who secretly marries the beautiful daughter of a vulgar but wealthy linen draper and is disinherited by his father as a result.

The novel opens with Basil's return to his family home after taking his college degree. Encouraged by his father to select a profession in the church, the army, or the navy, Basil instead chooses the law, which he feels will give him time to write fiction; at the outset of the story, he is engaged in writing a historical romance. Collins's opening chapters describe in detail the strained dynamics of Basil's family—the death of his mother during his early childhood, his troubled relationship with his elder brother, Ralph, his dealings with his distant and proud father, and his intimate and valued bond with his sister, Clara.

This bond is disrupted when Basil suddenly falls in love with Margaret Sherwin, whom he chances to see while traveling on a London omnibus. Pursuing Margaret, Basil learns of her lowly social origins, yet proposes marriage to her nonetheless. Knowing that his father, animated by family pride, will disinherit him for such a marriage, Basil stipulates that it must take place secretly, allowing him time to prepare his father for its disclosure. In turn, Margaret Sherwin's father stipulates that Basil's secret marriage to his daughter must remain unconsummated for a period of one year. Although Mr. Sherwin is anxious "to clench his profitable bargain" with the young gentleman, he is also distrustful of Basil's honor and wants to allow "for the formation of [Margaret's] constitution, and the finishing of her accomplishments" as well.[17]

Soon after his marriage to Margaret, Basil meets Robert Mannion, Mr. Sherwin's confidential clerk. Basil is told that Mannion has helped to educate Margaret, tutoring her during her school vacations. Befriending Basil, Mannion promises to use his influence with his employer in Basil's interests—to allow him more freedom in his chaperoned interviews with his wife. On the evening before Margaret is to become Basil's wife "in fact as in name," he follows her and Mannion from a party to a cheap hotel, and discovers their adultery: "I listened; and through the thin partition, I heard voices—*her* voice, and *his* voice. *I heard and I knew*—knew my degradation in all its infamy, knew my wrongs in all their nameless horror" (160). Later that night, Basil brutally assaults Mannion in the street and then collapses in a brain fever. Nursed back to health by Clara, he learns that Mannion has survived his attack but is grotesquely disfigured.

Revealing his secret marriage and its disgraceful outcome to his father, Basil is dramatically disinherited and expelled from their home, but he is then joined and supported by his brother. Learning that Margaret has contracted typhus while visiting her lover in the hospital, Basil heroically forgives her at her deathbed. He is then hunted down by Mannion, who follows him to a remote corner of Cornwall. Mannion considers Basil his enemy, we learn, not only because the clerk had planned to marry Margaret himself but also because Basil's father was indirectly responsible for the execution of Mannion's father for the crime of forgery. As the novel draws to its conclusion, Mannion accidentally falls to his death during a confrontation with Basil on the Cornish coast. Relapsing into unconsciousness, Basil is once again nursed back to health by his sister and is then fully reconciled with his father. Collins ends his story with a postscript of sorts—a letter written by Basil to a friend eight years after the central events of the novel take place. In this letter, Basil refers to the recent death of his father, identifies his brother, Ralph, as the new "head of our family," and describes his retired life with Clara on an estate she has inherited from their mother (341–42).

Basil is, first and foremost, a novel about inheritance and the ways in which the practices of a patriarchal culture privilege the few at the expense of the many. In an attempt to hand on the family property intact from one generation to the next, the landed English gentleman generally left his estate to his eldest son rather than dividing it among his children, a practice less common among the fathers of the middle class, whose liquid capital could be more easily divided among dependents.[18] At the beginning of his story, Basil identifies himself as "the second son of an English gentleman of large fortune" (2). This fact, Basil persistently reminds us, excludes him from any claim to the family property: "When I returned home, it was thought necessary, as I was a younger son, and could inherit none of the landed property of the family, except in the case of my brother's dying without children, that I should belong to a profession" (4). Justifying his reticence to displease his father to Mr. Sherwin, Basil again explains that he is a "younger son," and hence a "dependent" (67): "with the exception of a very small independence, left me by my mother, I have no certain prospects," he notes (70).

Rather than accepting his position within his family, Basil complains of its unfairness. Although his eldest brother will inherit the family property, Basil asserts, he is not deserving of "his birthright privilege" (12). In Basil's view, the system of primogeniture most commonly favors those who fail to merit or appreciate their elevated status: "When a family is possessed of large landed property, the individual of that family who shows least interest in its welfare; who is least fond of home, least connected by his own sympathies with his relatives, least ready to learn his duties or admit his responsibilities, is often that very individual who is to succeed to the family inheritance—the eldest son. My brother Ralph was no exception" (11). In effect, primogeniture creates a class system within the family, a system in which the elder brother plays the part of the undeserving yet titled lord, while his younger brothers and sisters play the role of commoners. Whatever their individual merits, their positions are unjustly determined for them by the arbitrary circumstances of their birth. Thus Basil's experience of patriarchal injustice within his family parallels his experience of social injustice at the university: "The most learned student in my college—the man whose life was most exemplary, whose acquirements were most admirable—was shown me sitting, as a commoner, in the lowest place. The heir to an Earldom, who had failed at the last examination, was pointed out a few minutes afterwards, dining in solitary grandeur at a raised table, above the reverend scholars who had turned him back as a dunce" (3).

Disinherited from the landed property of his family by the rules of primogeniture even before his father officially casts him out, Basil is a second-class citizen both at home and at college and allies himself with his sister, who is more broadly denied the rights and privileges that Basil desires by virtue of her sex. Basil is drawn to Clara, Collins suggests, because her dependent status as a woman is similar to his own as a younger son. Although Clara's exclusion is more complete than Basil's, Collins represents both siblings as exiles from patriarchy—children whose sole inheritance is bequeathed to them by their mother, on whose small estate they both eventually live. Indeed, Basil seems to feel that he has derived his identity from his mother rather than his father. Described by Clara as "my favourite brother" and "my poor mother's favourite son" (207), Basil assumes a matrilineal name once he is renounced by his father—"the name of a little estate that once belonged to my mother, and that now belongs to her daughter" (315)—and he takes refuge in Cornwall because his childhood nurse was a Cornish woman (307). Basil repeatedly develops a special feeling of camaraderie with women who have been victimized by patriarchal figures—with Mrs. Sherwin, the silenced victim of her husband's domestic tyranny, for example, who wishes to serve as Basil's second mother (218), and with the oppressed female domestic at the Sherwin's home. His "female" vulnerability is suggested by his recurring lapses into "nervous" excitement and mental instability, a condition from which the stereotypically weak Victorian woman was commonly thought to suffer.

Basil's status as younger son connects him to the female figures in Collins's novel, but it also ties him to his social inferiors—in particular, to Robert Mannion. Although Mannion is eventually revealed to be a villain, he is initially presented as a man whose talents and virtues have gone unrewarded because merit plays no role in the rigid class system. Recalling the "exemplary" and "admirable" man at Basil's college, who sits "in the lowest place," Mannion explains that he is forced to remain in a lowly position by the English "pride of caste," despite his extensive knowledge, his admirable work ethic, and his gentlemanlike acquirements, manners, and tastes (123). Collins uses Mannion's personal history to explode the Victorian myth of "self-help," according to which one's merits and virtues inevitably secure one's social rise. As Mannion himself asserts, his "high hopes" and "brave resolutions" of working his way "upward to high places" have been "persecuted and starved out of [him]" (233).

Introduced to us as a deserving man denied his rightful place by others' birthrights, Mannion resembles Basil, and Collins treats them as doubles. Not only was Mannion once an aspiring writer, as Basil is. He lives under an assumed name and has been wronged by Basil's father. Mannion's own father, he explains, "determined to live like a gentleman" and looked to Basil's father as his patron. Mistakenly expecting to receive a sinecure from him while incurring heavy debts, Mannion the elder ultimately forged a bond in his patron's name. Instead of forgiving him, Basil's father gave evidence against him, and he was executed in consequence (227–28). "You will now wonder no longer how I could have inherited the right to be his enemy," Mannion asserts (229).

However, Collins establishes the tie between Basil and Mannion only to sever it, insisting upon their class differences and paving the way for Basil's reconciliation with his father. If Basil and Mannion are "allies" (138), they are also antagonists, since the young gentleman is included in Mannion's vendetta against "all who are of his [father's] blood" (229) and remains a gentleman, though a second son. In Mannion's eyes, Basil has used his class privilege to unfair advantage, seizing the "prize" that belongs to him: "the man who, in his insolence of youth, and birth, and fortune, had snatched from me the one long-delayed reward for twenty years of misery, just as my hands were stretched forth to grasp it, was the son of that honourable and high-born gentleman who had given my father to the gallows" (242). Pairing Basil and his father as "high-born gentlemen," and revealing the treachery and class resentment of the clerk, Collins identifies Mannion as unfit for "social privileges" and "high places" (242, 233) and defends the social status quo.

Collins's characterization of Clara has much the same effect. Unlike Mannion, she proves to be deserving of praise—but because she willingly accepts her lowly status as a woman and does not insist upon her "rights" (22). In this regard, she not only differs from Mannion, the social upstart, but also from the "modern women" criticized by Basil. "We live in an age when too many women appear to be ambitious of morally unsexing themselves before society," Basil complains, "by aping the language and the manners of men": "Women of this exclusively modern order, like to use slang expressions in their conversation; assume a bastard-masculine abruptness in their manners, a bastard-masculine licence in their opinions; affect to ridicule those outward developments of feeling which pass under the general appellation of 'sentiment.' Nothing impresses, agitates, amuses, or delights them in a hearty, natural, womanly way" (19–20). In a novel about primogeniture and the disinheritance of the second son, Collins uses passages such as this to resolve Basil's problematic status. He suggests that those who are truly illegitimate—and hence justly disinherited—are those who fail to accept their "natural" place in the social order: the "modern woman," for example, characterized by Collins as a "bastard" man, and Mannion, whom he identifies as a "bastard" gentleman. Although Basil and Clara are denied the privileges of their elder brother, Collins offers them legitimacy of a different sort: he identifies Clara as a "womanly" woman, who gladly keeps her opinions to herself, and Basil as a real man. Obscuring the inferior status of his hero as a younger son, Collins solves a patrimonial crisis indirectly—by treating unruly women and upstart clerks as the social problem in his novel and shoring up his hero's sexual and class identity.

Collins does so largely through Basil's relationship with Margaret Sherwin, his unfaithful and ambitious wife. Even more menacing than Mannion, Margaret Sherwin challenges Basil's position as both a gentleman and a man, and she reveals the dangers of class mobility and female emancipation in Collins's eyes. Margaret's significance in the novel is suggested by the way she and Basil first meet—on a London omnibus, where class distinctions are blurred: "I know not any other sphere in which persons of all classes and all temperaments are so oddly collected together," Basil explains (27). One might expect Collins to defend such heterogeneous groupings, considering his critique of class segregation at Basil's college. Yet Basil's entrance into the democratic sphere proves to be his undoing, as he falls prey to the vulgar and grasping Sherwin family. A wealthy linen draper surrounded by "gaudy" objects that are "oppressively new" (61), Mr. Sherwin asserts that he can "hold his head up anywhere as one of the props of this commercial country" (68) and feels that he and his daughter are "worthy of any station" (244). Margaret herself wants to dress like a lady and ride in her own carriage, and she marries Basil because she believes he will enable her to do so, lifting her "out of her own class" (132–33, 244): "She was not wanting in ambition to ascend to the highest degree in the social scale," Basil observes (137).

However, Collins disappoints their hopes, punishing their greed and presumption, killing off the daughter, and exiling the father. Positioning them far beneath Basil and the "ancient" Norman stock from which he is descended (10), Collins justifies the class distinctions between the two families by suggesting that they are based on glaring moral differences that are "natural" or innate (239).

At the same time, Collins compounds the "vulgar ambition" (245) of the nouveau riche with the sexual ambition of a woman who rejects her proper place in the domestic sphere. Although Basil follows Margaret home and proposes marriage to her, she is clearly the sexual aggressor in their relationship. Unlike the demure and ladylike Clara, who exhibits no sexual feelings and looks "almost statue-like in [her] purity and repose" (39), Margaret is eroticized, and Basil describes "the fire in her large dark eyes" and their "voluptuous languor," and her lips that are "*too* full" (30): "The spell of the syren was over me," Basil asserts (34).

When Basil dreams of Margaret at night, she appears as a dark figure whose black hair is "unconfined," and whose eyes are "the eyes of a serpent": "looking intently on me with her wild bright eyes, she clasped her supple arms round my neck, and drew me a few paces away with her towards the wood . . . pressing her warm lips on mine" (45–46). Like the "modern women" criticized by Basil, Margaret "unsexes" herself by assuming the prerogatives of men and embracing and kissing her lover instead of passively receiving such attentions from him. In the process, she "unsexes" Basil as well, emasculating the hero. She forces him to live on "humiliating terms of dependence and prohibition" (143)—to wait a year before consummating his marriage—while she secretly conducts her adulterous affair with Mannion.

By threatening to seduce and "unsex" Basil, and then joining in Mannion's "foul plot" (160), Margaret enables Collins to recast the crisis that confronts his hero: "No woman had ever before stood between me and my ambitions, my occupations, my amusements. No woman had ever before inspired me with the sensations which I now felt . . . if I succumbed, as far as my family prospects were concerned, I should be a ruined man" (42). No longer identified as the characters who thwart the hero and ruin his prospects, Basil's father becomes a "loving" and forgiving figure (338), and his elder brother, Ralph, is morally transformed. Proving an exception to the general rule of irresponsible yet privileged heirs, he is "aroused by his new duties to a sense of his new position" and "emancipated from many of the habits which once enthralled and degraded him" (342). In *Basil,* as in *Antonina,* patriarchy is rehabilitated and restored.

By contrast, Margaret is fatally punished for her sexual promiscuity in a manner that fits her crime. She dies from typhus fever, which she contracts by "accidentally" visiting the wrong bed at the hospital: "she ran to the wrong bed, before the nurse could stop her," Mannion's physician explains (285). With Margaret's villainy exposed, Basil reclaims his masculinity by beating Mannion "savagely," an act that endows him with "raging strength" (164) while "destroying [Mannion's] very identity as a man" (249), and that gains him the approval of his manly and athletic elder brother: "He heard me almost with his former schoolboy delight, when I had succeeded, to his satisfaction, in a feat of strength or activity. He jumped off the bed, and seized both my hands in his strong grasp; his face radiant, his eyes sparking. 'Shake hands, Basil! Shake hands, as we haven't shaken hands yet: this makes amends for everything!' " (260). Perhaps more clearly than any other passage in the novel, Ralph's reaction to Basil's "feat of strength" reveals the unspoken function that Margaret and Mannion serve. Characterized by their sexual and social otherness, they are the scapegoats of the novel and enable two gentlemen and brothers to overlook their own differences and recognize their common cause.

Dickens and Collins

With its sensational and sexually explicit content, *Basil* received mostly hostile reviews when it appeared in November 1852. Complaining of Collins's "unfortunate selection of material," a number of critics found the novel "absolutely disgusting."[19] While admiring Collins's artistic skill, they objected in particular to his treatment of adulterous passion and betrayal: "There are some subjects on which it is not possible to dwell without offence; and Mr. Collins . . . has rather increased the displeasure it excited, by his resolution to spare us no revolting details."[20] "*Basil* is a tale of criminality, almost revolting from its domestic horrors," another reviewer complained. "The vicious atmosphere in which the drama of the tale is enveloped, weighs on us like a nightmare."[21]

Yet in the midst of these objections, Collins received praise from a new and valuable acquaintance, Charles Dickens, whom he had met the previous year, and to whom some critics believe he was indebted for the style and subject matter of *Mr. Wray's Cash Box*.[22] Thanking Collins for a copy of *Basil* in a letter written on 20 December 1852, Dickens assures him that he has "read the book with very great interest, and with a very thorough conviction that you have a call to this same art of fiction." "I think the probabilities here and there require a little more respect than you are disposed to show them," Dickens writes:

> But the story contains admirable writing, and many clear evidences of a very delicate discrimination of character. It is delightful to find throughout that you have taken great pains with it besides, and have "gone at it" with a perfect knowledge of the jolter-headedness of the conceited idiots who suppose that volumes are to be tossed off like pancakes, and that any writing can be done without the utmost application, the greatest patience, and the steadiest energy of which the writer is capable.
>
> For all these reasons I have made *Basil*'s acquaintance with great gratification, and entertain a high respect for him. And I hope that I shall become intimate with many worthy descendants of his, who are yet in the limbo of creatures waiting to be born. (*Letters*, 2:435–36)

Dickens had reason to admire *Basil*, a suspenseful novel written in a less-stilted prose style than *Antonina* and complicated by the inclusion of fictive newspaper accounts and letters written by characters from different social classes, a narrative strategy that anticipates such multivoiced novels as *The Moonstone* and *Armadale*. Even before the publication of *Basil*, Dickens had shown his approval of Collins's writing by accepting "A Terribly Strange Bed" for *Household Words*. A bizarre tale of attempted murder by means of a collapsing four-poster bed in a low gambling house in Paris, this story shows signs of Collins's growing interest in "the nervous . . . state of mind"[23] and was the first of dozens of his works to be published by Dickens in *Household Words* and *All the Year Round*.[24]

The first years of Collins's literary apprenticeship were dominated by his relationship with Richard Bentley, who published *Antonina* (1850), *Mr. Wray's Cash Box* (1851), *Rambles Beyond Railways* (1851), and *Basil* (1852) as well as a number of short stories. But Bentley was quickly displaced by Dickens, who serialized four of Collins's major novels in a little over 10 years: *The Dead Secret* in *Household Words* (1857); and *The Woman in White*, *No Name*, and *The Moonstone* in *All the Year Round* in 1859–1860, 1862–1863, and 1868, respectively. While publishing Collins's works, Dickens also collaborated with him on a number of stories that appeared in his journals, usually as special Christmas Numbers, including "The Wreck of the Golden Mary" (1856), "The Lazy Tour of Two Idle Apprentices" (1857), "The Perils of Certain English Prisoners" (1857), "A Message from the Sea" (1860), and "No Thoroughfare" (1867). Although Bentley published four of Collins's short stories in his *Miscellany* in 1851 and 1852,[25] and *Hide and Seek* in 1854, and was an influential figure whose list of "Standard Novels" was well known (*King*, 86), Dickens became what Bentley simply could not: the young writer's mentor.

Yet Dickens's role in Collins's life was not simply that of a teacher and guide. In his own ways, Collins gave support to Dickens, offering him companionship during his stormy marital separation, providing an unconventional example of domestic life, accompanying him on late nights out in Paris and London, and influencing a number of his novels as well. At the same time, Dickens's attitude toward the work of his protégé was sometimes more critical than admiring. Although he generally approved of Collins's writing, Dickens was wary of his subversive attitudes and served as Collins's censor as well as his guide. "I mark this note 'Immediate,' because I forgot to mention that I particularly wish you to look well to Wilkie's article about the Wigan schoolmaster, and not to leave anything in it that may be sweeping, and unnecessarily offensive to the middle class," Dickens wrote to W. H. Wills, his subeditor, in September 1858, about Collins's "Highly Proper." "He has always a tendency to overdo that" (*Letters*, 3:58). Although Collins's decision to write for *Household Words* and to become a salaried member of Dickens's staff seems to suggest his willingness to compromise his political principles to succeed as a professional writer,[26] Collins did not simply subordinate his views to those of Dickens, but tested the political limits of his editor and sometime collaborator.

Their work on "The Perils of Certain English Prisoners" amply illustrates this point and shows that Collins, while collaborating with Dickens, did not necessarily adopt his views or help to realize his intentions. Dickens conceived of "The Perils," the 1857 Christmas Number of *Household Words,* in reaction to the Indian Mutiny, which began in May of that year. The Indian sepoys who rebelled against their British officers were animated by economic and political grievances, but the immediate reason for their revolt was religious. Enfield rifles had been introduced into the army, and the sepoys believed that the new cartridges, which had to be bitten off for loading, were greased with pig and cow fat. The sepoys thus felt that the British were forcing them to commit sacrilege, and rebelled. British officers, as well as their wives and children, were killed, and a number of Englishwomen were allegedly raped by the Indians. Daily accounts of atrocities committed by the sepoys appeared in the British press and generated "calls for repression and revenge." "No episode in British imperial history raised public excitement to a higher pitch than the Indian Mutiny," Patrick Brantlinger notes.[27]

Sharing in this "excitement," Dickens called for the "extermination" of the Indian race and decided to write a story "commemorating . . . the best qualities of the English character that have been shown in India" (*Letters,* 2:894). Asking Collins to write the middle chapter of this story, Dickens wrote the first and third. He set the narrative in an English colony in Central America, an island where the silver taken from a mine in Honduras is temporarily stored, and represented the Mutiny as an assault on English men, women, and children by a band of pirates, who raid the island for the silver store. Dickens's first chapter portrays the leisurely life of the island before the attack and ends with the victory of the pirates over the colonists; Collins's chapter recounts the imprisonment of the British in the jungle; and Dickens's final chapter describes their escape and eventual victory over their captors.

What is most striking about "The Perils" are its inconsistencies in tone and characterization, which suggest that the intentions of the two writers are at odds. In the first chapter, Dickens reinforces racist stereotypes of the sepoys when he describes the martyrdom of the Englishwomen in the colony, who prefer death to sexual violation: "I want you to make me a promise," Miss Maryon tells Private Davis, "that if we are defeated, and you are absolutely sure of my being taken, you will kill me." "I shall not be alive to do it, Miss," Davis replies. "I shall have died in your defense before it comes to that."[28] But in the chapter that follows, Collins deflates Dickens's melodramatic account of British heroism, portraying the English prisoners struggling to suppress their laughter at the comic antics of the pirate chief, who plays his guitar "in a languishing attitude," "with his nose conceitedly turned up in the air" (281).

Whereas Dickens represents the pirate chief as an exotic figure, Collins highlights his English qualities, using him to depict imperial abuses rather than native treachery. Dickens models the pirate leader on the stereotype of the sadistic sepoy and shows him "playfully" mutilating his English captives with his cutlass (267). By contrast, Collins models him on the dandified British officers in India, known for their extravagant living and their inhumanity toward their native servants. Collins's pirate chief parades among his camp followers like one of "the dandies in the Mall in London" (269), in stiffened coat-skirts and a lace cravat. He abuses the natives under his command, using their backs as writing desks, and complaining of their stench, while covering his nose with "a fine cambric handkerchief," scented and edged with lace (270–71). Dickens adheres to the racist patterns of Mutiny literature in his portions of "The Perils," defining the evil natives against their innocent British victims. But Collins complicates matters by calling attention to the underlying abuses of power that generated the Mutiny in the first place.

Although Collins's attitude toward British imperialism is not consistently critical, and combines his sense of imperial wrongdoing with his fear of savagery among natives, he is considerably more wary of empire building than Dickens proves to be, and he defends colonized peoples against a host of racist allegations in his fiction and journalism. His political differences with Dickens over such matters may well have contributed to the increasing coolness between them in the 1860s, as did the marriage of Collins's brother, Charles, to Dickens's daughter Kate, a union of which Dickens disapproved. By the time of Dickens's death in 1870, he and Collins saw one another rarely. Although Dickens helped to launch Collins's literary career, and was for years his nearly constant companion, the relationship between mentor and protégé had been soured by their differences of opinion and their literary rivalry, for Collins had long since come into his own as one of the most popular writers of the day, a master of mystery and detection.

Chapter Three

Investigating Social Boundaries: Gender, Class, and Detection in *Hide and Seek, The Dead Secret,* and *The Law and the Lady*

Collins's critics have long credited him with inventing the genre of the detective novel in England,[1] and much of the scholarship devoted to his fiction in the twentieth century focuses on his treatment of crime and detection. Engaging in their own form of detective work, critics often identify actual criminal cases upon which Collins draws and read his novels in the context provided by his source material. The conspiracy launched against Lady Glyde in *The Woman in White,* they note, is based on a similar crime committed against the Frenchwoman Madame de Douhault in the 1780s, while the stained nightgown that figures prominently in *The Moonstone* and the dismissed detective, Sergeant Cuff, are based on elements of the Road murder committed by Constance Kent in 1860 and investigated by Inspector Jonathan Whicher. In representing bigamy in *Man and Wife,* Collins draws from the 1861 case of *Thelwall v. Yelverton,* and he makes use of Madeleine Smith's 1857 trial in *The Law and the Lady.*[2]

But while Collins was fascinated by annals of crime, and followed the notorious trials of his day with great interest, his use of such source material in his novels can be misleading and obscure his primary aims in writing them. Although thefts, murders, and suicides sometimes occur in his detective fiction, the transgressions that Collins most commonly describes involve violations of gender norms and class boundaries rather than criminal violence. More often than not, the transgressive characters in his novels prove to be the detectives themselves, working-class men and middle-class women who assume the prerogatives of their social superiors in the course of their investigations, and themselves become objects of scrutiny.[3]

Despite our association of detective fiction with sensational murders and thefts, such novels as *Hide and Seek* (1854), *The Dead Secret* (1857), and *The Law and the Lady* (1874–1875) have a different focus. Using transgressive figures to uncover family secrets, they call attention to acts of seduction and fraud, and enable Collins to investigate the grounds of social identity in Victorian England and to simultaneously challenge and reinforce gender boundaries and class lines. Bringing their detectives into contact with invalid figures, these novels examine the ties between physical handicaps and gender norms and explore the relationship between physiology and sexual identity. In their own ways, and to varying degrees, each of these works questions the assumption that gender and class distinctions are grounded in nature, while also treating sexual differences and class distinctions as innate and naturally determined.

Hide and Seek (1854)

Although *The Moonstone* is often cited as the first English detective novel, Collins began to experiment with this literary form from nearly the start of his career. Despite the absence of a policeman or inspector from its cast of characters, *Hide and Seek* can be considered Collins's earliest example of detective fiction. He began working on what was to become his third published novel in April 1853, describing it to George Bentley, the son and partner of publisher Richard Bentley, as a new and unexpected type of writing that would "make the readers of Antonina and Basil prick up their ears."[4] Completing it in May 1854, he dedicated it to Dickens, who praised its "great merit" (*Letters*, 2:570). The novel was published by Bentley on 5 June 1854, and Collins received the considerable sum of £150 for the first edition of 500 copies.

Like many of Collins's later novels, *Hide and Seek* begins with a prologue of sorts. Set in London in 1837, the "Opening Chapter" describes the tensions in the Thorpe family, as six-year-old Zachary is punished by his evangelical father for disobedience during a lengthy church service. Locked in an upstairs room, the boy is comforted by his mother and defended by his maternal grandfather, Mr. Goodworth, but he must submit to Mr. Thorpe's "restraint and discipline and punishment," and learns to "hate Sunday."[5]

The main narrative of *Hide and Seek*, set in 1851, is divided into two books, "The Hiding" and "The Seeking," and centers on the relationships within a second family, the Blyths, whose members are well known to Zachary. They include Valentine, a moderately successful painter who rejects a lucrative commercial partnership to pursue his artistic career; his invalid wife, Lavinia, confined to her bedroom by a spinal ailment; and their beautiful adopted daughter, named "Madonna" by Valentine, a 23-year-old deaf mute with whom Zachary forms a mutual attachment. Estranged from his father, who discovers that he has been sneaking out on "nocturnal tour[s] of amusement" (139), Zack runs away from home, determined to become an artist.

In a series of retrospective chapters, we learn that Madonna is the illegitimate child of Mary Grice, a young woman seduced in 1827 by a gentleman known as "Arthur Carr." Working as a dressmaker in Dibbledean, Mary runs away from home when her pregnancy is discovered. Although her father tries to find her and bring her back home, his efforts are thwarted by his vengeful sister, Joanna, who does not want her fallen niece to return and disgrace her respectable relations. Away on business in Germany, "Arthur" does not know of Mary's pregnancy. His letters are intercepted by Joanna Grice, and he never sees Mary again.

Robbed of her money during her confinement, the starving and homeless Mary is aided by Martha Peckover, the wife of a circus performer, who comes upon her on a roadside near Bangbury. Mrs. Peckover suckles Mary's infant along with her own, ensuring Madonna's survival. When Mary Grice dies the next day, leaving only a hair bracelet and a pocket handkerchief as keys to her identity, Mrs. Peckover and her husband adopt the baby. As a young child, "little Mary" earns her keep by performing in dangerous equestrian acts in the circus. Her deafness is the result of a fall from a horse, which she suffers at age seven, soon after which she ceases to speak, communicating instead by writing on a slate she carries with her.

Valentine Blyth first sees little Mary performing card tricks at the circus in Rubbleford in 1838, while he is visiting his friend Dr. Joyce. Drawn to the young girl because of her resemblance to the Madonnas of Raphael, he learns of her physical abuse at the hands of Mr. Jubber, the circus owner, and vows to protect her from further beatings. With the reluctant permission of Mrs. Peckover, whose "prior right" to the child's affections he fully acknowledges (104), he brings her to London, where she is happily incorporated into his family circle and often visited by her foster mother. However, Valentine's contentment is marred by fears that Madonna will be claimed by her unknown relations. In his anxiety, he hides Mary Grice's belongings and prohibits Mrs. Peckover from discussing with others what she knows of Madonna's early history. Mrs.

Peckover violates Valentine's prohibition at the end of Book I, when Zack mentions his plan to give Madonna a hair bracelet. Fearing that such a gift will bring bad luck to the young woman, she informs Zack that Madonna already has one, and he concludes that the bracelet is "mixed up somehow with the grand secret about Madonna's past history, which Valentine had always kept from him and from everybody" (176).

Book II introduces us to a mysterious stranger whom Zack assists during a drunken brawl. Darkly tanned, and scarred with old wounds, the man befriends Zack, introduces himself as "Mathew Marksman," and explains that he has just returned to England from America, where he has made his fortune in the gold diggings. Sharing Mat's lodgings, Zack introduces his new friend to the Blyths. Mat's startled reaction to Madonna's appearance identifies him to the reader as one of her unknown relations. Indeed, "Mathew Marksman" proves to be Mat Grice, Madonna's maternal uncle. Learning only now of his sister's pregnancy and death years before, he hopes to find, and exact his revenge on, the man who seduced and abandoned her.

Gathering together the evidence in the case, Mat confronts his aunt Joanna, learns of a hair bracelet given to Mary by "Arthur," and finds samples of her lover's hair. From Zack, he hears of the bracelet belonging to Madonna's mother. Entering the Blyths' home through a door he unlocks while modeling for a painting, and unfastening Valentine's bureau by means of a key he steals and duplicates, Mat takes the bracelet. Identifying the hair as that of "Arthur," he proves that Madonna is his niece; comparing "Arthur's" hair with Zack's, he realizes that Mary's lover—and Madonna's father—is the elder Mr. Thorpe. Out of brotherhood with Zack, Mat restrains his violence, but threatens Mr. Thorpe with exposure. Accompanied by his wife, Thorpe retreats to Wales. To Valentine's relief, both of Madonna's male relations want her to remain under his care. Mr. Thorpe dies in exile, and Mat returns to America, where he is joined by Zack. The novel ends after Zack's return and foretells Mat's reunion with Madonna in England. "Softened" by his contact with his niece and friends, he decides to "wander no more" (430).

Read as a detective novel in a literal sense, *Hide and Seek* presents us with a case of seduction and abandonment, and its amateur detective, Mat Grice, devotes himself to exposing the man who drove his sister to her death. Yet Collins seems considerably less interested in the problem of "Arthur Carr" than he is in the mysterious and transgressive qualities of Madonna and her uncle, and these two characters prove to be the central objects of scrutiny in the novel. From the beginning of Book I, Collins focuses the investigation on Madonna and her medical case. While he structures his plotline around the question of her parentage, and concludes with the revelation that Mr. Thorpe is "Arthur Carr," he identifies Madonna herself as the novel's underlying source of mystery:

> The keenest observers, beholding her as she at present appears, would detect nothing in her face or figure, her manner or her costume, in the slightest degree suggestive of impenetrable mystery, or incurable misfortune. And yet, she happens to be the only person in Mr. Blyth's household at whom prying glances are directed, whenever she walks out; whose very existence is referred to by the painter's neighbours with an invariable accompaniment of shrugs, sighs, and lamenting looks; and whose "case" is always compassionately designated as "a sad one," whenever it is brought forward, in the course of conversation, at dinner-tables and tea-tables in the new suburb. (48)

Indeed, it is the "incurable misfortune" of deafness and muteness—and the gender norms that these handicaps represent—that Collins proves most eager to investigate in *Hide and Seek*.

At various moments in the novel, this investigation seems doomed to failure by the traditional terms in which Collins describes sexual difference. Recalling *Antonina, Hide and Seek* draws on misogynistic conceptions of female nature, and it explains the inferiority of women to men by combining biblical references to the Fall with stereotypical notions of women's primitive condition.[6] Collins contrasts the vindictive rage of the spinster Joanna Grice—as "wild" as an "old tiger-cat" (208)—with the forgiving kindness of her brother, Joshua, making it seem as if Mary were victimized by her jealous aunt rather than her treacherous lover. In its own way, Collins's sympathetic portrait of Mrs. Thorpe is equally condemning. When she comforts young Zack, Collins attributes her behavior to maternal instincts as opposed to the higher thought processes of men. Modeling her actions on those of "all women . . . from the time of the first mother" (13), Collins contrasts her response to Zack's rebellion with those of the fathers in the household:

> If Mr. Thorpe had heard [the words "I won't!"], the boy would have been sternly torn away, bound to the back of a chair, and placed ignominiously with his chin against the table; if Mr. Goodworth had heard them, . . . he would instantly have lost his temper, and soused his grandson head over ears in the bath. Not one of these ideas occurred to Mrs. Thorpe, who

possessed no ideas. But she had certain substitutes which were infinitely
more useful in the present emergency: she had instincts. . . . His mother
opened her lips, stopped suddenly, said a few words, stopped again, hesi-
tated—and then ended her first sentence of admonition . . . by snatching
at the nearest towel, and bearing Zack off to the wash-hand basin.
(20–21)

Endowed with instincts but deprived of ideas, the kindhearted mother
comforts and grooms her son but cannot educate or discipline him. Representing Mrs. Thorpe in this way, Collins invokes the patriarchal logic
that associates the maternal with the natural, and argues that children
must dissociate themselves from their primitive if well-meaning mothers
in order to evolve.

Yet Collins qualifies this logic through his valorized treatment of Mrs.
Peckover and the "natural sustenance" that she provides for little Mary
(370). Her pivotal role suggests the primacy of the maternal rather than
its primitivism and highlights the impotence of the fathers in the novel,
expendable figures who either forsake their children or prove incapable
of assisting them. Furthermore, while Collins acknowledges the value of
the maternal and the natural in his treatment of Martha Peckover, he
also questions the very idea of natural or innate sexual distinctions in his
portraits of Madonna and Lavinia. In representing these female invalids,
he calls attention to the ways in which the physical and intellectual inferiority of women is culturally constructed.

As a primary source for *Hide and Seek,* Collins used John Kitto's *The
Lost Senses* (1845), an autobiographical work. Like Madonna, Kitto lost
his hearing in childhood, as the result of a fall, and Collins models the
medical treatment that his heroine receives as well as her injury and
symptoms on those of Kitto.

Yet in adapting *The Lost Senses* to his own ends, Collins makes deafness a female malady, associating it with the ideals that reduce Victorian
women to a condition analogous to that of a deaf mute. Although
Madonna is literally deaf in *Hide and Seek,* Collins gives her handicap a
metaphoric resonance that is absent from Kitto's book. Kitto is primarily concerned with describing the problems that deafness causes for
men, and the way it "disqualifies" them for an active life of business in
the public sphere (80–81). By contrast, Collins examines the ways in
which Madonna's deafness qualifies her for life in the domestic sphere;
her handicap serves as a metaphor for the plight of women unfairly
excluded from the public realm by the oppressive norms that force them

to remain "angels in the house."[7] "Deaf and dumb as [Madonna] was with the creatures of this world," Valentine Blyth muses, "she could talk with the angels, and could hear what the heavenly voices said to her in return" (143–44). Whereas Kitto describes the process by which he learned to talk in adulthood (22), Madonna remains largely mute throughout the novel, although she has the physical ability to speak, and Collins uses her deafness and silence to represent the enforced innocence and voicelessness of all Victorian women. Associating Madonna's deafness with Victorian constructions of womanhood, Collins notes that her knowledge and movements are restricted by Valentine. The only serious disagreement that occurs between Valentine and Zack centers on Madonna's presence in the male domain, when Valentine reprimands his young friend for bringing her downstairs, among men, after hours, "br[eaking] through all rule in doing so" (333). Significantly, Zack breaks the rules with the tacit approval of Valentine's wife, who has a "strong curiosity" to know about her husband's companions (330).

As Valentine's name for her suggests, Madonna embodies female perfection to the painter and his friends. Her features and expression remind them "of that image of softness, purity, and feminine gentleness, which has been engraven on all civilized memories by the 'Madonnas' of Raphael" (51). Yet Madonna's deafness and her silence also make her appear an ideal woman in Victorian eyes and complement her physical beauty. "She was always wonderful quiet and silent," Mrs. Peckover says of her "poor lamb," explaining that she "didn't wonder—at least at first—why [Madonna] never said a word, and never answered [her] when [she] spoke" (93). Nearly as quiet before her injury as she is after it, Madonna resembles those women intimidated into silence by men— Mrs. Thorpe, who meekly obeys her husband, and Mrs. Peckover, who "stifles her sobs" out of fear of Mr. Jubber (69). Revealing that the other female characters in his novel suffer from a muteness that recalls Madonna's own, Collins uses it to expose the pathology of the female norm, and to criticize a culture that places the highest value on a woman who "can hold [her] tongue" (123) and "not ask . . . a single question" (52)—who puts men at their ease with "the mute encouragement of a look" (330).

Collins deepens his investigation of Victorian gender norms and the construction of sexual difference through his portrait of Lavinia Blyth, another figure whose feminine perfection is oddly coupled with an "incurable malady" (117). Like Madonna's deafness and muteness,

Lavinia's invalid condition enables Collins to both represent and question the value of female domesticity. Although he praises the "innocence
and purity" of these two characters, he also suggests that they are
deformed by these feminine traits (119). Despite her painful spinal ailment, or rather, *because* of it, Lavinia proves to be the ideal wife and
housekeeper. Far from preventing her from performing her domestic
duties, her invalid condition makes her an exemplary wife and housekeeper by literally confining her to the house:

> From the studio to the kitchen, she managed every day, through channels
> of communication invented by herself, to find out the latest domestic
> news; to be present in spirit at least if not in body, at family consultations
> which could not take place in her room; to know exactly how her hus-
> band was getting on downstairs with his pictures; to rectify in time any
> omission of which Mr. Blyth or Madonna might be guilty in making the
> dinner arrangements, or in sending orders to tradespeople; to keep the
> servants attentive to their work, and to indulge or control them, as the
> occasion might require. Neither by look nor manner did she betray any
> of the sullen listlessness or fretful impatience sometimes attendant on
> long, incurable illness. Her voice, low as its tones were, was always cheer-
> ful, and varied musically and pleasantly with her varying thoughts. (142)

Emphasizing Lavinia's cheerfulness and efficiency, Collins suggests that
her invalidism—like Madonna's—cannot be easily detected. In so
doing, he not only normalizes her diseased condition, but also patholo-
gizes the female norm. It is business as usual in this middle-class home,
managed by a woman "doomed" to remain inside (37), "condemned to
. . . weary inaction" (117).

In his "Note to Chapter VII," Collins explains his reasons for representing these handicapped characters, providing us with a statement of
his "moral purpose": "I know of nothing which more firmly supports
our faith in the better parts of human nature, than to see . . . with what
patience and cheerfulness the heavier bodily afflictions of humanity are
borne, for the most part, by those afflicted; and also to note what elements of kindness and gentleness the spectacle of these afflictions con-
stantly develops in the persons of the little circle by which the sufferer
is surrounded" (431). Yet we should be wary of accepting an explanation
that, in Collins's own words, lies "so plainly on the surface" (431).
Despite his sentimentalized claims about "the ever bright side" of
"human calamity" (431), Collins uses the bodily afflictions of Madonna
and Lavinia to represent the impaired condition to which Victorian

women are reduced by gender inequities, and thus it is not surprising that these female invalids do not simply bear their afflictions patiently and cheerfully. Rather, they turn the tables on Valentine, "protecting" him from anxiety by preventing him from hearing of Madonna's nocturnal adventures downstairs (350–51), and using their handicaps to a subversive end: to resist the overprotective "kindness" that contributes to their disabled, feminine condition.

Collins first suggests the subversive potential of Madonna's deafness in the days that follow her injury, when she speaks with the "hoarse and low, and deep" voice that sounds like a man's and that leads Mrs. Peckover to think the young girl is "trying to imitate Mr. Jubber" (94). Although Madonna altogether ceases to speak with a voice that elicits only "shocked" and "frightened" responses (93), she continues to use her deaf muteness as an occasion to imitate men. Prevented by their handicaps—and by the dictates of female propriety—from attending Valentine's private exhibition of paintings in the studio below, Madonna entertains the painter's wife by "doing the visitors" (234), physically mimicking each of the guests as they arrive, and violating both gender and class boundaries in the process. Like the transgressive figure of the spiritual medium, possessed by the departed souls of both sexes and all social ranks,[8] the mute Madonna becomes male as well as female, working-class and aristocratic, by means of her mute pantomime—to the delight of the bedridden Lavinia:

Mrs. Blyth . . . smiled as she saw the girl puckering up her fresh, rosy face into a childish imitation of old age, bending her light figure gravely in a succession of formal bows, and kissing her hand several times with extreme suavity and deliberation. These signs were meant to indicate Mrs. Blyth's father, . . . whose old-fashioned habit it was to pay homage to all his friends among the ladies, by saluting them from afar off with tremulous bows and gallant kissings of the hand. . . .

While Mrs. Blyth was thinking about her father, Madonna signalised the advent of two more visitors. First, she raised her hand sharply, and began pulling at an imaginary whisker on her own smooth cheek—then stood bolt upright, and folded her arms majestically over her bosom. . . . The one represented Mr. Hemlock, the small critic of a small newspaper . . . The other pourtrayed Mr. Bullivant, the aspiring fair-haired sculptor. . . .

Close on the Dowager Countess followed a visitor of low degree. Madonna—looking as if she was a little afraid of the boldness of her own imitation—began chewing an imaginary quid of tobacco; then pretended to pull it suddenly out of her mouth, and throw it away behind her. It was all over in a moment; but it represented to perfection Mangles, the gardener. (232–33)

Gallantly kissing her hand to the ladies, pulling her whiskers, and chewing her tobacco, Madonna parodies a host of masculine behaviors and objectifies the very men who treat her as a beautiful feminine object. Her clever pantomime debunks the idea of natural and ineradicable sexual distinctions, an idea that Valentine promotes in the painting his visitors have come to see: *Columbus in Sight of the New World.* In this painting, Valentine celebrates the masculine conquest of a "tawny" female "Genius of America," who willingly submits to "her great discoverer" (239). The painter makes her subordination appear natural by aligning sexual with racial differences and invoking conceptions of imperial progress.

Rather than endorsing this analogy, however, and the natural subordination of women, Collins provides female versions of Blyth's "manful" explorer, whose highly developed "muscular condition" and "bursting . . . Biceps" are the subject of the painter's studio talk (241). Describing Mat Grice's adventures in South America, Collins refers to the Amazons, a domineering race of female warriors (188), and he represents Miss Florinda Beverley, a circus performer, as an "Amazonian Empress of Equitation" (55) as well as a "Conquering Hero" (58). The "imperial legs" (58) of this Amazon bear comparison with the muscular arms of Blyth's Columbus and suggest that women are as naturally capable of conquest and domination as men.

In *Hide and Seek,* Collins develops the theme of womanly domination in a domestic rather than an imperial context—through his treatment of the matrilineal and his suggestion that mothers may have a greater claim to their children than fathers do. Collins sets little Mary's birth and subsequent adoptions between 1828 and 1838, the decade immediately preceding passage of the first Infant Custody Act (1839), which modified the absolute rights of fathers to their children by enabling mothers to appeal for custody to the Court of Chancery. Despite his absolute right to little Mary, however, "Arthur" does not know of his daughter's birth and learns of her existence only to waive his paternal rights to her. In the absence of her father, little Mary is given to her foster mother, Martha Peckover, by her birth mother, Mary Grice, as a third woman, Peggy Burke, serves as witness (85). After Mary's death, these women tell the local clergyman that "the child's not to be took away" (86). As Mrs. Peckover explains, "having suckled the baby myself, and kissed its mother before she died, I couldn't make up my mind to the chance of its being took away from me . . . I know no more who its father is now than I did then. And glad I am that he's never come forward—though, perhaps, I oughtn't to say so" (87–88).

But while "Arthur Carr" never comes forward to claim his daughter, Valentine Blyth does, and Collins treats his benevolence ambiguously. On the one hand, Mary's adoption by Valentine satisfies the patriarchal logic invoked by Collins at the outset of the novel, according to which children must move from mothers to fathers in order to develop properly. But on the other hand, her second adoption is a coercive act that reveals the power an affluent gentleman wields over a working-class woman. Told that Valentine "*must* take the child home with [him]" (101), and "invited" to give her up by the rector Dr. Joyce, Mrs. Peckover has little choice in the matter. Neither does little Mary, whose intended use by the painter—to reconcile his wife to her hard lot—further complicates his "honourable" intentions (101). Devoting himself to "the sacred preservation of her purity," and "defending" her with "watchful kindness" (105), Valentine unwittingly incarcerates his adopted daughter in the same domestic prison occupied by his wife. Renaming her, he places her among the gentle beauties of patriarchal tradition.

However, Mrs. Peckover refuses to call little Mary by her new name, and Collins leaves us with the sense that the identity Valentine constructs for his adopted daughter is just that—a construction. Lacking any legal right to Madonna, Valentine suppresses her history and lives in "morbid dread that [she] might be one day traced and discovered by her father, or by relatives, who might have a legal claim to her" (122). His fears are realized by means of Mrs. Peckover, whose unwillingness to forget the dead mother leads to Madonna's discovery by her "mother's brother" (379). Mat Grice, who is Madonna's sole surviving relation on her mother's side, differs from Valentine in respecting rather than distrusting Mrs. Peckover. His gratitude to her reflects the value he places on the maternal. He settles his property on Mrs. Peckover in recognition of her mothering, explaining that "she earned it from Mary's brother, the day she stopped and suckled Mary's child by the road-side" (421).

At first glance, Mat's alliance with Martha Peckover seems unlikely. Judging from his pioneering experiences in the wilds of North and South America, and his physical resemblance to Blyth's Columbus, one would expect him to befriend Madonna's adoptive father rather than her foster mother. Despite his rough-hewn masculinity, however, Mat Grice—like his niece and his sister—proves to be a transgressive figure who belongs to opposing social categories and thus serves to undermine them. When Mrs. Peckover meets the dying Mary Grice, she comments on the ambiguity of her class status: "We saw somehow that she was a lady—or, if she wasn't exactly a lady, that no workhouse was proper for her, at any rate" (80). "So like a lady" (82)—yet "only a dressmaker," as her new friends discover (83)—Mary and her seeming gentility leave us with the sense that such categories are inadequate, approximations or similes at best.

The identity of Mat Grice seems equally ambiguous: he is a "Hercules" (324) who speaks for the matrilineal; an English adventurer and pioneer characterized by "barbarism" and "Moorish" otherness (181) and associated with the subjugated female "Genius of America" as well as the figure of Columbus. When representing Mat's relationship to Valentine, Collins compares him to the Native American squaw well known for her resistance to white settlement and control. To overpower the painter and steal his key to the bureau in which he hides Mary's bracelet, Mat serves him a potent concoction known as "Squaw's Mixture," playing on Valentine's mistaken belief in female weakness and native subordination when persuading him to drink (304–5). In a novel that describes the elaborate stratifications of the English class system, Mat is both wealthy and working class. Stealing into the Blyths' home in his search for evidence, he appears to violate its sanctity, aligning himself with a grotesque "hunchback" from the criminal underworld in order to duplicate Valentine's key and accomplish his ends (323). Yet he discovers that the members of the middle class have an underworld of their own. Like Sergeant Cuff, the working-class detective in *The Moonstone,* Mat Grice investigates his social superiors—the Blyths as well as the Thorpes—and finds them wanting. Uncovering their secret moral lapses, he challenges the logic of the class system.

In his next novel, *The Dead Secret,* Collins again creates an amateur detective whose investigation disrupts social boundaries, and whose own transgressions become the subject of the story. Conflating the traits of Mat Grice with those of Madonna, Collins introduces his first female detective, an illegitimate child who uncovers the secrets of her own past, and in so doing undermines the concepts of womanly subordination and class identity.

The Dead Secret (1857)

Collins started working on *The Dead Secret* in the spring of 1856, when he read a "sketch of the plot" to Dickens and discovered that "even *he* could not guess what the end of the story was, from the beginning": "He prophesies that I shall get more money and more success with it than I have got by anything else I have done," Collins told his mother in April.[9] The first of his novels to appear in serialized form, in Dickens's weekly journal *Household Words, The Dead Secret* began its half-year run on 3 January 1857 and was published in book form in June by Bradbury and Evans.

Divided into six books, *The Dead Secret* tells the story of Sarah Leeson, lady's maid to Mrs. Treverton, the wife of a navy captain. The novel begins in 1829, as the dying mistress calls Sarah to her room at Porthgenna Tower, the Trevertons' Cornwall estate. As Mrs. Treverton dictates a confession to her maid, we learn of a secret she has kept from the captain, one that concerns their young daughter, Rosamond, and in which Sarah is somehow an accomplice. Threatening to haunt Sarah after death unless she does her bidding, Mrs. Treverton makes her maid swear not to destroy the confession or to remove it from Porthgenna Tower, but dies before she can exact Sarah's oath to give it to the captain. Adding her own statement to the paper, Sarah hides it in the Myrtle Room of the uninhabited north wing. Leaving a note for the captain, in which she admits to keeping a secret from him, Sarah flees. After visiting the nearby grave of a miner, Hugh Polwheal, she travels to the home of her uncle Joseph, and he helps her to escape from Cornwall undetected.

The main narrative opens in 1844, with the marriage of Rosamond Treverton to Leonard Frankland in Long Beckley. Their marriage is privately performed by the vicar because of the groom's blindness, and Captain Treverton is the only witness. An old friend of Leonard's father, the captain sold Porthgenna Tower to the elder Mr. Frankland soon after his own wife's death rather than offering it to his misanthropic younger brother, Andrew Treverton, from whom he is estranged. Leonard has inherited the estate from his father. At the urging of his bride, he plans to repair its north rooms and take up residence there.

After Captain Treverton drowns at sea later that year and Rosamond inherits his fortune, the couple delay their trip to Cornwall. They finally set out for Porthgenna in May 1845, but their journey is interrupted when the pregnant Rosamond goes into labor en route and gives birth to a son. Attended by Mr. Orridge, Rosamond remains in confinement in West Winston, when her nurse becomes ill. At the recommendation of the local squire's wife, Mrs. Jazeph assumes the duties of Rosamond's nurse. In the figure of Mrs. Jazeph, strongly interested in Rosamond and her baby, the reader recognizes the former Sarah Leeson. Learning of

Rosamond's plans to live at Porthgenna Tower and to repair the north rooms, Mrs. Jazeph warns her to *"keep out of the Myrtle Room."*[10] Concluding that her new nurse is mad, Rosamond summons her husband to her room, and Mrs. Jazeph is dismissed. Only later do Leonard and Rosamond associate Mrs. Jazeph with the mysterious Sarah Leeson, of whom Rosamond was told by her father. Anticipating that she will visit Porthgenna, the couple instruct their housekeeper to admit her, but to watch her carefully, and they plan to follow as soon as Rosamond can travel, locating and searching the Myrtle Room themselves.

As predicted, Sarah arrives at Porthgenna with her uncle Joseph and requests a tour. She slips away from the housekeeper and steward, hoping to retrieve the confession, but faints before she can do so. It is thus left for Rosamond to find the document and learn that she is the illegitimate child of Sarah Leeson and Hugh Polwheal, a posthumous baby claimed by the childless Mrs. Treverton in order to retain her husband's love. Telling Leonard of her discovery, and returning her fortune to Andrew Treverton, to whom it rightfully belongs, Rosamond locates her ailing birth mother and is reunited with her shortly before the woman's death. Learning that Rosamond is not the daughter of his brother and his sister-in-law, a woman he detested, Andrew Treverton gives her back Captain Treverton's fortune. The novel concludes with Sarah Leeson's burial at Porthgenna, and with Leonard's praise of his illegitimate but truthful wife.

Recalling *Hide and Seek* while also reworking it, *The Dead Secret* is a novel in which an amateur detective investigates a family secret, only to discover her own illegitimacy. What seems most surprising about the revelation in the later novel is that it makes little difference in the outcome of the story. Identified as the daughter of unwed, working-class parents, Rosamond keeps the fortune she inherited when Captain Treverton died intestate and, as Leonard's wife, remains mistress of Porthgenna Tower. In *Hide and Seek,* the revelation that Mr. Thorpe is "Arthur Carr" forces him into hiding and prevents the romance between Madonna and Zack from developing, since their relationship is identified as an incestuous one. But in *The Dead Secret,* Sarah Leeson has been hiding since the beginning of the story, and the truth about Rosamond does not alienate the heroine from her husband, a man characterized by his class pride; instead, it provides him with an important "lesson": "The highest honors," he tells his wife, "are those which no accident can take away—the honors that are conferred by Love and Truth" (359). Read with these final words in mind, *The Dead Secret* seems to deliver an explicit social message—that one's class rank should be a matter of merit rather than birth, since birth is an "accident" that says little about one's character or value. While Collins appears to retain his faith in class differences, he redefines the grounds of gentility to account for and reward the noble nature of characters like Rosamond.

Yet Collins's revaluation of class categories is more complex and far-reaching than the novel's final lines suggest. Instead of supporting the concept of a meritocracy, Rosamond's detective work reveals the instability of class lines and social identities, whether these are determined by birth or by merit. While Rosamond herself continually violates class boundaries in the course of her investigation, she also uncovers situations in which masters and servants have exchanged places without being detected, treating their social positions as mere constructions—a matter of outward appearances rather than inner worth.

Married to a man conscious of his elevated class position, and "given to overrate the advantages of birth and the importance of rank" (60), Rosamond continually violates Leonard's sense of class boundaries in the course of her investigation, and Collins uses her behavior to highlight the democratic bent of the Victorian detective, who draws from all available sources in her search for truth. "Surely, we have all got very much the same feelings, whether we are high or whether we are low," Rosamond remarks (71).[11] Leonard repeatedly accuses his wife of being "too familiar" with her inferiors (70, 241), and he reprimands her for "trafficking" with Mr. Shrowl, the servant of Andrew Treverton, who offers to sell them a copied plan of the north rooms: "It is out of the question to traffic with a servant for information that has been surreptitiously obtained from his master's library," he tells her (252).

Yet Collins discredits Leonard's view by reminding us that gentility itself can be bought and sold. Rather than inheriting Porthgenna Tower, Leonard's father purchased it because he desired the prestige associated with a landed estate, having made his own fortune by trade: his "great ambition was to sink the merchant in the landed grandee, and to leave his son to succeed him in the character of a squire of large estate and great county influence" (55). Collins complicates matters further by representing this tradesman as a figure descended from "landed gentry of importance," who lost their class status and wealth during the English Civil War (55). Collins thus reminds us that class boundaries are continually subject to historical, political, and economic redefinition.

While the elder Mr. Frankland "metamorphose[s] himself from a plain merchant into a magnificent landed gentleman" (56), Mrs. Treverton accomplishes the reverse in her plot to present Rosamond to the world as her own daughter. Sarah Leeson conceives her child before her marriage banns are published and is left a single woman when Hugh Polwheal is killed in the mines. To save her servant from shame, and to provide her own husband with the child he longs for, Mrs. Treverton proposes that she and the pregnant Sarah travel north and exchange places on the way. Waiting upon her own lady's maid, she assumes the role of "a fine, buxom, comely servant-woman," supplying Sarah with "good linen" and herself with "coarse": "You are the married lady, Mrs. Treverton, and I am your maid who waits on you, Sarah Leeson," she tells her servant (327). In staging this successful masquerade, the two women do not simply obscure their class identities. Instead, like the elder Mr. Frankland, they collapse the distinction between social masquerades and social realities. While Mrs. Treverton is identified as the gentlewoman in the novel, she works as an actress before her marriage, and her class origins remain unknown; Sarah Leeson, although working-class, has the natural "grace" associated with gentility (23). "Quiet," "delicate," and "lady-like," characterized by "extreme propriety and neatness" (172), her imposture seems oddly convincing and apt. "Few men, at first sight of [Sarah], could have resisted the desire to find out who she was," the narrator notes, and "few would have been satisfied with receiving for answer, She is Mrs. Treverton's maid" (8).

In the midst of the social inversions that characterize *The Dead Secret,* and the conflicting definitions of class that it presents, one thing seems clear—the fixity of sexual difference. When the housekeeper of Porthgenna Tower catches her first glimpse of Sarah Leeson, a stranger whose class identity is ambiguous, she nonetheless categorizes her as "a woman"—that much "at least" appears to be self-evident: "There is a stranger waiting at the door at this very moment! a lady! or, at least, a woman—and dressed neatly, dressed in dark colors!" (174). At various points in the novel, Collins and his characters fall back on the categories of sexual difference, relying on their explanatory power in the face of class uncertainties. While Sarah's genteel traits conflict with her working-class status, her timidity and helplessness are explained by and heighten her femininity: "The trouble and fear in her voice, as she spoke, seemed to add to its sweetness; the agitation of her manner took nothing away from its habitual gentleness, its delicate, winning, feminine restraint" (10).

Rosamond herself invokes another type of female weakness—female curiosity—to explain her role as the novel's detective. "How can you doubt what will happen next?" she asks her husband: "Am I not a woman? And have I not been forbidden to enter the Myrtle Room?" (135). Rosamond's success as a detective, like her curiosity, is markedly "feminine" and illustrates "the marvelous minuteness of a woman's observation" (248), the "womanlike" manner of "looking . . . straight on to the purpose she had in view, without wasting a thought on the means by which it was to be achieved" (252).

But although Collins uses Sarah's timidity and Rosamond's curiosity to demonstrate their quintessential womanhood, he also uses these traits to subvert such categorizations—to show how these presumably natural characteristics are produced by the women's oppression. For example, he attributes Sarah's chronic fear and helplessness to the domestic tyranny she endured as the wife of Mr. Jazeph, not simply to the idealized gentleness of her womanly nature: "He followed me, he frightened me, he took away from me all the little will of my own that I had. He made me speak as he wished me to speak, and go where he wished me to go" (149). At the same time, Collins suggests that Rosamond's curiosity is a defense mechanism of sorts, one that enables her to resist such treatment. Restricting the new mother to her room for weeks after she gives birth, Rosamond's doctor and her husband infantilize her in the interests of her well-being. "Leaving [her] in quiet," they "expatiate on the evils of over-excitement," darkening her chambers and discouraging her from talking: "As soon as she has quieted the baby, she ought to go to sleep," her doctor warns (120). Rejecting such advice, and escaping her incarceration, the curious Rosamond violates codes of feminine propriety. Interviewing and investigating her fellow characters, she relegates her infant to a servant's care in the nursery while she pursues her "voyage of discovery" in the manner of a male explorer (242).[12]

Treating the idea of women's constitutional weakness as a medical misconstruction, Collins includes a number of male invalids in his novel, suggesting that men are as subject to physical infirmity as their mothers, wives, and daughters. Collins characterizes Mr. Phippen, a friend of the vicar, as "A Martyr to Dyspepsia" (39) and describes his palpitations and "shattered" nerves (58), and he represents Leonard Frankland as a man with "great constitutional weakness," whose "delicacy" ultimately manifests itself in blindness (45–46). In effect, Collins uses Leonard's invalid condition to invert the traditional relation between husband and wife. His blindness makes possible Rosamond's gender transgressions, by placing the husband in a subordinate and wifely position of dependence.

When Collins first describes the couple on their way to be married, he focuses on the "inexplicable" helplessness of the bridegroom (37), and the autonomy it grants to the bride: "Instead of holding the gate open for the lady to pass through, he hung back, allowed her to open it for herself, [and] . . . allowed her to lead him through the entrance, as if he had suddenly changed from a grown man to a helpless little child" (37). Ostensibly, Rosamond treats her husband's blindness as a call to increased wifely vigilance and duty—when, for example, the couple first enter the Myrtle Room, and she watches his "vain attempt . . . to guess at the position in which he was placed": "the mute appeal which he made so sadly and so unconsciously to his wife's loving help, . . . recall[ed] her heart to the dearest of all its interests, to the holiest of all its cares" (259). But while Rosamond refuses to hear Leonard talk "as if there was any . . . superiority in [her] position over [his]" (263), her husband's handicap allows her to appropriate his powers and determine what he does and doesn't know. "I am but a helpless adviser," her husband concedes after they enter the Myrtle Room: "I must leave the responsibilities of decision, after all, to rest on your shoulders" (263). Although she promises to see for her blind husband, and let her eyes "serve for both" (64), Rosamond *speaks* for him as well—as his "mute appeal" in the Myrtle Room suggests. Reprimanding the landlady's daughter for spying on the newlyweds, Rosamond tells her to "fetch the bill" in terms that make her ventriloquism clear: "We give you warning. Mr. Frankland gives you warning—don't you, Lenny? . . . Mr. Frankland says he won't have his rooms burst into, and his doors listened at by inquisitive women—and I say so too" (68).

Having found the confession, however, Rosamond tells her husband of it rather than keeping him in the dark. Although she considers destroying it without telling Leonard of its contents, and has "the power of keeping it a secret from her husband with perfect impunity," she overcomes this "fearful temptation," and in so doing restores her husband to his proper place as her guide and comforter (280, 284). With this turn in his plotline, Collins reinscribes the sexual differences and the gender roles he suspends or inverts in earlier scenes. A reformed Rosamond notes her inability to think like a man, asserting that women are "not competent to decide" questions that involve "a man's nature" (280), while Leonard asserts his property rights as her husband, reminding her that she cannot return her fortune to Andrew Treverton without his consent: "My consent, as your husband, is necessary, according to the law, to effect this restitution. If Mr. Andrew Treverton was the bitterest enemy I had on earth, . . . I would give it back of my own accord to the last farthing—and so would you!" (289). As Leonard exhibits his new-found ability to "speak for [Rosamond] as well as for [him]self" (353), his wife willingly accepts her revised role in mute submission, "look[ing] at him admiringly [and] in silence" (289).

Like *The Dead Secret, The Law and the Lady* reveals the "ideological doubleness" of Collins's fiction, presenting us with a female detective, but one who marries and gives birth in the course of the story, ultimately resigning her investigative role and returning to her place at her husband's side. Yet while Rosamond Frankland subordinates her duties as wife and mother to her detective work for much of *The Dead Secret*, only to realize the error of her ways at its end, Valeria Macallan manages to combine these two functions in the later novel. Heralding a "new generation" of women, Collins's heroine rejects the advice of her male relations by reopening a murder case tried three years before her own story begins, investigating the evidence and the witnesses for herself, and threatening to become a "lawyer in petticoats."[13] But she does so in order to be a "good wife": because her own husband is the accused party, and their domestic happiness depends on his exoneration. As Mr. Play-more, a Scottish lawyer, tells her, "it is a duty towards Justice, as well as a duty towards your husband, to bring the truth to light" (356–57).

The Law and the Lady (1874–1875)

Collins wrote *The Law and the Lady* in 1874, after returning to London from a seven-month reading tour in the United States, and nearly two decades after *The Dead Secret* was first published. In June 1874 he told his friend Charles Ward that he had borrowed "a copy of the Trial" from William Tindell, his solicitor and agent[14]—presumably referring to the Scottish trial of the alleged poisoner Madeleine Smith, upon which he draws in the novel. *The Law and the Lady* was serialized in the *Graphic,* a weekly illustrated newspaper, from 26 September 1874 to 13 March 1875, during which time Collins and his publishers had a serious dis-agreement. When Arthur Locker, the literary editor of the *Graphic,* took offense at what he perceived to be Collins's representation of a sexual assault, and deleted portions of a paragraph from the manuscript with-out Collins's permission, his unauthorized censorship led to an exchange of hostilities. Forced to print the original passage in a subsequent issue, in accordance with the terms of Collins's contract, the newspaper's own-ers did so reluctantly, and they ultimately disavowed the novel—"not

one which we should have voluntarily selected to place before our readers," they asserted in a note to the last number.[15] This statement led, in
turn, to rebuttals by Collins and his friend Edmund Yates in the *World*.
Yates accused the publishers of violating "the rules . . . [of] literary courtesy" by attacking their author after profiting from his work, and
Collins attributed the impropriety of which he stood accused to his editor and publishers. "Simmering together in a moral miasma of their own
dirty raising," Collins claimed, they misread his novel, "plac[ing] a nasty
interpretation" on a "perfectly innocent passage" and mistaking a character's attempt to *kiss* his heroine for an "attempted violation" of her.[16]

With its striking mixture of the conventional and the transgressive,
The Law and the Lady invites such interpretive conflicts. The novel
begins by describing the London wedding of Valeria Brinton and
Eustace Woodville, in a private church ceremony performed by Valeria's
uncle Starkweather, a north-country vicar, and witnessed by her aunt
and her elderly friend Benjamin, "the faithful old clerk" (8) of her dead
father. The wedding is overshadowed by a number of ominous signs: by
the absence of Eustace's mother, who refuses to sanction the marriage;
by the disapproval of Valeria's aunt and uncle, who receive an unsatis-
factory character reference for Eustace from a mutual acquaintance,
Major Fitz-David; by Eustace's attempt to release Valeria from her
engagement in consequence, an offer she strenuously rejects; and by the
mistake she makes after the ceremony, when she signs the marriage register under her "married instead of [her] maiden name" (8).

On her honeymoon in Ramsgate, Valeria discovers a photograph of
Eustace's mother in a hidden compartment of his dressing case and then
accidentally meets the woman on the beach. From their encounter, Valeria learns that her husband has married her under a false name, but neither he nor his mother, Mrs. Macallan, provides her with a satisfactory
explanation of his reasons for doing so. Instead, her mother-in-law
expresses pity for Valeria, while warning her to remain satisfied with her
husband's love, and "abstain from attempting to know more than you
know now" (43), advice that Eustace himself reiterates: "A good wife
should know better than to pry into affairs of her husband's with which
she has no concern" (54).

But Valeria finds her state of ignorance unendurable and resolves to
discover the secret that her husband is keeping from her. Visiting Major
Fitz-David, her husband's friend, she soon makes her painful discovery.
Given permission to search the library in the Major's house, assured that
the clue can be found there, Valeria proceeds in her investigation, but

she is ultimately enlightened by Miss Hoighty, the Major's protégée, who hands her a volume of trials. When Valeria learns from the title page that her husband was tried for the alleged poisoning of his first wife at Gleninch, their Scottish estate, she faints. Told that his wife has discovered his secret, Eustace leaves her, declaring that Valeria's discovery "has fatally estranged [her] from him" (99). Although Valeria has complete faith in his innocence, Eustace believes that she will soon begin to distrust him if they continue living together, since the Scottish verdict of "Not Proven" failed to fully exonerate him.[17]

Valeria soon realizes that, to save her marriage, she must reopen her husband's murder case and prove his innocence: "What the Law has failed to do for you, your Wife must do for you" (116). To the dismay of her relations and friends, who fear she will become a "lawyer in petticoats" (121), she reads the report of the trial, pursues new leads, and repeatedly interviews Miserrimus Dexter, one of the key witnesses in her husband's defense. A "deformed" and legless figure—"literally the half of a man" (173)—Dexter responds to her inquiries with a mixture of aggression and hysteria. While confirming Valeria's mistaken suspicions of Eustace's cousin, the widow Mrs. Beauly, Dexter himself excites the suspicion of Mr. Playmore, the Scottish lawyer whom Valeria consults and to whom she describes her strange interviews with the "half-man" (179). Based on certain details that Dexter lets slip, Mr. Playmore and Valeria realize that he knows more of the first "Mrs. Eustace" and her death than he will admit: that he was in love with Sara and secretly hated Eustace; that he showed Sara entries from her husband's diary, in which Eustace expressed repugnance for his wife and love for Mrs. Beauly; and that he entered Sara's bedroom soon after her death, stealing and ultimately disposing of a letter she wrote to Eustace on her deathbed.

In the midst of her investigation, Valeria is called to the sickbed of Eustace, badly injured while working as a Red Cross volunteer in Spain. She nurses her husband back to health with the help of her mother-in-law, who advises her to remain at Eustace's side. Valeria reluctantly agrees, "saying adieu to the one cherished ambition" of her life (312)— attaining proof of her husband's innocence. But she reverses her decision almost immediately, when she realizes that she is pregnant, resolved to vindicate her husband's good name for the sake of their child.

Returning to London and obtaining one last interview with Dexter, Valeria gathers evidence that leads to the discovery of Sara Macallan's missing letter, which Dexter tore into fragments and the housemaid

deposited in the dustheap at Gleninch. As the remorseful Eustace makes
his way back to England, Valeria is once again called to his bedside and
forced to resign her role in the investigation. But her work is carried on
by Benjamin and Mr. Playmore, who piece together Sara Macallan's
torn confession with the help of a chemist from London and realize that
she committed suicide. Already consuming small doses of arsenic in the
hope of improving her "muddy, blotchy" complexion (130), Sara
explains in her letter, she despairs of her husband's love and decides to
take a lethal dose. She leaves her letter where Eustace will find it, but
because Dexter steals and suppresses it, her husband is accused of her
murder.

Assisted by Benjamin and Mr. Playmore, Valeria possesses indisputable evidence of her husband's innocence and tells him of his first
wife's suicide and his own vindication. But she urges him to leave Sara's
confession unread and sealed for his own well-being, and out of respect
for the memory of his first wife, and to allow their children to make the
document public at some future date, if they see fit. The novel concludes
soon after the death of Dexter in a lunatic asylum, and the birth of Valeria's son, as Eustace accepts his wife's judgment, leaves "the seal of the
letter unbroken" (412), and hence agrees to remain in the dark.

In *The Law and the Lady,* Collins again uses his female detective to
explore conceptions of sexual difference and gender norms and to dramatize their construction and violation. He does so, in part, by bringing
Valeria into contact with the male invalid Miserrimus Dexter and by
having her investigate the fate of her bedridden predecessor, the first
"Mrs. Eustace." In *The Dead Secret,* Collins uses Leonard Frankland's
blindness to blur the distinction between feminine dependence and masculine guidance. In *The Law and the Lady,* he uses Dexter's physical
deformity to examine the grounds of male sexual identity and to raise
the question of what makes a man. Like Rosamond at the end of *The
Dead Secret,* Valeria conceptualizes the world in terms of sexual polarities,
defining the members of one sex against those of the other: "Women
alone can estimate what it cost me to be silent," she asserts. "And men
alone can understand how irritating my silence must have been" (52);
"A man in my place would have lost all patience, and would have given
up the struggle in disgust. Being a woman, and having my end in view,
my resolution was invincible" (65). At one and the same time, Dexter,
the "half-man," confirms these polarities and casts them in doubt, as
Collins defines and redefines his sexual status.

The initial portrait of Dexter, drawn from the record of Eustace's trial, reveals the complexities of his "many-sided . . . character" (326). "Gliding" through the crowded courtroom in his wheelchair,

> a strange and startling creature—literally the half of a man—revealed himself to the general view. A coverlid, which had been thrown over his chair, had fallen off during his progress through the throng. The loss of it exposed to the public curiosity the head, the arms, and the trunk of a living human being: absolutely deprived of the lower limbs. To make this deformity all the more striking and all the more terrible, the victim of it was—as to his face and his body—an unusually handsome, and an unusually well-made man. . . . Never had Nature committed a more careless or a more cruel mistake than in the making of this man! (173)

With "the eyes and hands of a beautiful woman" on a legless trunk of "manly proportions" (173), Dexter seems a grotesque and incomplete composite of male and female body parts. Yet his appearance signifies more than a "cruel mistake" on Nature's part, since his case is far from exceptional in the novel. On the contrary, all of the figures associated with Dexter exhibit some form of bisexuality. To Valeria's surprise, Dexter's "rough" gardener treats him with the "gentleness" of a woman (300), while Ariel, the female cousin who attends him, is easily "mistake[n] . . . for a man" (203). Ariel speaks with "a rough, deep voice," which Valeria "should certainly never have supposed to be the voice of a woman" (203), and is "clad in a man's pilot jacket" (210). Valeria can only "tell . . . that she [is] a woman" by means of her petticoat and hair comb (210), and even these clues to sexual identity, Valeria learns, can be deceptive. Dressed in pink silk for one of Valeria's visits, and adorned with gold bracelets, Dexter provides her with a brief history of male costume, explaining the extent to which categories of masculinity and femininity can overlap, depending on how they are constructed by particular cultures: "I have dressed, expressly to receive you, in the prettiest clothes I have. Don't be surprised. Except in this ignoble and material nineteenth century, men have always worn precious stuffs and beautiful colours as well as women. A hundred years ago, a gentleman in pink silk was a gentleman properly dressed" (232).

But while Dexter argues that gender norms are as changeable as fashions, his characterization also confirms traditional conceptions of sexual identity and is based, in part, on a physiological model of sexual difference—a model that opposes masculinity and femininity, according to the presence or absence of the organs unique to each sex.[18] Whether described as emasculated or hypersexual—and Collins describes him as both—Dexter confirms Valeria's belief in innately determined sexual differences. On the one hand, Collins associates Dexter's "effeminacy" and "hysteria" (208) with physical emasculation, leading us to suspect that the "absolute" absence of Dexter's legs signifies another, more private, deformity. On the other hand, Collins represents Dexter's attempts to intimidate and master Valeria as sexual assaults, attributing Dexter's will-to-power to male sexual aggression. During each of Valeria's interviews with Dexter, he physically "insults" his guest and takes "liberties" with her (299, 240), and she learns not to "trust . . . [her]self alone with him" (237): "He caught my hand in his, and devoured it with kisses. His lips burnt me like fire. He twisted himself suddenly in the chair, and wound his arm round my waist. In the terror and indignation of the moment, vainly struggling with him, I cried out for help" (299).

Like Dexter, Sara Macallan is an invalid whose portrait both confirms and undermines traditional conceptions of sexual identity. The crucial revelation of the novel—that Sara was not murdered by her husband but committed suicide—supports numerous stereotypes of female nature and is taken to illustrate the innate vanity and artfulness of women, and the way in which these traits imperil men. Arguing that Sara dosed herself with arsenic to improve her looks while hiding the fact from her husband, Eustace's lawyer defends his client by suggesting that Sara acted like a typical woman: "Is it in [our] experience of the sex, that a woman who is eagerly bent on making herself attractive to a man, would tell that man . . . that the charm by which she hoped to win his heart—say the charm of a pretty complexion—had been artificially acquired by the perilous use of a deadly poison? . . . And there you see her husband, in peril of his life, because a woman acted *like* a woman— as your wives, Gentlemen of the Jury, would, in a similar position, act towards You" (181).

But while Sara's artful behavior confirms stereotypes of female nature, it also reveals the destructive effects of the sexual double standard, which literally leads her to poison herself in an attempt to establish her worth. A woman who assumes male prerogatives by courting Eustace and following him to London (154–55), only to find herself married to a man who staunchly supports social proprieties, Sara becomes the inmate of Gleninch, which Valeria describes as "a prison" (286). Although Sara is not killed by her husband in any literal sense, she is destroyed by the ideals of feminine behavior that he enforces, with his "strait-laced" (267) insistence that his wife act "properly," suppress her anger and her sexual feelings, and "control [herself]" (129).[19] While he treats Sara, "a plain woman," as "the next worst thing . . . to a deformity" (380), he also uses her income to keep Gleninch "in splendour" because his own resources are "inadequate fitly to defray the expenses of living at his splendid country seat" (176). A woman with literary ambition, surrounded by writing materials, Sara composes poetry, but she is denied literary as well as economic agency and finds no audience or publisher for her works (130–31, 143). Thus it is not surprising that she is best remembered for "her temper"—"easily excited to fly into a passion, and quite reckless, in her fits of anger, as to what she said or did" (128).

Restrained and ladylike in her behavior, Valeria seems the reverse of Sara Macallan, yet Collins treats them as doubles throughout the novel. Sharing the same title, "Mrs. Eustace" (210, 330, 357), they also resemble one another in build, as Dexter and Mr. Playmore both note (216, 316). Even more to the point, both women occupy subordinate positions in their marriages and culture, and Collins uses Valeria to investigate the implications of Sara's fate as a woman and a writer—to examine, in particular, the issue of women's knowledge, its desirability, and its dangers. Subtitling the first book of his novel "Paradise Lost," Collins reworks Milton's epic in such a way that the wife's desire to know is justified. For Valeria, as for Milton's Eve, knowledge is forbidden, yet this prohibition seems unjust in Collins's novel, as virtually all the characters in the know agree. Eustace's mother refuses to attend her son's second wedding because he disregards her advice to tell Valeria about his past (66, 197), and the major considers it "monstrous" of Eustace "to expect that a woman placed in [Valeria's] situation will consent to be left for the rest of her life in the dark" (71). As Valeria herself explains when her husband tells her to "control [her] curiosity" and "know better than to pry," his secrecy places her in an "unendurable position":

> "Is it no concern of mine," I asked, gently, "when I find that my husband has not married me under his family name? Is it no concern of mine when I hear your mother say, in so many words, that she pities your wife? It is hard, Eustace, to accuse me of curiosity, because I cannot accept the unendurable position in which you have placed me. . . . Your cruel silence is estranging us from each other, at the beginning of our married life. . . . Oh, my darling, why do you trifle with our love and our confidence in each other? Why do you keep me in the dark?"
> He answered with a stern and pitiless brevity,

"For your own good."
I turned away from him in silence. He was treating me like a child. (54)

Valeria's desire to be enlightened does not stem, simply, from the unique and mysterious circumstances that surround her marriage to Eustace. As the terms of their marital dispute suggest, Valeria's curiosity, like Rosamond Frankland's, marks her resistance to infantalization as a woman and wife, and to the various constraints placed on her by the male characters in the novel. Although Collins does not foreground the issue of women's rights in *The Law and the Lady*, it informs the novel nonetheless, and Valeria's behavior is often taken as a threatening sign of her desire for equality, professional employment, and financial autonomy. Dismayed by the plans of his niece, the vicar angrily attributes them to her "conceit" and professional ambition—her desire to become a "lawyer in petticoats" (121)—while Benjamin associates them with the "new ideas" of a "new generation," in which women are content to live apart from their husbands or to remain unmarried (117, 321). Put on the defensive by Valeria's investigation, Dexter tells her that women will never "ris[e] equal to . . . men" because of their intellectual inferiority, whatever the changes in the law or in social institutions (246–47), and he reminds her that "ladies are not generally in the habit of troubling their heads about dry questions of law" (239).

Read in this context, Valeria's acts of detection signal her rebellion and allow her to subvert the restrictive gender norms and wifely constraints that indirectly led to the death of the first Mrs. Eustace. Enjoined to "subjection" by "the Marriage Service of the Church of England" (7)— unable to go for a walk or on household errands without her husband's permission (26, 44, 45)—Valeria begins to investigate Eustace even before she learns that he has married her under a false name—when, suffering from a feeling of "confinement" at the start of their honeymoon, she enters his dressing room, searches his dressing case, and discovers "a secret compartment for letters and papers" (24). Whether or not one's husband has an allegedly criminal past, Collins suggests, he will secrete much from his wife on the grounds of her innocence or incapacity. For this reason, Valeria's wifely ignorance and her suspicions of her husband make their relationship seem ordinary rather than exceptional. "On our way to London," Valeria observes, "nobody noticed us; nobody would have doubted that we had been married for years" (45).

In reopening her husband's murder case, and discovering his secrets, Valeria learns of the limits imposed on her by virtue of her sex, and simultaneously oversteps them, gaining the education and experience she has been previously denied. Valeria's discoveries often tell us more about herself than they do about her husband, providing us with proof of what she doesn't know—when, for example, she finds the broken vase that directs her attention to the bookcase in the major's library. Rather than demonstrating her expertise and her breadth of knowledge, in the familiar manner of a Sherlock Holmes, Valeria lists her subjects of ignorance when describing her find: "I was too ignorant of the subject to be able to estimate the value of the vase, or the antiquity of the vase—or even to know whether it was of British or of foreign manufacture. . . . Upon the space within one of the medallions was painted with exquisite delicacy a woman's head; representing a nymph, or a goddess, or per- haps a portrait of some celebrated person—I was not learned enough to say which" (81). Although Valeria does not gain a classical education in the course of her investigation, or learn about market values, she "turns her studies" to the law, a subject "sufficiently wide of the ordinary limits of a woman's thoughts and actions" to merit astonishment and disap- proval in those around her (243–44). "Are you surprised at the knowl- edge of the law which this way of writing betrays in an ignorant woman?" Valeria asks her husband in a letter:

> I have been learning, my dear: the Law and the Lady have begun by understanding one another. In plain English, I have looked into Ogilvie's Imperial Dictionary; and Ogilvie tells me: "A verdict of Not Proven only indicates that, in the opinion of the Jury, there is a deficiency in the evi- dence to convict the prisoner. A verdict of Not Guilty imports the Jury's opinion that the prisoner is innocent."—Eustace! that shall be the opin- ion of the world in general, and of the Scotch Jury in particular, in your case. To that one object I dedicate my life to come, if God spares me! (116)

As a result of her learning, Valeria turns the tables on her husband, placing him in the position of ignorance that she occupied at the outset of the novel. "Am I to know no more than I know now?" Eustace asks his wife near the conclusion (398). Using the same terms employed by men to justify their secrecy toward women, Valeria explains that Eustace must not read his first wife's letter to ensure his own "tranquility" (382)—she asks him to remain ignorant "out of compassionate regard for his own peace of mind" (410). Although the pregnant Valeria would seem to be the one who needs tranquility and rest, her prospective motherhood provides yet another reason for her to pursue her detective work—to protect their child's inheritance, and better "face the glorious perils of childbirth" (314). Adopting the role of benevolent protector generally assigned to husbands, Valeria tells Eustace to trust her and to believe that she is "doing [her] duty towards [him] . . . in making [her] request" (384), and he complies in order to "please" her (412).

Nonetheless, Collins suggests that Valeria's transgressive behavior and learning serve a conventional purpose, enabling her to "dedicate [her] life" (241) to her husband, and reach a traditional goal: a happy marriage. Despite her legal education, Valeria does not become a "lawyer in petticoats," but remains a dutiful wife whose gender transgressions provide the means of best serving her husband.[20] Her "dearest interests as a wife," she explains, depend on her ability to penetrate the mystery and discover the truth (37): "Nothing will bring him back to me—nothing will persuade Eustace that I think him worthy to be the guide and companion of my life—but the proof of his innocence . . . He, and his friends, and his lawyers all despair of ever finding that proof, now. But I am his wife; and none of you love him as I love him. I alone refuse to despair; I alone refuse to listen to reason" (241). Far from demanding equality with men or complaining of "the defective institutions of the age," as her "mistaken sisters" do (247), Valeria accepts her subordinate position. "Only a friendless woman," she hopes to "win back" her husband so that he can serve as her "guide" (241). While Valeria transgresses gender norms in her role as detective, her methods and her motives reinforce our sense of her ineradicable femininity. "There are signs that never deceive a woman," Valeria tells Mr. Playmore, "when a man is talking to her of what is really near his heart" (278).

Motivated by romantic love, guided by female intuition, and superior to reason, Valeria succeeds where men have failed by virtue of her sex. Instead of demonstrating women's promise as professionals, her success highlights the very traits associated with women's inferiority and dependence. "The light which the whole machinery of the Law was unable to throw on the poisoning case at Gleninch, has been accidentally let in on it, by a lady who refuses to listen to reason and who insists on having her own way" (277). While Valeria gathers the incriminating evidence against Dexter, she proves incapable of interpreting it, and mistakenly believes that it "set[s] interpretation at defiance" (349). When Mr. Playmore tells her that he "understand[s] perfectly what the words mean," she implores the Scottish lawyer to "make [her] understand them too," and he graciously complies (353). And when Valeria arrives at "right conclusions," she often does so by following her "jealous instinct" (90)—

because the best detective is "a woman who can watch her ['prey'] with the patience of a tigress in a state of starvation" (252).

To the extent that Collins exempts Valeria from such misogynistic stereotypes, he does so by virtue of her class identity—by underscoring her status as a respectable, middle-class woman. Although Valeria is credited with cracking the poisoning case, and although Mr. Playmore asserts that "but for her resolution, . . . we should never have seen so much as a glimmering of the truth" (381), her success as a detective is modest at best, and her inability to make important discoveries becomes the sign of her gentility. Indeed, most of the important revelations that lead Valeria to the truth are made by the working-class women with whom she associates, yet against whom she is defined. On the beach at Ramsgate, for example, Valeria notes that her mother-in-law fails to recognize the name Woodville, but only learns that her husband's surname is Macallan from her landlady. While Valeria remains "helpless" in her room, this second woman "degrades" herself by secretly following Eustace's mother back to her lodgings and making inquiries of the landlord there (39–40). Valeria benefits from her discovery, yet remains free from the taint of spying.

This pattern is repeated at Major Fitz-David's, when Valeria's dirty work is once again performed for her by a working-class woman. Valeria searches the major's library systematically, but before she can examine the bookcase, the major's mistress, Miss Hoighty, intrudes upon her with "coarse questions" and "uncultivated manners" (91), completing the search that "the lady" only begins. While Valeria watches, "helpless as a baby," Miss Hoighty retrieves and opens the volume of trials, which she has already read with relish "twice over" (92–93). Her unflinching response to the shocking story highlights Valeria's ladylike refinement. Merely glancing at the title page, Valeria is "swallowed up" by a "black swoon" (94), while Miss Hoighty remains fully conscious, shouldering the blame for procuring this forbidden knowledge. "Not one of the fainting sort" (97), she defends herself in terms that associate her detective powers with her sexual fall: "Didn't you tell me you were looking for a book?" she asks Valeria. "And didn't I present it to you promiscuously, with the best intentions?" (97).

Exempt from the "promiscuity" of knowledge in *The Law and the Lady*, Valeria learns the truth without moral taint, but she does so at the expense of Miss Hoighty and others—her working-class surrogates in the novel. In *The Woman in White* (1859–1860), *No Name* (1862–1863), and *Man and Wife* (1869–1870), Collins also examines class relations among women, representing a set of female doubles from different social classes in each one. But rather than emphasizing their moral differences, or using these working-class figures to maintain the purity of their social superiors, he establishes their largely common interests—as victims of English marriage law.

Chapter Four

Sensation Fiction and Marriage Law Reform: Wives and Property in *The Woman in White, No Name,* and *Man and Wife*

Although twentieth-century readers often identify Collins as the father of detective fiction, his contemporaries were more likely to associate him with a second, less reputable, subgenre: that of the "sensation novel." Applying this pejorative term to a host of novels written in the 1860s, critics speaking for the literary establishment labeled such works as *The Woman in White* "sensational" on two grounds—their scandalous revelations, which center on acts of adultery, bigamy, and domestic abuse; and the physiological effects these novels allegedly produced in readers, whose pulses were quickened and whose nerves were electrified with every new twist in the plotline. These effects were heightened, critics claimed, by the disturbing "proximity" of the stories, which domesticated and modernized the horror of Gothic fiction, bringing it home to Victorian England from medieval and Renaissance Italy. "Proximity is, indeed, one great element of sensation," Henry L. Mansel notes in an 1863 review. "It is necessary to be near a mine to be blown up by its explosion; and a tale which aims at electrifying the nerves of the reader is never thoroughly effective unless the scene be laid in our own days and among the people we are in the habit of meeting."[1]

A clergyman and Oxford don, Mansel wholeheartedly disapproves of sensation novels, which he considers "mere trash." Yet his judgment—like that of many Victorian critics—is based on a misunderstanding of the preoccupations and aims of sensation novelists. In Mansel's view, writers such as Collins merely desire to "electrify the nerves." His explanation is no more satisfying than that provided by a writer for the *Westminster Review,* who compares the "sensation mania" in literature to a "virus . . . spreading in all directions":

There is no accounting for tastes, blubber for the Esquimaux, half-hatched eggs for the Chinese, and Sensational novels for the English. Everything must now be sensational. . . . Just as in the Middle Ages people were afflicted with the Dancing Mania and Lycanthropy, sometimes barking like dogs, and sometimes mewing like cats, so now we have a Sensational Mania. Just, too, as those diseases always occurred in seasons of dearth and poverty, and attacked only the poor, so does the Sensational Mania in Literature burst out only in times of mental poverty, and afflict only the most poverty-stricken minds.[2]

But if sensation fiction is an "affliction" of sorts, it is symptomatic of something other than the "mental poverty" of mid-Victorian writers and readers. Products of the 1850s and 1860s, sensation novels dramatize marital strife and domestic horror within the middle-class Victorian home, which is itself diseased. Undermining the ideal of middle-class domesticity, they represent the private sphere as a place of Gothic strife and suffering rather than a healthy and harmonious refuge from the conflicts of public life. Out of "the commonest consideration for Lady Glyde's safety," Walter Hartwright notes in *The Woman in White,* she must be removed "at once from the place of all others that was now most dangerous to her"—"her own home."[3] Like Mrs. Henry Wood's *East Lynne* (1861) and Mary Elizabeth Braddon's *Lady Audley's Secret* (1862), Collins's sensation novels "burst out" during the 1850s and 1860s because these were the decades in which Victorians began to debate and reform the laws governing marriage and divorce in England, years in which the reading public became increasingly aware that domestic strife was endemic to their society, and that the victimization of wives by their husbands was a legally sanctioned phenomenon.[4]

The decade in which Collins published his first novels began with the appointment of a royal commission whose members were to consider the possibility of civil divorce in England. At that time, divorces were granted by the ecclesiastical courts and, on very rare occasions, in combination with a private act of Parliament, which then allowed those divorced to remarry. The Parliamentary investigation and debates that began in 1850 culminated in the Divorce and Matrimonial Causes Act of 1857, which established a civil divorce court in London, allowed husbands to divorce their wives on the grounds of adultery, and granted wives the right to divorce adulterous husbands if their adultery was compounded by cruelty, bigamy, incest, or bestiality.[5]

Equally Gothic material concerning middle-class husbands and wives was brought to the fore in the 1850s as liberal Members of Parliament

(M.P.s) attempted to reform the laws governing married women's property. Inspired by the notorious case of Caroline Norton, whose writings about the plight of wronged and disempowered wives helped sway public opinion, politicians began to question the common-law doctrine of coverture, the basis for a woman's loss of property rights upon marriage. According to the doctrine of coverture, a husband and wife were considered "one person"—that person being the husband. As Sir William Blackstone explains in his standard work of English jurisprudence, *Commentaries on the Laws of England* (1765–1769), "the very being or legal existence of a woman is suspended, or at least it is incorporated or consolidated into that of the husband, under whose wing, protection and cover she performs everything, and she is therefore called in our law a *feme covert*" (Holcombe, 25). Widows and single women had the same property rights as men, but wives did not; instead, they exchanged their property rights for the "cover" extended to them by their husbands. Under English common law in the mid-Victorian period, a man gained possession and control of his wife's earnings, her personal property, and whatever property she might inherit, upon their marriage. A wife retained legal possession of whatever "real property" (property in land) she brought to her marriage, since her husband could not dispose of it without her consent. But he was entitled to whatever income she might receive from it.

In theory, coverture provided wives with privileges and protection that unmarried women did not enjoy. But in practice, as Victorian feminists pointed out, it deprived wives of their freedom and autonomy and left them utterly dependent on their husbands, who might or might not choose to protect them in the manner described by common law. When a woman "unites herself to a man," Barbara Leigh Smith argued in her 1854 summary of English marriage laws, "she finds herself legislated for, and her condition of life suddenly and entirely changed. Whatever age she may be of, she is again considered as an infant . . . loses her separate existence, and is merged in that of her husband."[6]

Despite the efforts of Smith, Norton, and those M.P.s sympathetic to their cause, the first married women's property bill to be introduced into Parliament was defeated in 1856. Although a clause was added to the Divorce Act, stipulating that wives legally separated from their husbands were entitled to the same property rights as single women, wives who lived with their husbands were not granted a measure of financial autonomy, and given control of their own earnings, until the first Married Women's Property Act was passed in 1870.

In his sensation fiction, Collins responds to these debates over the institution of marriage and the respective rights of husbands and wives, and he does so in a characteristically mixed way. Reacting to the defeat of the married women's property bill in such novels as *The Woman in White* and *No Name*, he dramatizes the losses inflicted on his female characters when they become wives legally subject to victimization. At the same time, however, these works also express cultural anxieties about the sexual and economic autonomy granted to women by the 1857 Divorce Act, and they persistently represent adulteresses who threaten to disrupt patriarchal order by producing spurious heirs. Indicting the laws governing marriage, Collins demonstrates that women lose their property rights and their legitimacy when they marry, and undergo a type of "civic death."[7] But he also suggests that coverture may be a necessary evil, a means of providing for innately dependent women and counteracting the dangers of female emancipation.[8]

The Woman in White (1859–1860)

The Woman in White was the first of Collins's novels to be labeled "sensational"—indeed, the term was initially applied to Victorian fiction in an 1861 review of *The Woman in White* and *Great Expectations*.[9] Collins began working on what was to become his most famous book in the summer of 1859, after Dickens asked him to provide a novel for the newly launched *All the Year Round*. Dickens planned to publish it in weekly installments as soon as *A Tale of Two Cities* had ended. As events proved, the first installment of Collins's novel appeared alongside the final number of Dickens's, on 26 November. The last of the novel's 40 parts was published on 25 August 1860. By that time, it had become an immensely popular success, boosting the circulation of Dickens's journal to three times that of *Household Words*. Published in book form in August 1860, in a first printing of 1,000 copies, *The Woman in White* sold out on publication day. One of the most widely read novels in the Victorian period, it helped to establish Collins's reputation as "the ablest representative" of "the sensation school" of fiction.[10]

As a primary source for his novel, Collins used a volume of records of French crime that he bought in a Paris bookstall in 1856, Maurice Méjan's *Recueil des Causes Célèbres*, second edition (1808–1814). In particular, Collins drew from Méjan's account of the 1788 conspiracy against Madame de Douhault, the daughter of a marquise. The conspiracy was planned by her greedy brother, who wanted the money she had inherited from their father, and it robbed Madame de Douhault of her identity. Confined in a Parisian lunatic asylum under a false name, Madame de Douhault was presumed dead, and her estate was inherited by her brother and nephew. Although she was released from the asylum in 1789, Madame de Douhault never succeeded in proving her identity and regaining her property, and she died in poverty in 1817.

In *The Woman in White,* Collins adapts Méjan's account of crime in ancien régime France to his own contemporary purposes. He transforms a story of sibling rivalry on the verge of the French Revolution into a tale of marital oppression in England in the years 1849 and 1850. While retaining many of Méjan's details, he reworks his source material so that the conspiracy launched against Madame de Douhault by her brother becomes a conspiracy launched against Lady Glyde by her husband. Méjan's tale becomes the vehicle by which Collins considers the status of married women's property rights in England in the 1850s and dramatizes a wife's loss of legal identity under the rules of coverture.

Collins's story centers on the relationships that develop among six primary characters, three of whom serve as narrators in the novel: Walter Hartwright, a struggling drawing master; Laura Fairlie, the young heiress with whom he falls in love; Marian Halcombe, Laura's half-sister on her mother's side; Anne Catherick, Laura's illegitimate half-sister on her father's side; Sir Percival Glyde, the baronet to whom Laura is engaged; and Count Fosco, Sir Percival's closest friend. The novel opens in 1849, as Hartwright prepares to leave London for Limmeridge House in Cumberland, where he is to serve as drawing master to Laura Fairlie and Marian Halcombe. Late on the evening before his departure, as he walks back to London from Hampstead, Walter encounters a "strange" and "solitary" woman dressed in white, who claims to have "met with an accident" and asks for his assistance in reaching London (15–16). Ignorant of her identity and purposes, yet impressed by her helplessness, Hartwright complies; his interest in her is fueled by her "chance reference" to Limmeridge House, and her fond memory of the dead Mrs. Fairlie (19). Immediately after the two reach London and "the woman in white" disappears, Hartwright overhears two men in her pursuit and learns that she has escaped from a private lunatic asylum.

Once at Limmeridge House, Hartwright identifies the woman in white as Anne Catherick, a slow-witted woman in whom Mrs. Fairlie once took a kind interest because of Anne's striking resemblance to her own daughter Laura. While Walter, too, is struck by the "ominous likeness" between the two women, he can only account for it in the way

that Mrs. Fairlie had—as "one of those extraordinary caprices of acci-
dental resemblance which one sometimes sees" (51).

Hartwright is soon forced to leave Limmeridge House because of the
mutual attachment that has developed between himself and Laura.
Their relationship is perceived as hopeless on the grounds of class differ-
ence, but also because Laura is engaged to marry the baronet Sir Percival
Glyde, the man chosen for her by her father Philip before his death.
When Laura receives an anonymous note warning her not to marry Sir
Percival, a man "without pity and without remorse" (68), Walter and
Marian discover that it was written by Anne Catherick, and that Sir Per-
cival is the man responsible for her incarceration. Justifying his behavior,
Percival explains that he has sent Anne to the asylum for her own good,
as a favor to her mother. Laura, Marian, Walter, and the family lawyer
are all troubled by misgivings, and Laura tries to convince him to release
her from their engagement by confessing her love for another man.
Nonetheless, their marriage takes place in December 1849.

Laura soon discovers that Percival is, indeed, the sinister figure
described by Anne. Heavily in debt, he has married her for her money.
Sir Percival proves anxious to find Anne Catherick and return her to the
asylum because he believes she knows his secret, a mysterious fact that
he wishes to remain concealed. Jealous of Hartwright, he hires men to
persecute the drawing master, who takes refuge on an archaeological
mission to Honduras. Failing in his attempt to force Laura to sign a
document that would give him access to the trust money settled upon
her—a document that he will not allow her to read—Sir Percival
engages in a conspiracy with his friend Count Fosco to falsify her death
and inherit her estate. Percival will gain 20,000 pounds by staging her
death, and Fosco stands to inherit 10,000 through his wife, Eleanor,
Laura's aunt. As Marian lies ill with a fever she contracted while spying
on the two men and discovering their scheme, Percival and Fosco lure
Anne Catherick to London. Already ill of heart disease, she dies in
Fosco's home. Her death certificate falsely identifies her as Lady Glyde.
The real Lady Glyde travels to London the next day, where she is
drugged and admitted to the asylum under the name of Anne Catherick. Mentally shaken by her experiences, Laura escapes with Marian's
help; the two women are joined and supported by Walter upon his
return to England.

Walter soon finds that Laura's relations and friends believe her to be
Anne Catherick, since her sufferings have strengthened her resemblance
to the woman in white. Confronted with disbelief about Laura's identity,

Walter undertakes his own investigation: he finds that Anne was the
illegitimate daughter of Philip Fairlie and Jane Anne Catherick, and
hence Laura's half-sister; that Sir Percival is himself illegitimate, has
forged the record of his parents' marriage in the register of the Old
Welmingham Church, and has no claim to the estate or the title he
inherited from his father; and, finally, that Count Fosco is a traitorous
member of an Italian brotherhood dedicated to the liberation of Italy
from Austrian control, a spy whose death has been decreed by the patri-
ots he has betrayed. Imperiled by Walter's knowledge of his crime, Percival burns to death in an attempt to destroy the forged register. Soon
afterward, Walter and Laura marry. Threatening Fosco with exposure,
Walter forces the count to provide him with a signed narrative of the
conspiracy against Lady Glyde. Fleeing from England, Fosco is assassi-
nated by the brotherhood in Paris. With the evidence he has gathered,
Walter legally establishes his wife's identity, although her fortune has
been squandered. The novel concludes six months after the birth of their
first son, as Walter, Laura, and Marian prepare to move from their London lodgings to Limmeridge House, which Laura has inherited through
the death of her uncle Frederick.

Writing a novel about an Englishwoman's loss of identity and property in marriage, Collins begins his analysis of marriage law by addressing, more generally, the issues of gender relations and sexual difference.
Ostensibly, Collins intends the opening encounter between Walter
Hartwright and Anne Catherick to leave us wondering about Anne's
identity and her plight. Yet he uses their encounter to raise a larger
question central to this work: what right, if any, do men have to control
women?

Anne approaches Walter because she is a helpless woman who needs
aid in reaching London, knowing nothing of its geography or its ways:
"I have only been in London once before," she tells him, "and I know
nothing about that side of it, yonder. Can I get a fly, or a carriage of any
kind? Is it too late? I don't know" (17). Despite her helplessness, however, what Anne really desires from Walter is autonomy—freedom from
interference. "If you will only promise not to interfere with me," she
repeatedly implores him: "Only say you will let me leave you when and
how I please—only say you won't interfere with me. Will you promise?"
(17). Although Walter promises, he does so begrudgingly, troubled by
"self-distrust" and "something like self-reproach" (18), "distressed by an
uneasy sense of having done wrong" (21): "What could I do? Here was a
stranger utterly and helplessly at my mercy—and that stranger a forlorn

woman. No house was near; no one was passing whom I could consult; and no earthly right existed on my part to give me a power of control over her, even if I had known how to exercise it. I trace these lines, self-distrustfully, with the shadows of after-events darkening the very paper I write on; and still I say, what could I do?" (17).

While Walter characterizes as "ill-considered" his "promise to leave [Anne] free to act as she pleased" (22), his regret does not stem, simply, from his knowledge that she has escaped from a lunatic asylum. Indeed, he finds her "quiet and self-controlled" (15), and immediately suspects that she may be "the victim of the most horrible of all false imprisonments" (22). Rather, his "self-distrust" stems from his sense that, in promising not to interfere with her, he has failed in his duty as a man.[11] In declining to exercise his control over a helpless woman, Walter has, in effect, violated the gender norms of his day. According to these norms, as Collins satirically describes them, it is the job of men to confine women in the domestic sphere and to thwart their desires—to "say nay" to their wishes, as Anne's foster mother, Mrs. Clements, puts it (87). Instead of treating Anne as a special case, and representing her incarceration as necessary if unpleasant, Collins connects her to the other, healthy women in his novel, and he conflates the lunatic asylum from which she escapes with the imprisoning "asylum" of the home (316). Like Anne Catherick, Marian Halcombe desires independence, complaining that, as a woman, she has been "condemned to patience, propriety, and petticoats, for life" (178), and she praises Walter for "giving [Anne] her liberty": "she seems to have done nothing . . . to show herself unfit to enjoy it" (29). Subjected to her husband's control, Lady Glyde later echoes Anne's plea for autonomy: "I will sign with pleasure . . . if you will only treat me as a responsible being" (223).

Despite such pleas, the men in Collins's novel persistently exercise their right to control the members of the female sex, a right they base on the "natural unfitness" of women to make decisions and act as adults. "Women . . . are nothing but children grown up" (295), Count Fosco asserts, while Percival tells Laura that "others"—that is, her husband—must do her thinking for her (353). "I wait to be instructed . . . before I venture on giving my opinion in the presence of well-informed men," Countess Fosco tells Laura and Marian, after her advocacy of "the Rights of Women" is beaten out of her by her husband (210, 200).

Calling attention to the coercive and violent means by which women's subordination is achieved, Collins undermines ideas of their innate incapacity and dependence. Eroding the distinction between masculine and feminine traits, he undermines the justification for coverture. Indeed, virtually all of Collins's characters are sexual hybrids of a sort—either effeminate men or masculine women—and Walter's conventional beliefs about natural sexual difference continually prove inadequate to explain his experiences in the novel. Despite her helplessness, for example, Anne Catherick is "unwomanly" in Walter's view—unaccountably forward and aggressive in her behavior. She touches Walter's arm rather than calling to him and doesn't seem vulnerable or tearful enough to suit his tastes. When Anne thanks Walter for his help, and acknowledges his kindness, he describes "the first touch of womanly tenderness that [he] had heard from her," yet remains disappointed that she hasn't shed any tears (17).

Similarly, Walter finds Marian Halcombe an unwomanly woman, whose tears, like Anne's, "do not flow so easily as they ought" (147). Struck by "the rare beauty of her form"—"perfection in the eyes of a man"—he registers his surprise at her masculine features, which "flatly contradict" the "old conventional maxim, that Nature cannot err": "The lady's complexion was almost swarthy, and the dark down on her upper lip was almost a moustache. She had a large, firm, masculine mouth and jaw; prominent, piercing, resolute brown eyes; and thick, coal-black hair, growing unusually low down on her forehead. Her expression—bright, frank, and intelligent—appeared, while she was silent, to be altogether wanting in those feminine attractions of gentleness and pliability, without which the beauty of the handsomest woman alive is beauty incomplete" (25). Initially repelled by Marian's appearance, Walter attributes the "masculine form and masculine look of [her] features" to an error of nature. Yet Collins himself does not, since all of his characters appear both male and female, Walter included. While Walter views Marian as manly, Marian views Walter as womanly (51, 61), and she repeatedly urges him to act "like a man" (61). In explaining that he can "sigh over [his] mournful confession [of love] with the tenderest woman who reads it and pities [him]" and "laugh at it as bitterly as the hardest man who tosses it from him in contempt" (53), Walter calls these very distinctions into question.

So, too, do the other male characters in the novel, all of whom possess feminine traits. With small feet and hands, dressed with "womanish" accessories, Laura's uncle Frederick has "a frail, languidly-fretful, over-refined look," which Walter finds "singularly and unpleasantly delicate in its association with a man" (32). More importantly, Frederick suffers from "nerves," a disorder that Victorians found particularly troubling because it undermined sexual distinctions and brought its male victims "perilously close to the feminine condition."[12] "I am nothing but a bundle of nerves dressed up to look like a man," Frederick confesses (319). Like Laura's uncle, Walter repeatedly complains of his "nerves" (139), and Sir Percival seems "almost as nervous and fluttered, every now and then, as his lady herself" (350). Even Count Fosco, who prides himself on his ability to tame the female characters in the novel, is a sexually hybrid figure, "nervously sensitive" despite "his look of unmistakable mental firmness and power" (197). "As noiseless in a room as any of us women" (197), he "has all the fondness of an old maid for his cockatoo," and his "nerves are so finely strung that he starts at chance noises" (199). Marian repeatedly remarks on the count's "effeminate tastes and amusements" (200) and describes him as "a fat St. Cecilia masquerading in male attire" (205).[13]

Collins begins *The Woman in White* by claiming that the story of Laura and Walter will illustrate the sharp distinction between women and men: "This is the story of what a Woman's patience can endure, and of what a Man's resolution can achieve" (1). Having drawn this distinction, however, Collins proceeds to break it down, dramatizing the resolute behavior of his female characters. Despite her "womanly" sweetness and delicacy (54), Laura speaks both "patiently and resolutely" to her first husband and the count (153, 209), and when patience fails her, she becomes "resolute" (441). While Marian "tr[ies] to be patient" (415), she finds it easier to act "resolutely" (258, 264), and Count Fosco berates Sir Percival for failing to see that "Miss Halcombe . . . has the foresight and the resolution of a man" (296). While Collins's female characters demonstrate their resolve, his hero exhibits the virtues of manly patience: "I am not rash enough to measure myself against such a man as the Count before I am well prepared for him," Walter explains. "I have learnt patience; I can wait my time" (510).

At his most subversive moments, Collins disappoints the conventional expectations raised by his opening sentence and suggests that the differences between resolute men and patient women are merely constructions of an inequitable legal system. In so doing, he undermines the grounds on which men justified their protection of women. Developing his critique, he directs our attention to the two principal forms in which such protection was offered to Victorian wives—that of the marriage settlement, and of coverture itself—legal practices that work against each other, and thus discredit the authority and logic of the law.

For women of the middle and upper classes, the injustice of marriage law was mitigated by the practice of settling separate property on daughters, a costly expedient based on the law of equity. Drawn up by a lawyer, a woman's marriage settlement limited the common-law rights of her husband by stipulating that certain properties were to remain her own, under the management of a trustee. The separate property placed in trust for a married woman could include real or personal property of any kind and was overseen by the Court of Chancery.

In *The Woman in White*, Collins focuses considerable attention on the negotiations involved in drawing up Laura's marriage settlement, and he highlights the crucial importance of a wife's separate property to her future well-being. Twenty years old at the outset of the novel, Laura will inherit from her father's estate a trust worth £20,000 on her next birthday, in addition to a life interest in an additional £10,000, a sum that is to go to her aunt Eleanor, Count Fosco's wife, should Laura die first. She is also the heiress to the family property, with its annual income of £3,000. In negotiating Laura's marriage settlement, her lawyer, Vincent Gilmour, stipulates that her fortune is to be settled upon her, and the income from her personal and real property left at her disposal; that her husband is to inherit her income in the case of her death, and the principal to be left to their children, or to the parties she names in her will. "This was the clause," he explains, "and no one who reads it, can fail, I think, to agree with me that it meted out equal justice to all parties" (134).

Yet "equal justice" proves elusive for Laura Fairlie. Despite the fairness of Mr. Gilmour's stipulations, they are rejected by Sir Percival, who insists, through his lawyer, that Laura's fortune must go to him in the event of her death (135). To Gilmour, this "audacious proposal" reveals Sir Percival's "mercenary motive" in marrying the heiress (135). Nonetheless, when Gilmour appeals to Laura's legal guardian, her uncle Frederick, telling him that "Glyde has no shadow of a claim to expect more than the income of the money" and that "the money itself . . . ought to be under her control" (142), Frederick refuses to argue the point with Sir Percival. Laura's uncle forces the lawyer to sacrifice "the just rights of [his] niece, and of all who belong to her," although "it is against all rule to abandon the lady's money entirely to the man she marries" (142–43). Ironically, Laura's marriage settlement leaves her even more vulnerable than she would have been without it. Although the contract requires Sir Percival to obtain "his wife's permission" to use her income, it also gives him "an interest of twenty thousand pounds in [her] death" (143).

Rather than protecting Laura, her marriage settlement inspires the conspiracy against her, encouraging Sir Percival and the count to substitute the dead Anne Catherick for the living Lady Glyde in order to inherit her fortune. Blocking what Victorians generally considered a married woman's escape route from the inequities of common law, Collins highlights Laura's vulnerability and emphasizes the need for legal reform. At the same time, he criticizes the wife's protected status as a *feme covert* by staging the fictitious death of Lady Glyde. In robbing his wife of her identity, Sir Percival commits a crime that is punishable by law. Yet thefts similar to his, Collins astutely suggests, are legally sanctioned by coverture, and committed daily, every time an Englishwoman marries.

In staging Laura's death, Sir Percival and Count Fosco exhibit their own villainy; yet they also expose the criminality of the common law, which forces a woman to suffer a civic death upon her marriage, depriving her of her property rights and her legal personality.[14] As Count Fosco notes in describing his own marital relations, he and his wife "have but one opinion between us, and that opinion is mine" (219). Paraphrasing Blackstone, and repeatedly alluding to the principle of coverture in defense of his behavior, Fosco describes the figurative death sentence imposed on English wives by common law, and the "self-immolation" (570) demanded of them in what he ironically terms "the land of domestic happiness" (557): "I remember that I was married in England—and I ask, if a woman's marriage-obligations, in this country, provide for her private opinion of her husband's principles? No! They charge her unreservedly, to love, honour, and obey him. That is exactly what my wife has done" (570). Laura's identity, like that of her aunt Eleanor, is destroyed by virtue of her "marriage-obligations." As "the wife of Percival Glyde," she is "torn in her own lifetime from the list of the living" (380) and undergoes a fictitious and wrongful death long before Anne Catherick's death certificate is issued under her name—for, as Marian Halcombe observes, "writing of [Laura's] marriage" is equivalent to "writing of her death" (166).

In his treatment of Lady Glyde's death, Collins offers his readers a radical critique of Victorian marriage law. Yet he undermines the radical implications of his novel by suggesting that Laura's identity can be recovered through her second, happy marriage. According to the logic of Collins's central metaphor, Laura cannot regain her selfhood as long as she is a married woman. But having dramatized a wife's civic death under common law, Collins suggests, conversely, that Walter can help Laura recover her identity by marrying her—that he can "have her publicly received and recognised" for the person she really is, once she has become his wife (573). Assembling Laura's relatives, friends, and tenants at Limmeridge House toward the end of the novel, Walter describes the conspiracy launched against her and identifies her to the satisfaction of the crowd: "I was there present (I informed my hearers) to declare . . . that my wife, then sitting by me, was the daughter of the late Mr. Philip Fairlie" (576). Ostensibly, Walter reveals "Laura herself" to those assembled in this dramatic scene (577). Yet she is still identified solely in terms of others. No longer "Laura, Lady Glyde," she is now "my wife," and "the daughter of the late Mr. Philip Fairlie." Thus the scene in which Walter appears to strike "the last fetters of the conspiracy . . . off Laura herself" and to resolve the problem of her identity only mystifies it further—by concealing her fetters as his wife.

Indeed, Laura seems even more childlike and dependent in her second marriage than she was in her first, when she feared and resisted her husband. Carried in Walter's arms (577), and amused with "children's games" (401), Laura is infantalized, yet Collins renders her dependence on Walter palatable by suggesting that he covers her as a husband should: "She was mine at last! Mine to support, to protect, to cherish, to restore" (381). Whereas the mercenary Sir Percival robs Laura of her property by staging her death, Walter kindly recognizes her incapacity as a wage earner. When Laura expresses her wish to earn a living shortly before their marriage, and objects to being "treat[ed] . . . like a child" (441), Walter humors her desire for financial autonomy, encouraging her to draw, while noting that the artwork she produces has no market value:

> "You know that I work and get money by drawing," I said. "Now you have taken such pains, now you are so much improved, you shall begin to work and get money, too. Try to finish this little sketch as nicely and prettily as you can. When it is done, I will take it away with me; and the same person will buy it who buys all that I do. You shall keep your own earnings in your own purse." . . . Her drawings, as she finished them, were placed in my hands; Marian took them from me and hid them carefully; and I set aside a little weekly tribute from my earnings, to be offered to her as the price paid by strangers for the poor, faint, valueless sketches, of which I was the only purchaser. It was hard sometimes to maintain our innocent deception, when she proudly brought out her

purse to contribute her share towards the expenses, and wondered, with serious interest, whether I or she had earned the most that week. I have all those hidden drawings in my possession still: they are my treasures beyond price—the dear remembrances that I love to keep alive . . . that my heart will never part from. (442)

When Walter promises his future wife that she shall "keep [her] own earnings in [her] own purse," he appears to satisfy one of the foremost demands of those who championed married women's property rights in the 1850s and 1860s—the demand that a wife's wages or earnings be considered her separate property, over which she retains control. As Walter himself explains, however, his promise is a hoax. While leading Laura to believe that she is earning money and competing with him in the public sphere, Walter actually supports her. Yet his conspiracy, unlike Sir Percival's, is an "innocent deception," and Laura's exclusion from the marketplace not a sign of her oppression but the consequence of her incapacity for business.

Insofar as Collins grants Laura a form of independence, he does so in a paradoxically confining way—by excluding her from public life. As Mrs. Walter Hartwright, Laura assumes a position similar to that of Walter's mother and sister, women left "independent" by Walter's thoughtful father: "His affectionate anxiety to provide for the future of those who were dependent on his labours, had impelled him . . . to devote to the insuring of his life a much larger portion of his income than most men consider it necessary to set aside for that purpose. Thanks to his admirable prudence and self-denial, my mother and sister were left, after his death, as independent of the world as they had been during his lifetime" (2). According to the strained logic of such thinking, female autonomy is simply impossible, since women can only secure their independence by remaining in the home, dependent on men's labors. Evading the political issues raised elsewhere in his novel, Collins suggests that Laura's second marriage gives her the autonomy that she has desired all along. Obscuring her economic subordination with what he represents as her newfound emotional freedom, Collins unites her with a good provider, a man who sees to it that she can remain comfortably sequestered in the "asylum" of the home. Shoring up sexual differences, Collins returns his male and female characters to their proper places: Laura becomes the childlike woman that Percival and Fosco originally made her out to be; the resolute Marian becomes "a useless, helpless, panic-stricken creature" in whose behalf Walter must act (306);

and Walter finds his "resolution returned to [him] with tenfold strength" (524).

While Collins evades the issue of married women's property rights by satisfying Laura in her second marriage, he devalues the demand for female autonomy by sexualizing it, through his treatment of Jane Anne Catherick. A more fully developed character than Cecilia Jane Elster, the mother of the illegitimate Percival, who squanders the estate of his father's rightful heir (503), Mrs. Catherick is an adulteress in whom Collins conflates the desire for financial independence with sexual license.[15] Palming her spurious offspring upon her unsuspecting husband, whom she marries only after learning she is pregnant, she shoulders the blame for Anne's illegitimate birth. In representing her, Collins draws on misogynistic fears of patrilineal disruption, reinforces the sexual double standard of adultery, and indirectly suggests that those who wanted divorce to remain a male prerogative may well have been correct.

Collins returns to the subject of illegitimacy in *No Name,* the novel he started writing soon after completing *The Woman in White,* yet he uses it to a very different end in the second work. Like Anne Catherick and Sir Percival Glyde, the two central figures in *No Name,* the Vanstone sisters, are born out of wedlock. But rather than suggesting the need to control unruly women whose adultery threatens patrilineal order, Collins's treatment of illegitimacy in *No Name* bolsters his critique of English marriage law and provides an effective metaphor for the disinherited condition of married women in England.

No Name (1862–1863)

Collins began working on *No Name* in the summer of 1861 and showed early sections of the novel to Dickens in January 1862, rejecting the 26 titles his friend suggested for the new work. The first number of *No Name* was published on 15 March 1862 in *All the Year Round,* and in *Harper's Weekly* in the United States. Suffering from rheumatic gout and drugged with laudanum, Collins struggled to complete the novel by December. He finished it on Christmas Eve, and the last of its 44 weekly numbers appeared on 17 January 1863.

The plot of *No Name* centers on Magdalen and Norah Vanstone, wealthy young women who are disinherited from the family fortune. Having introduced the sisters, their parents, and their former governess, Miss Garth, Collins focuses on 18-year-old Magdalen, whose physical beauty and talent for acting set her apart from the subdued and conventional

Norah. Soon after their parents return to Somersetshire from a mysterious trip to London, Magdalen becomes engaged to marry the ne'er-do-well Frank Clare. Her father, Andrew, promises to give his daughter a dowry of £20,000, but he is killed in a railway accident, and his wife, her health already impaired by a pregnancy, dies within two days of her husband.

Left parentless, Magdalen and Norah soon learn from William Pendril, the family lawyer, that they are penniless as well. Disclosing the story of their father's early life, Mr. Pendril explains that, as a young army officer stationed in Canada, Andrew Vanstone married a disreputable woman whom he was unable to divorce. Saved from suicide by his superior officer, Major Kirke, Andrew returned to England, falling in love with one Miss Blake. Sacrificing her marriage prospects to his well-being, Miss Blake agreed to live with Andrew as if they were husband and wife, and the two were accepted as such by friends and neighbors.

Norah and Magdalen are the two surviving children of this union. Although they are illegitimate, their father has amply provided for them in his will. But when he learns of the death of his wife, and secretly marries their mother in London, he unwittingly disinherits them. As Mr. Pendril explains, a man's marriage "destroys the validity of any will which he may have made as a single man."[16] Despite the existence of his will, therefore, Andrew Vanstone dies intestate, as does his wife, and because their daughters were born out of wedlock, they are denied the property to which legitimate children are entitled under the same circumstances. Andrew's estranged elder brother, Michael, who was himself disinherited by their father, receives his brother's fortune, as does his sickly son, Noel, upon Michael's death. Although wealthy, neither Michael nor Noel Vanstone proves willing to share Andrew's fortune with his two daughters.

Norah and Magdalen respond to their plight in antithetical ways. Norah patiently accepts her misfortunes, moves to London with Miss Garth, and earns her living as a governess, but Magdalen seeks vengeance against her uncle, who possesses the money that would have enabled her to marry Frank Clare. She hopes to cheat Michael Vanstone out of her father's property through fraudulent investment schemes, and when her uncle dies she plots against his son and heir instead. Suppressing her feelings for Frank, who breaks their engagement, Magdalen plans to regain her father's fortune for herself and her sister by hiding her identity and marrying her detestable cousin Noel under a false name. With the help of Captain Wragge, a rogue distantly related to her mother by marriage, Magdalen perfects her acting abilities, earns hundreds of pounds in a one-woman show, and then passes herself off to Noel as a young woman named Miss Bygrave, with Captain and Mrs. Wragge as her uncle and aunt. Despite the counterplots of his wily housekeeper, Mrs. Lecount, who sees through Magdalen's disguise, Noel falls into the trap set for him and marries his cousin. Infatuated with her, yet ignorant of her identity, the failing Noel offers to leave her his entire fortune. But Magdalen asks him to limit his bequest to £80,000—the value of her father's estate—and to leave the remainder of his property to their cousin George Bartram.

Although Magdalen attempts to elude Mrs. Lecount, the house-keeper tracks them to Scotland. In Magdalen's absence, she reveals the conspiracy to Noel and encourages him to cut his wife from his will while including his housekeeper in it. Having written a new will, Noel dies later that evening, leaving the bulk of his estate to his friend Admiral Bartram. In a separately written secret trust, he stipulates that the admiral is to give the money to his nephew George Bartram, but only if George marries within six months of Noel's death. This last condition is intended to protect George from Magdalen, whom Noel fears will marry his heir if given enough time for scheming.

Learning of her second disinheritance, Magdalen trains as a parlor maid under the guidance of her own maid, Louisa, and enters the household of Admiral Bartram as a domestic servant. Surprised in the act of reading Noel's secret trust, she is forced to flee to London. Unable to support herself, and unwilling to burden Norah with her own troubles, she collapses in a fever in a poor lodging house. She is nursed back to health by Captain Kirke, the son of the army major who rescued her own father from suicide.

Meanwhile, Norah is courted by her cousin George Bartram, whom she meets while searching for her missing sister, and accepts his marriage proposal. Although their wedding takes place after the six-month period stipulated in the secret trust, George inherits Noel's money upon the death of the admiral because the document cannot be found. Soon after Magdalen recovers, however, Norah finds it among some ashes at the admiral's estate. Because its conditions were not met, half of Noel's fortune reverts to Magdalen. But the repentant heroine refuses to claim her inheritance as Noel Vanstone's widow. Explaining to her sister that their "shares" of their father's money "come to [them] in very different ways" (545), Magdalen destroys the document and asserts that she will only accept a portion if she receives it from Norah and her husband, whose virtue and mutual love render them "deserving" (537). Having confessed her story to Captain Kirke, Magdalen is engaged to marry him at the conclusion of the novel. While "narrow people" will only remember Magdalen's sins, the narrator tells us, Kirke recognizes "the priceless value, the all-ennobling virtue, of a woman who speaks the truth" (547–48).

Ostensibly, Collins uses *No Name* to criticize the law governing inheritance and illegitimacy, which categorizes Norah and Magdalen as "Nobody's Children" (98). Unlike "the more merciful and Christian laws of other countries," under which the subsequent marriage of parents legitimizes their children, English law does not. As Mr. Pendril asserts, "the law of England, as it affects illegitimate offspring" is "a disgrace to the nation" (98). Although Norah and Magdalen would not be legitimized by their parents' marriage even in the "more merciful" countries of Europe, since their father was already married at the time of their birth, virtually all the characters in *No Name* consider them to be victims of a "cruel law" (103). The sole exception is their uncle Michael, who conveniently adopts a high moral tone and speaks of their disinheritance as a "Providential interposition" (110).

But while Collins is concerned with illegitimacy as a social and legal problem in *No Name,* he uses it to an ulterior end: to address the issue of married women's property rights and legal status. In effect, his treatment of the illegitimacy of Norah and Magdalen and the "cruel law" governing it serves as a displaced critique of English marriage law and the disinherited condition of English wives. Even if the death of her father had not deprived Magdalen of her property, Collins observes, she would nonetheless have been partly disinherited upon her marriage to Frank Clare, since the marriage settlement envisioned by her father would give her husband half her fortune, to be used to further his career (63).

Like the illegitimate daughters of Andrew Vanstone, the married women of *No Name* discover that they have no claim to their own property or earnings. Stripped of their legal personalities and property rights by the doctrine of coverture, they appear to be as nameless and penniless as illegitimate children. Born out of wedlock, Norah and Magdalen have "no name" or money; as married women, they must "part with" their property and their names (535). Developing this analogy, Collins fills his novel with women whose property is unjustly, yet legally, appropriated by their husbands. Collins dwells on the "shocking story" of Magdalen's landlady, for example, who is forced to evict the ailing Magdalen from her lodgings by her brutal husband, until Kirke intercedes:

But not half an hour since, her husband—who never came near the house, except to take her money—had come to rob her of her little earnings, as usual. She had been obliged to tell him that no rent was in hand for the first floor, and that none was likely to be in hand until the lady recovered, or her friends found her. On hearing this, he had mercilessly insisted—well or ill—that the lady should go. There was the hospital to take her to; and if the hospital shut its doors, there was the workhouse to try next. If she was not out of the place in an hour's time, he threatened to come back, and take her out himself. (518)

Although neither Captain Wragge nor Frank Clare physically abuse their wives, they, too, use them as a lucrative source of income. Breaking his engagement with the penniless Magdalen, Frank marries an elderly widow, using her money to purchase a fine estate (541). Captain Wragge "mercilessly squander[s]" his wife's earnings and her small inheritance "to the last farthing" (18) and remains in her company only because she continues to have expectations from an aging aunt. "Speaking purely in a pecuniary point of view," Wragge explains, "I can't afford a total separation from her," since she "will prove a second time profitable to me, on that elderly relative's death" (258).

Magdalen's own relationship to Captain Wragge reinforces our sense that wives are simply a source of profit to their husbands. While their partnership is not literally that of a married couple, Magdalen and the captain exchange vows that parody those of a wedding service:

"Say the word—do you take me?"
    Her heart beat fast; her lips turned dry—but she said the word.
"I do."
    There was a pause. Magdalen sat silent, struggling with the vague dread of the future which had been roused in her mind by her own reply. Captain Wragge, on his side, was apparently absorbed in the consideration of a new set of alternatives. His hands descended into his empty pockets, and prophetically tested their capacity as receptacles for gold and silver. (164)

Treating Magdalen much as he treats Mrs. Wragge, the captain swindles his partner out of her earnings, accumulating his own "private surplus" from her performances while pretending to give her a "fair share of profit" (178, 373). Acting as if in collusion with Noel Vanstone, he arranges for Magdalen to marry her cousin without a separate marriage settlement, "trust[ing] him" to "provid[e] for her pecuniary future"

(314). While Magdalen contrasts her outcast condition as "Nobody's Child" to what she naively presumes will be her "protected" status as "Somebody's Wife" (436), she learns that there is little to choose between the two positions. Like both her landlady and Mrs. Wragge, Mrs. Noel Vanstone is married under English common law, without a separate settlement, and thus remains as penniless and disempowered as she had been as a disinherited child.

In *The Woman in White,* Collins represents Sir Percival's successful scheme to marry Miss Fairlie for her money, but in *No Name,* he cleverly inverts this formula, depicting Miss Vanstone's failed attempt to regain her father's fortune through marriage. Magdalen's counterplot, Collins suggests, is doomed to failure by the gender inequities of common law. While Magdalen hopes to make her father's fortune "change owners again" (119), the means she employs to do so—matrimony—necessarily defeat her ends. Until widowed, no woman can be said to have married her husband for money because, in marrying, she becomes a *feme covert,* without property by definition. Furthermore, while a wife regains her property rights upon the death of her husband, she does not necessarily inherit her husband's wealth or regain the property she brought to her marriage. When a husband dies intestate, Collins notes, a third of his property goes to his widow (79, 97). But the husbands in *No Name* often leave their widows a much smaller fraction of their estates—if anything at all. As Magdalen's attorney explains, English law, unlike Scottish, "allow[s] a husband the power of absolutely disinheriting his wife" (442), and Noel Vanstone chooses to exercise this power.

Wishing to recover her lost inheritance and put "Norah's fortune into Norah's hand" (437), Magdalen finds herself denied economic agency as a widow and a wife. Unlike Miss Garth, who retains control over her own "pecuniary interests" by remaining a spinster (116), Magdalen mistakenly looks to marriage to recoup her legacy, only to learn that fortune hunting is a male prerogative. Although women may seem to have their "pick" of husbands, they are only free to decide which of their suitors will exploit them: "I had my trifle of money, and I had my pick, and I picked the captain," Mrs. Wragge explains. "He took care of me and my money. I'm here, the money's gone" (149). Despite her brilliant ability to act and plot, which enables her to marry her uncle's heir, Magdalen loses Andrew Vanstone's property to yet another male cousin, George Bartram, and is left wishing to "be a man" (533).

In *No Name,* as in *The Woman in White,* Collins ultimately suggests that such desires are illegitimate. Just as the masculine Marian learns the virtues of female subordination and seeks protection under Walter's wing, so the "resolute" Magdalen (52) abandons her methods and goals. Renouncing her "perversity" and "pride," she willingly submits to the authority of her cousin George, who marries her sister: "What your husband thinks right, Norah, you and I will think right, too" (545). Punished with a near-fatal fever, she comes to admire the conventionally feminine "courage" of her sister—"the courage of resignation":

> Norah, who had patiently accepted her hard lot; who, from first to last, had meditated no vengeance, and stooped to no deceit—Norah had reached the end which all her sister's ingenuity, all her sister's resolution, and all her sister's daring, had failed to achieve. Openly and honourably, with love on one side and love on the other, Norah had married the man who possessed the Combe-Raven money—and Magdalen's own scheme to recover it, had opened the way to the event which had brought husband and wife together! (537)

Comparing Magdalen's failure to Norah's success, and suggesting that the patient sister achieves "the end" desired by the daring one, Collins elides the crucial difference between them: Norah's husband possesses their fortune, but Magdalen wanted to possess it herself.

In *No Name*, as in *The Woman in White*, Collins blunts his critique of common law by suggesting that both Magdalen and Norah can be happily married, with their fortune regained for them by Norah's husband. The problems with marriage lie with individuals rather than with laws, it seems. Nonetheless, Collins gives considerably less weight to this conventional resolution in *No Name* than he had in the earlier novel. Unlike the second, happy marriage of Laura Fairlie and Walter Hartwright, that of Magdalen and Captain Kirke is never represented, and her unconvincing reformation is relegated to the brief "Last Scene" of the novel—less a sign of Collins's mixed feelings about his aggressive heroine than a half-hearted attempt to draw a moral lesson from a subversive story to soothe ruffled readers. Despite Collins's remarks on Magdalen's "serpentine" appearance and the "dangers" of her strength (29, 104, 470), his moralistic conclusion has a peculiarly hollow ring, and the daring Magdalen rather than the resigned Norah is his central and heroic figure.

In *The Woman in White* and *No Name*, Collins conveys his critique of English marriage law in largely metaphorical ways: through the criminal conspiracy launched against Lady Glyde, which stages her death, and through the illegitimacy and disinheritance of the Vanstone sisters.

In *Man and Wife,* by contrast, Collins directly confronts the problem of marriage law, claiming it as his primary theme and producing his "first full-blown *roman à thèse*" (*King,* 316).

Man and Wife (1869–1870)

Man and Wife was written and published as Members of Parliament debated and revised what would soon become England's first Married Women's Property Act. Defeated in 1856, proponents of married women's property rights renewed their efforts to change the law in 1868, when a new married women's property bill was introduced to Parliament. This bill was intended to give married women the same property rights enjoyed by the *feme sole,* and M.P.s supporting the measure emphasized the disjunction between common law and equity in making their case. They noted that while women from the upper classes were able to sidestep coverture by having separate property settled upon them, working-class women could not. Neither they nor their family members could afford to pay the legal fees required to do so. Reworked over the next two years, the bill became increasingly narrow in its scope. Many M.P.s were willing to grant married women control of their earnings, but they were not willing to recognize the property rights of wives in any general sense, or to concede that common law was unjust in its premises. The bill had originally stipulated that wives should retain the same control over their "real and personal estate" as single women. But as passed in August 1870, the first Married Women's Property Act treated only a wife's earnings, certain types of investments, and small legacies as her own separate property, and thus "the friends of married women's property reform scarcely knew whether to regard the . . . Act of 1870 as a victory or a defeat" (Shanley, 68).

Collins himself knew that the 1870 act was a mixed success. Although he acknowledges that "it is . . . better than no law at all" in his 1871 preface to *Man and Wife,* he complains of the opposition encountered by the bill and criticizes the House of Lords for substantially altering it (*King,* 320). His tone is more optimistic in the original preface, written in June 1870, while the bill was still under debate. Here, he expresses his hope that Parliament is "bestirring itself" to grant property rights to married women and to remedy the "cruel abuses" of the common law: "There is a prospect, at last, of lawfully establishing the right of a married woman, in England, to possess her own property, and to keep her own earnings."[17]

Using the 1868 *Report of the Royal Commission on the Laws of Marriage* as a primary source for *Man and Wife,* Collins refers skeptical readers to specific pages in the *Report* in his appendix, identifying it as "the book which first suggested to [him] the idea of writing the present Novel" (645). In particular, Collins notes, the *Report* criticized the Scottish practice of "irregular marriage," a union established solely on the basis of mutual consent, without any need for formal ceremony or authorization. While relying on the findings of the 1868 *Report,* Collins also drew from a well-known bigamy case of 1861—*Thelwall v. Yelverton*—in which a marriage was declared "null and void" on the basis of discrepancies between the laws of England and Ireland.

Serialized in *Cassell's Magazine* from December 1869 to September 1870, and also in *Harper's Weekly, Man and Wife* centers on the experiences of Blanche Lundie and Anne Silvester. Their mothers, also named Blanche and Anne, are introduced in the prologue, set in 1831. In that year, the elder Blanche is sent to India as a governess, where she marries the baronet Sir Thomas Lundie. Returning to London in 1855, she finds her old friend in a state of collapse. The latter woman has just been deserted by her husband, John Vanborough, who leaves her for Lady Jane Parnell, a wealthy and aristocratic young widow whom he believes can further his political career. Vanborough's reprehensible desertion of his wife and his subsequent marriage to Lady Jane are legally sanctioned by "the Irish Statute of George the Second." As his unfeeling lawyer, Mr. Delamayn, points out, Vanborough converted to Catholicism, his wife's religion, but failed to wait a full year before marrying her, and thus their union is considered "null and void," and their daughter illegitimate (27). Resuming her maiden name of Silvester, the first Mrs. Vanborough soon dies as a result of the "merciless injury inflicted on her" (41). Her daughter, Anne, is then raised by Blanche (the elder), who sees to it that she is trained as a teacher and happily established as governess to little Blanche.

The central story of *Man and Wife* begins at a Scottish estate in 1868. Anne is still Blanche's governess and friend, but she is now employed by the widowed stepmother of her pupil, the second wife of Sir Thomas, whose title and estates have descended to his eccentric brother Patrick. While Blanche is engaged to marry Arthur Brinkworth, Anne has been seduced and betrayed by Geoffrey Delamayn. The second son of the lawyer introduced in the prologue, Anne's lover is an unscrupulous young athlete whose physical prowess has made him a national hero. Estranged from his wealthy father, now known as Lord Holchester,

Geoffrey is nonetheless dependent on him "for every farthing" of his income (79) and unwilling to irritate him further by marrying a lowly governess. Both he and Anne are anxious to hide their past alliance, but because Anne is pregnant, she must be married to save her reputation. Having repeatedly promised to make her his wife, Geoffrey finally agrees to meet her at a nearby inn, where they can marry without a formal ceremony of any kind. As Anne knows, the laws of Scotland allow for "irregular marriages." All she and Geoffrey must do to marry is mutually declare themselves husband and wife in the hearing of others. But before Geoffrey can meet Anne and make his declaration, he is called to the bedside of his ailing father. Entrusting Arthur Brinkworth with his secret, Geoffrey sends his friend to Anne in his place, with the necessary explanations in writing. But because the landlady will not give Anne a room before her husband arrives, Arthur is forced to assume that role, and the two spend the night in the same quarters, taken for man and wife.

Required to marry the wealthy young widow Mrs. Glenarm to be reinstated in his father's will, Geoffrey uses Arthur's masquerade to his own advantage. To Anne's horror, he tells her that he cannot marry her because she is already Arthur's wife according to Scottish law, since Arthur declared himself to be her husband at the inn. Fainting at Geoffrey's declaration, Anne is brought back to consciousness by Hester Dethridge, a mute cook dismissed by the unfeeling Lady Lundie. A mysterious and frightening figure, Hester seems to understand Anne's plight. Fleeing from Blanche and Arthur, Anne takes refuge in Glasgow, where she gives birth to a stillborn infant and falls dangerously ill. Estranged from Geoffrey, yet unaware of his villainous claim, Arthur marries Blanche before Anne can recover and tell him of the conspiracy against them. Arthur is thus unwittingly placed in the position of an alleged bigamist. Meanwhile, Mrs. Glenarm and the Delamayn family learn of Anne's claims on Geoffrey by means of a blackmailer, Mr. Bishopriggs, who possesses letters they have exchanged. Geoffrey extricates himself from this difficulty by acknowledging that he flirted with Anne, but claiming that he did so only to learn that she was the wife of Arthur Brinkworth.

It is left to Anne and Sir Patrick Lundie, a renowned Scottish lawyer, to extricate Arthur and Blanche from their difficulties. Retrieving her letters from Bishopriggs, Anne presents them to Sir Patrick, who sees that they contain "a written promise of marriage" and thus furnish proof that she and Geoffrey were already married under Scottish law when

Arthur arrived at the inn (522–23). Although Sir Patrick is unwilling to see Anne married to Geoffrey, whose physical and moral decline have been grossly accelerated by his excessive athletic training, she insists that the lawyer produce the letters when they convene with the others to determine the legal status of Arthur's marriage to Blanche. To the horror of those assembled, Anne sacrifices herself to the happiness of Blanche and Arthur by declaring herself to be the wife of Geoffrey Delamayn, despite his "devouring hatred" of her (517).

Geoffrey takes Anne home to his lodgings in Fulham, which he rents from the mute Hester Dethridge. Since leaving Scotland, Hester has inherited the secluded house in which she and her lodgers live. Learning that he cannot divorce Anne, Geoffrey decides to murder her and marry Mrs. Glenarm. He finds Hester's confession, which describes the physical abuse and economic exploitation she suffered at the hands of her drunken husband, and the means she used to murder him, and decides to adopt Hester's own means in killing Anne, suffocating her in her sleep. Blackmailing Hester, Geoffrey obtains her reluctant aid. But as he is about to suffocate his wife, he suffers a paralytic stroke and is attacked by the mute woman. Anne awakens to find Hester strangling Geoffrey's corpse. The novel's epilogue makes a series of disclosures—Hester, hopelessly mad, has been incarcerated in a lunatic asylum, Blanche and Arthur are expecting their first child, and the widowed Anne has become the wife of Sir Patrick Lundie.

Like the sensation novels that precede it, *Man and Wife* brings home the horrors of Gothic fiction in its representation of married life and the helplessness of married women. The lawful victimization of three wives—Anne Vanborough, Anne Delamayn, and Hester Dethridge—provides the novel with its structure. Once again, Collins centers his story around the troubling ironies of marriage law, which legalizes the oppression of women while ostensibly protecting them from misfortune and mistreatment. But in *Man and Wife,* he illustrates these ironies, in part, through Scottish marriage law. Designed to protect seduced women against desertion, it compounds the injuries they have already suffered by forcing them on resentful men who are then deemed their masters. Stipulating that men are actually married to the women they have seduced under false promises of marriage, the Scottish law makes these women legally and permanently dependent on those who have betrayed them. Collins makes this point in the scene that unites Anne to Geoffrey, when Sir Patrick objects to the defense of Scottish marriage law offered by a fellow solicitor: "The persons here present, Mr. Moy, are now about to see the moral merit of the Scotch law of marriage . . . in operation before their own eyes. They will judge for themselves of the morality (Scotch or English) which first forces a deserted woman back on the villain who has betrayed her, and then virtuously leaves her to bear the consequences" (523).

In a scene that adapts the conventions of the Gothic to the 1860s, Anne Silvester "bears the consequences" of the law, to the common "horror" of those assembled (524). Claiming Geoffrey Delamayn as her husband to establish the validity of Blanche's marriage to Arthur, Anne is forced to submit to the authority of the man who wants her dead. "Is it settled?" Geoffrey asks his solicitor:

> "Has the law of Scotland made her my wife?"
> "The law of Scotland has made her your wife". . . .
> "Does the law tell her to go where her husband goes?"
> "Yes."
> He laughed softly to himself, and beckoned to her to cross the room to the place at which he was standing.
> She obeyed. . . . "I am here," she said to him. "What do you wish me to do?"
> A hideous smile parted his heavy lips. He offered her his arm.
> "Mrs. Geoffrey Delamayn," he said. "Come home." (525–26)

Whereas Sir Percival merely stages the death of his wife, Geoffrey Delamayn plots to kill Anne, yet his behavior, like the baronet's, seems to have official sanction, since the law denies property rights, security, and legal identity to married women and permits what courts now consider the crime of spousal rape: "There were outrages which her husband was privileged to commit, under the sanction of marriage, at the bare thought of which [Anne's] blood ran cold. . . . Law and Society armed her husband with his conjugal rights. Law and Society had but one answer to give, if she appealed to them:—You are his wife" (550).

Collins challenges the justification commonly offered for a husband's conjugal rights by questioning conceptions of natural sexual differences—not by peopling his novel with masculine women and effeminate men, as he does in *The Woman in White,* but by grotesquely exaggerating these differences, which come to seem pathological rather than natural. The athleticism of Geoffrey Delamayn, for example, reduces masculinity to a dangerously overdeveloped muscular strength, stripping "manly virtue" of any moral or intellectual substance. In "Muscular England," the ideal man is simply "a magnificent human animal" (61), indistinguishable from a "savage" or a "wild beast" (68, 495). At the same time, the patience and endurance of Anne Silvester take the feminine ideal to a dangerous extreme and illustrate the pitfalls of that "noble abnegation of Self" commonly perceived as "one of the grandest . . . virtues of the sex" (168). Collins treats Anne's self-sacrifice as a "dreadful" act (520), itself a source of horror in the novel. Appropriately, the "virtues of the sex" are most clearly embodied by the voiceless and exploited Hester Dethridge: "A woman who *can't* talk, and a woman who *can* cook—is simply a woman who has arrived at absolute perfection," Sir Patrick facetiously observes (271).

In choosing Hester, a mute domestic servant, to epitomize wifely oppression, Collins reveals the importance of class identity to the workings of marriage law. In *The Woman in White* and *No Name,* the class status of his heroines makes little difference in their plight as married women. Although Laura Fairlie is an heiress who receives the best legal advice, her marriage settlement fails to protect her from her husband and gives him a hefty financial interest in her death. The genteel Magdalen Vanstone seems equally vulnerable, marrying without any marriage settlement at all. Reminding readers of *No Name* that a lady is still a woman, albeit one who wears silk (453), Collins develops Magdalen's allegiance with her landlady and her maid and suggests that their class differences are negligible when compared with their shared oppression as English wives.

In *Man and Wife,* however, Collins highlights the class differences that divide married women. Both John Vanborough and Geoffrey Delamayn are assisted by upper-class widows in victimizing their working-class wives, and many of the women from the upper class seem to act in complicity with the mercenary men in the novel. Those who do not are still set apart from working-class women by their economic and legal privileges, and their access to the law of equity. Rich and highborn, Blanche Lundie can afford to be happily married, Collins suggests, but Hester Dethridge cannot, knowing nothing of "lawyers and settlements" (299). Abused and exploited by her husband, Hester discovers that she cannot prevent him from selling her household furniture and goods, although she paid for them with her own savings, as the local magistrate explains:

> "Is your furniture settled on yourself?" he says, when I told him what had happened.
> I didn't understand what he meant. He turned to some person who was sitting on the bench with him. "This is a hard case," he says. "Poor

people in this condition of life don't even know what a marriage settlement means. And, if they did, how many of them could afford to pay the
lawyer's charges?" Upon that, he turned to me. . . . "In the present state
of the law, I can do nothing for you. . . . The law doesn't allow a married
woman to call anything her own—unless she has previously (with a
lawyer's help) made a bargain to that effect with her husband, before
marrying him. You have made no bargain." (586)

Unable to afford a legal separation, despite her husband's physical cruelty (588), Hester is followed by him from place to place and legally
robbed of her earnings. As a poor woman, she finds that "there is no
limit, in England, to what a bad husband may do" (590). After she "suffer[s] the last and worst of many indignities at [her] husband's hands"
(599)—spousal rape—Hester murders him. Although Collins does not
exonerate her, he treats her crime as the logical outcome of her own victimization under common law. Like the Victorian feminist Frances
Power Cobbe, who noted in 1869 that "the property of the woman who
commits Murder, and the property of the woman who commits Matrimony, [are] dealt with alike" under English law,[18] Collins suggests that
the working-class wife, treated as if she were a felon under common law,
may very well become one.

In *Man and Wife,* as in the sensation novels that precede it, Collins
qualifies his critique. He notes that Blanche is "improved by her marriage," which "quiets" her (387)—an ominous achievement when one
considers the mute Hester—and he supplies Anne Delamayn with a second husband, Sir Patrick, whose protective kindness compensates her
for the cruelty of her first. Nonetheless, this happy marriage, like Magdalen's to Captain Kirke, is never represented, and the novel ends, simply, with its announcement. While Collins suggests that Laura Fairlie
cannot earn a living, and idealizes her loving and unwaged labor as Walter's wife, he proves less willing to endorse such ideals in his 1870 novel.
Instead, he emphasizes the ability of Hester Dethridge to support herself, an ability that her husband fully exploits—by pocketing her wages,
and by employing her without pay himself: "He was not going to call in
a man or a boy, and then have to pay them. He was going to get it done
for nothing, and he meant to make a journeyman of *me*" (598), Hester
explains.

Although a number of passages in *Man and Wife* seem to belie
women's abilities as wage earners, and promote the idea of their natural
dependence on men, these passages not only describe but criticize the
natural state, and they emphasize the need to evolve beyond it. If the

"past history of the sexes" leads us to believe "that the natural condition of a woman is to find her master in a man," that fact alone is not an argument in its favor. Rather, such natural desires are driven by "primitive instinct," encourage women to "throw themselves away" on unworthy men, and are best repressed and resisted (336).

In Collins's novel, the strongest case against women's natural subordination is provided by "natural man" himself (236)—by the savage Geoffrey Delamayn, whose position as a national hero reveals the latent barbarism of the English, in Collins's view. As Sir Patrick explains, "there is far too much glorification in England, just now, of the mere physical qualities which an Englishman shares with the savage and the brute": "And the ill results are beginning to show themselves already! We are readier than we ever were to practise all that is rough in our national customs, and to excuse all that is violent and brutish in our national acts. Read the popular books; attend the popular amusements—and you will find at the bottom of them all, a lessening regard for the gentler graces of civilized life, and a growing admiration for the virtues of the aboriginal Britons" (68 – 69).

Invoking the image of "aboriginal Britons" in the context of marriage law reform, Collins criticizes the lawful yet primitive mastery of husbands over their wives. He develops the image of British savagery in *Armadale* (1864–1866), *The Moonstone* (1868), and *The New Magdalen* (1872–1873), in the context of imperial rule and race relations, questioning assumptions about civilization and savagery and criticizing the Englishman's mastery over the subject races as well as over his wife.

Chapter Five

Reverse Colonization and Imperial Guilt: Representations of Empire in *Armadale, The Moonstone,* and *The New Magdalen*

When Collins alludes to the aboriginal Britons in his novel *Armadale,* his allusion seems an idle one—much less pointed in its significance than his attack on the primitive English "virtues" of Geoffrey Delamayn in *Man and Wife.* As the characters in *Armadale* embark on their outing to the Norfolk Broads, Pedgift Jr. calls attention to the relics of Roman Britain—to "the remains of a Roman encampment," a place he believes will prove "very interesting" to Major Milroy, "a military man."[1] Ostensibly, Pedgift Jr. uses these archaeological remains to distract the major from the courtship of his daughter Neelie by Allan Armadale. Yet the context in which Pedgift Jr. makes his remarks suggests that the imperial relics of Roman Britain, and the image of England as a conquered land, are not incidental to Collins's aims. Setting the main narrative of *Armadale* in 1851, the year in which the English celebrated their imperial progress at the Great Exhibition in London (337), Collins sends his characters to the "wild regions" of England (247)—to an area "pretty nearly wild enough . . . to be a prairie" in the American West (253). In so doing, he blurs the boundary between the civilized and the primitive, compares the English to an aboriginal and subject race, and challenges their faith in "the progress of [their] national civilization" (506). Placing his characters under the leadership of Pedgift Jr.—a "patriotic" Englishman named "Augustus" (243), who learns Latin and studies "the Pagan writers" (337)—Collins compares the British Empire with the Roman and reminds his readers that empires rise only to fall. Once the members of a subject race, the English imperialists, like the Roman, can become so again.

With their attention to imperial history and the rise and fall of empires, *Armadale* (1864–1866), *The Moonstone* (1868), and *The New*

100

Magdalen (1872–1873) are sensation novels with a difference. Like such works as *The Woman in White* and *Man and Wife,* these novels dramatize the legalized exploitation of English wives, the dangers of coverture, and the horrors of marital relations. Yet they also provide imperial frameworks for their tales of domestic horror. *Armadale* begins with a prologue set on the eve of the Emancipation Act (1833), a narrative about race relations and the enslavement of Africans by the British in the West Indies. *The Moonstone* includes a prologue that describes the Siege of Seringapatam (1799) and the murder of three Hindu priests by an English officer, while *The New Magdalen* opens with a scene from the Franco-Prussian War (1870) that highlights the violence of imperial powers in Europe. Responding to such disturbing events in Britain's colonial possessions as the Indian Mutiny (1857) and the Jamaica Insurrection (1865), and registering his sense of the savagery of European nations, Collins dramatizes imperial crimes in each of these works and acknowledges his feelings of imperial guilt. Punishing the imperialists for their misdeeds, Collins stages the reverse colonization of England by the Creoles and Hindus who invade the home country and threaten to colonize it.[2]

In these novels, Collins's interest in domestic "sensation" is as much the means to an end as an end in itself. Describing the enslavement of wives and the emancipation of widows in *Armadale,* for example, Collins develops the analogy between imperial and sexual conquest in order to criticize Britain's colonial practices, and to compare the exploitation of the subject races with that of disempowered Englishwomen. Thus Collins's sensational representation of his character Mrs. Waldron, horsewhipped by her brutal husband, bolsters his critique of British imperialism and its legacy of slave trading.

At the same time, however, Collins's domestic sensationalism allows him to displace imperial conflicts with sexual ones. He transforms political and cultural differences into those that seem natural and inevitable to his readers, and he suggests that women conscious of their rights pose as great a danger to the empire as rebellious natives. Assuaging his sense of British guilt, Collins feminizes native insurrection, redefining the nature and the origins of crime among his characters in the process. Although he does so to varying degrees in the three works, he consistently displaces the rage of exploited natives with that of independent and treacherous women, and at times attributes the outbreak of seemingly racial violence to sexual jealousy and feminist anger instead of colonial oppression. In this way, he partly obscures the injuries suffered by the conquered peoples and discredits as well as acknowledges their desire for self-rule.

Armadale (1864–1866)

Although *Armadale* did not begin its monthly serialization in the *Cornhill* until November 1864, Collins agreed to write the novel for the publisher George Smith in 1861, for the impressive sum of £5000. At that time, Collins had already promised his next novel, *No Name,* to Dickens, but Smith was willing to wait for the work of the now-famous novelist. Writing to his mother in July 1861, Collins expressed his delight over his agreement with the publisher: "Endeavour to consider me (if life and health last) in the light of a wealthy novelist," he told her. "Smith and Elder have *bought* me away from All the Year Round under circumstances which *in Dickens's opinion* amply justify me in leaving. . . . Five thousand pounds for nine months or, at most, a year's work—nobody but Dickens has made as much."[3]

With *No Name* published in volume form in 1862, Collins began gathering material for *Armadale* the following year, visiting Wildbad, Germany, in April 1863, and the Isle of Man in August. Telling his friend Charles Ward in January 1864 that he was "sketching the outline" of his new book,[4] he began to write it in April and generally managed to stay several months ahead of the printers after the first monthly number appeared in November. He finished the novel in April 1866, and its last installment was published that June.

Armadale opens with a prologue set in Wildbad in 1832, but recalling events in the British West Indies in the 1820s, and it contains the deathbed confession of one of the five characters named "Allan Armadale" in the novel. These characters include the first Allan Armadale, who lives in England but owns the largest estates in Barbados; the disreputable son he disinherits, who appears in the West Indies under the name "Felix Ingleby"; Armadale's godson, Allan Wrentmore, who lives in Barbados and changes his surname to "Armadale" to inherit his godfather's estates; and the sons of "Felix Ingleby" and Allan (Wrentmore) Armadale, identified as Allan Armadale and Ozias Midwinter, respectively.

As Allan (Wrentmore) Armadale lies dying of a paralytic affliction in Wildbad, he dictates a letter he intends his son to read when a grown man. The letter tells of his conflict with, and murder of, "Felix Ingleby" in 1829. After inheriting his godfather's estates, he explains, he was befriended by the disguised "Ingleby," who traveled to Barbados and became his clerk to exact revenge. Fired for "unpardonable misconduct" (24), "Ingleby" married Jane Blanchard, a woman (Wrentmore) Armadale had never met but planned to wed. "Ingleby" did so by masquerading as (Wrentmore) Armadale, in a scheme that involved fraud and forgery, and that led Miss Blanchard to deceive her own father, with the help of her 12-year-old maid. In turn, (Wrentmore) Armadale murdered his successful rival by locking him in the cabin of a sinking timber ship, *La Grâce de Dieu*. Although he confesses his crime to his son, (Wrentmore) Armadale does not do so out of remorse, but because he fears that "Ingleby's" accomplices, as well as his posthumous son, pose a danger to his own.

The main narrative of the novel begins in Somersetshire, England, in 1851, as the Reverend Decimus Brock reminisces about his relationship with "Ingleby's" widow and son, now known as Mrs. Jane and Allan Armadale. Mr. Brock meets Mrs. Armadale in 1837, when he becomes Allan's tutor. Mr. Brock, who knows that Mrs. Armadale is keeping painful secrets from him, learns that she has been blackmailed by a veiled woman, later identified as her former maid, Lydia Gwilt. But he respects her silence and agrees to protect her son against strangers—including a second, slightly younger, Allan Armadale. Mrs. Armadale's suspicions center on an impoverished and dark-skinned young man named Ozias Midwinter, whom her son befriends. Only after her death in 1850 does Mr. Brock learn that Midwinter is, indeed, the second Allan Armadale whom she fears—the son of Allan (Wrentmore) Armadale. Having heard Midwinter's story, however, and read his father's confession, Brock advises him to stay with his friend. Offering a Christian interpretation of (Wrentmore) Armadale's "fatalism," and of a menacing vision that comes to Allan Armadale while on board the wrecked remains of *La Grâce de Dieu*, Brock suggests that Midwinter may be sent to protect Allan rather than to harm him: "If danger ever threatens Allan, you, whose father took his father's life—YOU, and no other, may be the man whom the providence of God has appointed to save him" (503).

These rival interpretations of their relationship are soon tested by the schemes of Lydia Gwilt, who assisted in the plot against (Wrentmore) Armadale by forging a letter for Jane Blanchard and "Felix Ingleby" in 1829. Now 35, the beautiful Miss Gwilt is a convicted murderess pardoned by the Home Secretary and previously imprisoned for theft. After Allan Armadale inherits his family estate in Norfolk, she becomes the governess of Miss Milroy, whose parents live nearby, in the hopes of marrying the wealthy squire—the son of her former mistress. Although Allan has already begun to court Miss Milroy, he is easily seduced by Miss Gwilt, but learns that she is associated with the procuress Mrs. Oldershaw in London, and with the abortionist Doctor Downward as well. Falsely assuming that Miss Gwilt is a fallen woman seduced and abandoned by a lover, Allan severs his connection with her. But Midwinter has fallen in love with her in the meantime, violently argues with Allan over her respectability, and privately marries her in London. In love with Midwinter herself, Miss Gwilt knows his history and marries him under his legal name. As "Mrs. Allan Armadale," she plans to kill the wealthy squire and present herself as his widow to inherit an annual income of £12,000, renouncing her own husband to do so.

Reconciling Midwinter and Allan Armadale, Miss Gwilt unsuccessfully tries to poison the squire soon after her marriage takes place. She then arranges for him to take a cruise with her former lover, the Cuban Captain Manuel, who plans to murder Armadale in the Adriatic. After an erroneous notice of Allan's death appears in the papers, Lydia leaves Midwinter under the pretense of a family emergency and makes her claim as Armadale's widow, assisted by the legal advice and the false testimony of Doctor Downward. Downward now runs an unlicensed sanatorium for "nervous" patients in Hampstead, under the name Doctor Le Doux. When the two learn that Armadale has survived Manuel's murder attempt, the doctor shows Lydia how to suffocate the squire by means of poison gas, piped into a room in the sanatorium through a fumigating apparatus. After Midwinter confronts his wife, and she renounces him, she and the doctor lure Armadale to the sanatorium by telling him that Miss Milroy is a patient there. But he arrives with Midwinter, who changes rooms with Armadale, and fulfills Mr. Brock's prophesy when he is gassed in his friend's place. His wife, however, realizes that he has changed rooms before he is fatally poisoned. Writing a confession to Midwinter, the remorseful Lydia enters the poisoned room herself, committing suicide. The novel ends by describing the forgiveness of the two men she has wronged, as well as the wedding plans of Allan Armadale and Miss Milroy, and the promising career of Midwinter, a literary man.

Although much of the action of *Armadale* unfolds in England, Collins is preoccupied with colonial and race relations—not surprising in a novel composed between 1864 and 1866, years that overlap with the American Civil War and that were characterized by unrest and violence in Britain's "sugar colonies." Collins sets his prologue in 1832, on the eve of Britain's Emancipation Act, yet his representations of racial conflict and of West Indian affairs reflect a more contemporary imperial crisis—the Jamaica Insurrection of 1865. The Insurrection did not take place until October 1865, almost a year into the novel's serialization. But Collins wrote the novel amid the conflicts and controversies that culminated in the armed revolt. Discussions of native insurrection, and imperial rise and fall, are interspersed among its monthly numbers, in the articles that appeared alongside the novel in the *Cornhill,* and these reveal the cultural anxieties that Collins and his readers felt over the administration, aims, and strength of the empire in the 1860s.[5]

A British possession since 1655, Jamaica was used for the cultivation of sugar cane and the production of sugar, a commodity that required an unusually intensive amount of labor, which was supplied by slaves until 1834. Throughout the eighteenth and early nineteenth centuries, the island was a crucial point in the British slave triangle. Slaves from the west coast of Africa were shipped to Jamaica, where they were sold to British plantation owners. Sugar and sugar products were shipped from Jamaica to England, and textiles and weapons from England to Africa in exchange for more slaves. Growing moral indignation in England over the slave trade, as well as changing economic structures and needs, led Parliament to pass the Emancipation Act, under which slaves became free apprentices throughout the British West Indies, and the planters were paid 20 million pounds in compensation for their property losses.

Three decades later, Jamaica was once again brought to the attention of the British public by events that resulted in native insurrection, widespread massacres, and the dismissal and trial of Governor Edward Eyre. The early 1860s were marked by economic distress and growing discontent among the black peasantry of Jamaica, Barbados, and other West Indian islands, as sugar prices reached an all-time low in 1863, and wages fell. Suffering from agricultural distress and an economic depression, discouraged from obtaining their own freeholds, and punished with the whip and the treadmill for petty offenses, the ex-slaves of Jamaica were inspired by George William Gordon, himself an ex-slave and Baptist Churchwarden, who advocated political reform. After the Jamaicans were told to be "industrious" and "prudent" in an ill-judged letter from the Colonial Office, entitled the "Queen's Advice," and a deputation was turned away by Governor Eyre in Kingston, an angry mob attacked the courthouse in St. Thomas-in-the-East on 11 October. After 7 blacks were killed by the militia, the mob murdered the 14 white vestrymen of the parish. In response, the governor declared martial law and authorized the massacre of hundreds. Although George Gordon had no connection with the attack on the courthouse, he became Eyre's scapegoat and was hanged.

Criticized for his repressive measures, Eyre was recalled by the British government and put on trial. Although he was ultimately acquitted of murder, the royal commission that investigated his actions criticized his prolonged declaration of martial law and found his use of executions and corporal punishments reckless and excessive.[6] Because of the role the island had played in the slave trade, Jamaica's colonial history had already produced feelings of imperial guilt among the British. The reprehensible actions of Governor Eyre served as a reminder of the crimes committed in the name of empire.

To many of Collins's friends and contemporaries, however, such reminders were unwelcome. Comparing the Jamaica Insurrection with the Indian Mutiny of 1857, Dickens, Thomas Carlyle, and other prominent literary men justified the use of martial law against the "inferior" races, and as members of the Eyre Defense Committee praised the actions of the governor. By contrast, John Stuart Mill, Charles Darwin, and other liberal writers and philosophers formed the Jamaica Committee and called for Eyre's criminal conviction. In formulating his own response to the crisis in the West Indies, Collins draws on the views of both camps, representing the conflict in a typically mixed way. Depicting the violence and corruption of white colonists and slave owners in *Armadale,* he acknowledges the guilt of the British in the West Indies and evokes sympathy for the oppressed blacks. Yet he does so indirectly—by detailing events of the 1820s and 1830s rather than the 1860s—and he defends the aims of the empire as well. He champions the Christian mission of the Reverend Decimus Brock, who desires to convert the "heathen"; he reveals the threat posed to the British by violent and unruly natives; and he discredits the cause of the ex-slaves by conflating them with female savages back home—with the emancipated and "strong-minded" Englishwomen whose political wrongs seem equivocal at best, and against whom both Armadale and Midwinter rally, despite their racial differences.

Collins expresses his sense of Britain's imperial guilt most directly in his prologue, which describes the "wild . . . and vicious life" of Allan (Wrentmore) Armadale, the largest plantation owner in Barbados (7), and introduces the character of a female slave, traveling with the Armadales in Europe. "My boyhood and youth were passed in idleness and self-indulgence," the plantation owner confesses, "among people—

slaves and half-castes mostly—to whom my will was law" (20–21). Violent and tyrannical, (Wrentmore) Armadale describes the "base pleasures" of his "animal-self" and refers to his seduction or rape of Negro women, "wronged beyond all forgiveness" (23–24). Nearly killed by "a known negro-poison," he is unsure whether to attribute the murder attempt to "Felix Ingleby" or to resentful natives, "whose vengeance might well have reached [him] at that time" (24). While Collins seems more concerned with the corrupting effects of slavery on the plantation owners than with the suffering of the slaves, he dramatizes the mute obedience of the enslaved Negress in the Armadale household, who stands "grim, and old, and silent" at her owner's bedside (15). The paralysis that afflicts (Wrentmore) Armadale, and over which the slave symbolically presides, serves as a metaphor for the corruption of the imperial body politic and the well-deserved "ruin of West Indian property" "at the time of . . . emancipation" (38, 91), and it reduces the slave owner himself to a "fettered" and mute condition (19).

Collins extends this critique of empire by challenging the association between dark skin and the primitive, so often used by the British to justify their acts of conquest and subjugation in the colonies. Introducing the figure of an "aboriginal Briton" into his prologue—that is, a Celt— Collins compares the conflict between white colonists and black slaves with the antagonism between (Wrentmore) Armadale and "Felix Ingleby," a character with a Gaelic (Celtic) name. As one of the *Cornhill* articles published beside *Armadale* reminds us, the Celts were members of Britain's aboriginal "tribes," a people continually subject to invasion and conquest—by the Romans, Danes, Normans, and English.[7] In his uncertainty over the identity of his would-be assassin, (Wrentmore) Armadale conflates "Ingleby" with the "vengeful" Negroes, and the resentment of the disinherited Celt, whose name suggests the "flame" ("ingle") of native revolt, with that of the enslaved Africans. Both a Briton and the member of a subject race conquered by the English, "Ingleby" erases the color line separating master from slave, colonizers from colonized, calls into question polarized conceptions of racial difference, and suggests that imperial conquest is a matter of political and military might, not a consequence of racial destiny or a moral burden borne by whites. Like the Celtic Manxman described by Collins in his main narrative, whose Isle of Man is "explored" by Englishmen "eager for adventure in unknown regions" (76), the members of the subject races outside the British Isles desire political autonomy and "laws of [their] own" (108).

While Collins recognizes the desire for self-rule among the subject races, however, he tends to strip imperial relations of their political content. He centers the conflict between (Wrentmore) Armadale and "Ingleby" on sexual jealousy, despite their seemingly racial differences, emphasizing their rivalry over Jane Blanchard instead. Throughout the novel, Collins echoes the language used to describe native insurrections in the newspapers and periodicals of the day, but he does so to portray the sexual rage of his characters—that of the major's wife, for example: "the smouldering fire of Mrs. Milroy's jealousy had burst into flame, in the moment when she and the handsome stranger first set eyes on each other" (303).

In Collins's hands, even the resentment and rage of his African characters become sexual matters, their anger attributed to spurned love and romantic rivalry rather than to racial exploitation or political oppression. The violent altercation between the "fair" Englishman, Allan Armadale, and the "dark" Creole, Ozias Midwinter, has all the trappings of a racial conflict, as Midwinter, already troubled by "sourly-savage" feelings of resentment (187), turns on Allan, "his eyes aflame, and his hot Creole blood rushing crimson into his face" (387). Despite Midwinter's racial otherness and resentment, however, Collins attributes his attack on Armadale to male rivalry. "Your violence quite takes me by surprise," Allan asserts. "I can't account for it . . . unless you are sweet yourself on Miss Gwilt" (387). When Midwinter later turns against Lydia Gwilt with "savage suddenness," and "the savage blood that he had inherited from his mother [rises] dark and slow in his ashy cheeks," this "black flush" is brought into his face by his belief that she has been unfaithful (613–14). Once again, Collins represents Midwinter's "black" rage, but does so out of context, displacing the historical and political causes of his behavior with sexual ones.

This pattern of displacement is apparent from virtually the start of the novel, when (Wrentmore) Armadale marries a "dusky" woman of African descent. Collins represents their relationship as a form of slavery in which the wife "sacrifice[s] . . . her freedom" to her husband (38). Yet the anger that makes her "hot African blood burn" does not stem from her sense of enslavement to a plantation owner, but from her knowledge that he does not love her—that he loves "the fair" Jane Blanchard instead:

> Mrs. [(Wrentmore)] Armadale . . . sat with her face steadily turned away from him. The hot African blood burnt red in her dusky cheeks as she obstinately repeated the question, "Was she a fair woman—or dark, like me?"

"Fair," said her husband, without looking at her.

Her hands, lying clasped together in her lap, wrung each other hard—she said no more. (24)

In her anger, Mrs. (Wrentmore) Armadale registers her sense of inequities between "the fair" and "the dark." But she is concerned with the romantic and not the political consequences of this racial difference—with the way in which her darkness renders her undesirable in her husband's eyes. Portraying her as willingly submissive, if only her husband would love her, Collins uses the jealous African wife not only to obscure racial politics but also to suggest that the colonized naturally desire to be subjugated. Conflating racial and sexual differences, he makes imperial rule seem natural by emphasizing its manliness: for, as Lydia Gwilt later observes in regard to her own husband, men are natural masters: "He spoke in a new voice—he suddenly *commanded,* as only men can" (410).

While stereotypes of men's natural mastery allow Collins to justify imperial rule, misogynistic conceptions of women's sexual power enable him to defend the empire by suggesting that it is imperiled by reverse colonization of the female kind, and that men rather than women occupy a position analogous to that of the subject races. Despite her darkness—or rather, because of it—Mrs. (Wrentmore) Armadale "conquers" the Scotsman, Alexander Neal, at first sight:

> He turned on the instant, and saw before him, with the pure midday light shining full on her, a woman of the mixed blood of the European and the African race, with the northern delicacy in the shape of her face, and the southern richness in its colour—a woman in the prime of her beauty, who moved with an inbred grace, . . . whose little dusky hand offered itself to him in mute expression of her thanks, with the welcome that is given to the coming of a friend. For the first time in his life, the Scotchman was taken by surprise. Every self-preservative word that he had been meditating but an instant since, dropped out of his memory. His thrice impenetrable armour of habitual suspicion, habitual self-discipline, and habitual reserve, which had never fallen from him in a woman's presence before, fell from him in this woman's presence, and brought him to his knees, a conquered man. (14)

Initially cast as a dark-skinned victim, the dusky and "mute" woman gains ascendancy over Alexander Neal, who becomes her second husband and is "brought to his knees." In a subtle sleight of hand, Collins redefines the oppressed as the oppressor, depicting Midwinter's mother as a slave driver of sorts, who dresses her "swarthy" son in shabby clothes and locks him in the lumber room on a diet of bread and water, while her second husband horsewhips the child (83).

At various points in his novel, Collins redefines his female characters in this way, forcing them to bear the burden of guilt associated with British imperialism. Although (Wrentmore) Armadale brutalizes his slaves and murders his rival, his crimes seem to fade in comparison with that of Jane Blanchard, who betrays her father in order to marry "Ingleby." Learning that her suitor is not the "Allan Armadale" whom she and her father were expecting—that is, the son of Mrs. Wrentmore of Barbados—she passively assists in the hoax rather than exposing it to her father, permitting her maid to forge a letter that paves the way to her marriage. Although Collins initially suggests that Miss Blanchard only assists "Ingleby" because she has already been seduced (27), he quickly obscures her status as victim, magnifying her crime instead.

When Mr. Brock reads the confession of (Wrentmore) Armadale, for example, he is deeply troubled by Miss Blanchard's "treason," but not by the murder committed by the plantation owner: "All his heart . . . was with the memory of the woman who had been the beloved friend of his later and happier life; all his thoughts were busy with the miserable secret of her treason to her own father which the letter had disclosed" (79). Similarly, Midwinter seizes on Miss Blanchard's crime as a means of extenuating that of his father, while ostensibly protecting her memory: "If the story of the names is ever told, there can be no limiting it to the disclosure of my father's crime; it must go back to the story of Mrs. Armadale's marriage. I have heard her son talk of her; I know how he loves her memory. As God is my witness, he shall never love it less dearly through *me*!" (92). Providing us with a genealogy of crime, Collins places Miss Blanchard's at the very beginning, implicitly blaming her for all those that follow. Like *The Law and the Lady, Armadale* is a novel partially modeled on Milton's *Paradise Lost,* but one in which the modern Adam appears to bear little or no blame for the Fall: "The daughters of Eve still inherit their mother's merits and commit their mother's faults. But the sons of Adam, in these latter days, are men who would have handed the famous apple back with a bow, and a 'Thanks, no; it might get me into a scrape' " (251).

In *Armadale,* Miss Gwilt is Collins's most obvious Eve figure, and he uses her, like Miss Blanchard, to exonerate "the sons of Adam" in his novel—by transforming yet another enslaved woman into a criminal and slave driver. Developing the analogy between African slaves and married women, deprived of legal identity and property rights under English common law, Collins compares the relation between Lydia Gwilt and Mr. Waldron, her first husband, to that of slave and master. Waldron incarcerates his wife in his Yorkshire estate and treats her with "almost unexampled barbarity" (519). Like a plantation overseer, he punishes her with the whip, which he "laid . . . across [her] face" (533). Recalling the oppressed and vengeful blacks of the prologue, Lydia Gwilt gains her emancipation by poisoning her master. Although Collins extends less sympathy to Miss Gwilt than the Home Secretary in his novel, who pardons her after her conviction, he represents her crime as highly provoked, and he suggests, in the words of Mr. Bashwood, that her husband "deserved it" (517).

But if Collins uses Miss Gwilt to dramatize the crimes committed by British masters, both at home and abroad, he also uses her to displace these crimes, disavowing his sense of guilt. He does so by supplying her with a second, more sinister, oppressor and by blaming the victim herself for imperial decline. Although Lydia Gwilt is enslaved by the Englishman, Mr. Waldron, she is most brutally victimized by a Cuban, Captain Manuel. Having persuaded her to murder Waldron, supplying her with the necessary poison, Manuel commits bigamy in marrying the widow, quickly squanders the property of his new "wife," and then deserts her. In a novel about enslavement and empire, Collins identifies his arch villain as "a native of Cuba, and . . . an ex-officer in the Spanish navy" (516), and his choice of Spanish Cuba as the home of Manuel shifts blame away from the British at an especially troubling moment in their imperial history.

As Collins's readers knew, the economic distress from which Britain's West Indian islands suffered in the 1860s was produced, in part, by the cheapness of Cuban and Brazilian "slave sugar," still produced by slave labor in the Spanish colonies. Unlike the British, who willingly emancipated their slaves in 1834, the Spanish were forced to do so only after the American Civil War, and their slave ships were attacked by the British Navy for much of the nineteenth century. Their colonies served as "final refuges" for the institution of slavery,[8] and their horrific colonial practices provided a convenient foil for the British, a point that Collins exploits in identifying Captain Manuel as Waldron's rival and successor.

Collins not only casts Lydia Gwilt as Captain Manuel's victim but also as his accomplice, suggesting that she, too, poses a threat to the British Empire by participating in Spanish colonization. Although

Lydia's plan to "journey to the Brazils" and go into business there (204, 209) is a fabrication, she does enter into an alliance of sorts with the Cuban, using him as an "instrument" in her plot against "the rich young Englishman" (557). Yet in a novel about empire, the most pressing threat that Lydia Gwilt poses is not that of a colonist to Brazil but of an Englishwoman who desires legal and sexual autonomy. The "greedy" Spaniard may covet Britain's imperial wealth (555), but Lydia envies the "privileges of the men" in the novel (453). The consequences of her affair with Manuel are especially telling in this regard. Deserted by her Cuban lover, a suicidal Lydia Gwilt jumps into the Thames. Yet the female victim becomes the feminist victimizer when Arthur Blanchard, Allan Armadale's cousin, dies after saving her, and their uncle and cousin, next in line to the family estate, are killed by an avalanche while returning home. In effect, Miss Gwilt's suicide attempt leads to the death of the squire of Thorpe-Ambrose and his next two heirs, nearly eliminating the male line. Were Lydia to succeed in her plot against Allan Armadale, who next inherits the estate, a female heir, Allan's cousin Miss Blanchard, would finally possess Thorpe-Ambrose (584). Thus when Pedgift Sr. classes Miss Gwilt with "all the hungry single women in the community," to whom the wealthy bachelor appears their "natural prey" (352–53), he underestimates the threat she poses. More menacing than most "strong-minded . . . single ladies" (344), she hungers for mastery and wishes to become a widow rather than a wife.

Developing the dual meanings of emancipation in his novel, Collins calls attention to the enslavement of English wives and "the misery of being a woman" in a patriarchal culture (432), providing examples of women cut from their husbands' wills (518) and evicted from their homes when widowed by the rules of male succession (73). Criticizing a society that keeps women in ignorance to "protect" and "spare" them (33, 34), he parodies widely held assumptions about the weakness and purity of "the female constitution" (624). But Collins also uses his female characters as scapegoats for Britain's imperial woes, reinscribing the gender norms he criticizes by suggesting that emancipated English-women threaten the empire at home—as unnatural wives and mothers. Equating female emancipation with the emasculation of men and the destruction of children, Collins represents Lydia Gwilt as a "conqueror" who bends Midwinter to her will (415, 435) and who refuses to become a mother. While she refers to Midwinter's employers as his "slave-own-ers" (540), Collins reveals her drive to become his master. Characterized by her "extraordinary independence" and resolve (617), she dominates and ultimately renounces her husband, dressing in widow's weeds although he is alive. At a time in which the health of the empire was measured by census reports, the growth of the English population, and the competency of mothers, Lydia Gwilt dissociates sex from reproduction, fantasizes about "hav[ing] . . . a child to beat" (157), and consorts with an abortionist.[9]

Collins's interest in Dr. Downward may seem odd in a novel about race relations and imperial crime, yet abortion was understood as a sign of atavism and imperial decay by mid-Victorians—as a crime against the empire, threatening British hegemony and civilization from within.[10] Leading the British "downward"—on the path of decline and fall—Miss Gwilt enables Collins to trace an imperial crisis to what he suggests is its sexual source—away from tyrannical plantation owners, lawless colonial governors, and rebellious natives, to women who desire to abandon their proper roles, avoid motherhood, and "plunge into public life" (622). Diagnosing the sexual ills of the empire, and attributing them to female emancipation and promiscuity, Collins suggests that (Wrentmore) Armadale's paralysis is a symptom of venereal disease—"the terminal stage of syphilis" (Peters, Explanatory Notes, 664), an illness for which prostitutes ("public women") were held accountable by the Contagious Diseases Act of 1864.

Whether represented as a female savage or as a slave master, the emancipated woman enables Allan Armadale and Ozias Midwinter to overcome their racial differences by highlighting the primacy of sexual differences instead. When Collins introduces Midwinter into the main narrative, he emphasizes the Creole's racial otherness and repeatedly suggests that the part-African character brings the dangers of native insurrection to England's shores. With "[his] mother's negro blood in [his] face" (81), Midwinter leads "the life of a savage" (295), and acts in ways that resemble a rebel slave: "Young, slim, and undersized, he was strong enough . . . to make it a matter of difficulty . . . to master him," Collins remarks (51). Although he is describing the effects of "brain fever" on Midwinter in this passage, Collins seems to attribute such wild behavior to what he refers to as "negro blood." Endowing Midwinter with the stereotypical traits of the subject races, Collins depicts him as "tawny," "lean," and "lithe," with "long supple, sinewy fingers" that "look . . . like claws" (55–56). Grasped by Midwinter, Allan finds "those long claws of [his] . . . rather tight" (115), while the "healthy Anglo-Saxon flesh" of Mr. Brock "crept responsively" at the sight of the Creole's "yellow face" and "supple" movements (56). Even more alarm-

ing to Mr. Brock is Midwinter's "heathen belief" (94) that he is predestined to harm Allan Armadale. Responding to the Creole's "evil spirit of
Superstition" (501) as a missionary would, Mr. Brock struggles to convert him to Christianity—to banish "the paralysing fatalism of the heathen and the savage" from his heart and convince him "to look at the
mysteries that perplex, and the portents that daunt [him], from the
Christian's point of view" (502).

Midwinter's conversion does, indeed, take place, but not simply
through his acceptance of Christianity. Rather, he achieves an alliance
with the Protestant Anglo-Saxons by means of Miss Gwilt, whose sexual
otherness obscures the racial otherness of the Creole. Anticipating her
arrival on the scene, Collins displaces the threatening image of the mutinous native with that of the uncontrollable woman—by feminizing
Midwinter and his revolt. "Frenzied" and "feverish," Midwinter's "spirits
flame . . . out into sheer delirium" at the major's home, yet his behavior
is diagnosed as womanly—as a "hysterical paroxysm" symptomatic of
"his sensitive feminine organization" (212–17). With the appearance of
Miss Gwilt, however, Collins frees Midwinter from this womanly role,
while continuing to represent native insurrection as a form of hysteria
and female revolt.

The tensions between Midwinter and Armadale reach their breaking
point when they argue over Miss Gwilt, inflaming Midwinter's "hot
Creole blood" and leading him to violence (387). Yet the introduction of
Miss Gwilt redefines the nature of their disagreement, enabling them to
overcome it. Forcing the racial antagonists to become male rivals, she
provides them with common ground. Although Collins claims, in his
chapter title, that "she comes between them," Miss Gwilt actually
brings Armadale and Midwinter together by reminding them of their
shared manhood and by supplying them with a common enemy—the
emancipated woman herself. Even before they discover her plot against
them, which hinges on their identity as "Allan Armadales," the two men
become allies against Lydia Gwilt, as she herself complains: "Midwinter
finds in Armadale's company . . . a refuge from *me*" (540).

While Midwinter's racial status aligns him with the subject races in
the colonies, his sexual status defines him as a master in the home. "She
has denied her husband to-night," Midwinter observes when Lydia
renounces him: "She shall know her master to-morrow" (516). Midwinter asserts his prerogatives as husband and master toward the end of the
novel, and Lydia Gwilt assumes her proper, subordinate place. Renouncing her plot, invoking God's forgiveness, and sacrificing her life for that

of her husband, she becomes "womanly and lovely once more" (652). For both Miss Gwilt and Mrs. Milroy, womanly subordination proves fatal: the major's wife "is greatly altered," Pedgift Sr. tells his son, approvingly, "quiet and gentle, and anxiously affectionate with her husband and her child. But . . . this happy change is, it seems, a sign of approaching dissolution, from the medical point of view" (657). By means of this subplot, Collins wryly suggests that a wife's proper behavior may kill her. However, such insights do not keep him from sacrificing the emancipated women in his novel to an imperial cause. Transforming them into docile and subservient figures, while also representing their subordination as natural and appropriate, he defuses the threat of native insurrection and assuages his sense of imperial guilt.

In *The Moonstone,* his next novel about British imperialism, Collins proves considerably more willing to acknowledge the guilt of the British and hold them accountable for their crimes. As he does in *Armadale,* Collins opens *The Moonstone* in a British colony, only to bring his story back to England in a central narrative. But in the later novel, he includes an epilogue that returns us to India and redresses the wrongs inflicted on the Hindus by their British conquerors. Developing the analogy between mutinous natives and rebellious Englishwomen, Collins again uses his female rebels to sexualize and displace the threat of insurrection. Yet he seems primarily interested in exposing the common plight of subjugated women and subject races in *The Moonstone,* largely justifying their anger and resistance, and bolstering his critique of empire with a critique of patriarchy. Drawing an analogy between imperial and class relations as well, he compares the members of the subject races to those of the English working class and suggests that their pride in the British empire is misplaced. Whereas Collins repeatedly invokes *Paradise Lost* in *Armadale,* he reworks *Robinson Crusoe* in *The Moonstone,* arguing that English servants as well as colonized natives play the role of Friday in imperial Britain.

The Moonstone (1868)

Collins began work on *The Moonstone* in the spring of 1867, reading histories of British India and consulting John Wyllie of the Indian Civil Service for firsthand information about the colony. "I have been too busy to write before today," he told his mother on 11 May, "between my negotiation with *All the Year Round,* and my readings in the [Athenaeum] Club Library of works that I must consult for my new book."[11] By July he had written the first three numbers, to be serialized weekly in Dickens's *All the Year Round,* beginning in January 1868. Collins wrote the novel under notably adverse circumstances; he was bedridden in February by a severe attack of rheumatic gout, and grief stricken the following month by the death of his mother. In the midst of his sufferings, Collins turned to his novel as a source of relief, producing his most popular success since the publication of *The Woman in White* nearly a decade earlier.

The Moonstone opens with a prologue related by an English army officer in India, describing the Siege of Seringapatam in 1799. A member of the Herncastle family, the officer writes for the benefit of his relatives— to account for his estrangement from his cousin, a fellow officer named John Herncastle. As the narrator explains, the Muslim ruler Tippoo, Sultan of Seringapatam, possesses a Hindu diamond sacred to the god of the moon and secretly guarded by three Brahmins. During the siege, John Herncastle steals the diamond from Tippoo's palace, murdering its three Hindu guardians. Although the narrator does not see the murders committed, he finds Herncastle holding a bloody dagger and standing over a dying Brahmin. "The Moonstone will have its vengeance yet on you and yours," the Brahmin warns.[12]

The Moonstone exacts its vengeance in the central section of the novel, set in 1848 and 1849 and related by a host of narrators: these include the faithful steward at the Verinder estate, Gabriel Betteredge, an avid reader of *Robinson Crusoe;* an Evangelical spinster, Miss Clack; Franklin Blake, a cousin in the Herncastle family; and Mathew Bruff, the family solicitor. The story begins when John Herncastle, a family outcast, bequeaths his famous diamond to his niece, Rachel Verinder. Her cousin, Franklin Blake, brings it to the Verinders' Yorkshire estate from London, followed by three Indians descended from the Hindus murdered in India 50 years before. Courted by Blake, whom she loves and plans to marry, Miss Verinder receives the diamond on her 18th birthday, 21 June 1848. That night, it is stolen from an Indian cabinet in her bedroom, and Sergeant Cuff of Scotland Yard arrives to investigate the case.

Although many of the English characters initially believe that the Hindus have stolen the diamond, and Cuff suspects that Rachel Verinder has staged its theft with the help of the housemaid Rosanna Spearman, to pay off her debts, we eventually learn that Franklin Blake stole the jewel unconsciously, out of concern for its safety, while under the influence of an opiate secretly administered to him by the local doc-

tor, Mr. Candy, to prove a medical point. Later that night, still unconscious of his actions, Blake gives the diamond to another cousin, the
philanthropist Godfrey Ablewhite, for safekeeping at his father's bank.
The next morning, Ablewhite realizes that Blake has no memory of
these events and steals the diamond himself, hoping to restore money to
a trust fund he has embezzled. Rosanna Spearman finds an incriminating paint stain on Blake's nightgown, and realizes that he has stolen the
diamond, but conceals the evidence because she loves him. Rachel
Verinder also knows that Blake has stolen her jewel, having witnessed
the theft, but declines to expose him. Enraged at what she perceives to
be his dishonesty and dissimulation, she breaks off their relationship.
Unaware of Ablewhite's role in the crime, she agrees to marry him
instead, only to learn of his mercenary interests in her property and
income and end their engagement. Rejected by Blake in her various
attempts to reveal her knowledge of his crime, and win his gratitude
and love, Rosanna Spearman commits suicide, leaving him a note that
identifies him as the thief, in a package containing his stained nightgown.

Stunned by this evidence, Blake is aided by Ezra Jennings, Mr.
Candy's assistant, who reconstructs the events of 21 June. Although Mr.
Candy falls ill on the night of the theft, and loses his memory of the
trick he played on Blake, Jennings discovers the truth by piecing
together the doctor's incoherent ramblings. Administering opium to
Blake at the Verinder estate, Jennings restages the theft, exonerating
Blake and reuniting him with Rachel Verinder. Still tracking the Moon-
stone, the Hindus find it in Ablewhite's possession and murder him.
After disclosing the marriage of Franklin and Rachel, and the concep-
tion of their first child, the novel ends with an epilogue describing the
Brahmins' escape from England and the restoration of the diamond to a
Hindu shrine in the Indian province of Kattiawar, witnessed by Mr.
Murthwaite, an English expert on India.

Like Collins's earlier works of sensation fiction, *The Moonstone* exposes
a mercenary plot against a wealthy young woman, who learns that English marriage law makes her an object of financial speculation to men.
"Poor thing!" Mr. Bruff says of Rachel Verinder, before he tells her of
Ablewhite's scheme. "The bare idea of a man marrying her for his own
selfish and mercenary ends had never entered her head" (318). But like
the Mutiny novels of the 1860s—works written in response to the
Indian uprising of 1857[13]—*The Moonstone* also represents a military conflict in British India and examines the political and cultural differences

between colonizers and colonized. Throughout the novel, Collins combines his interest in domestic "sensation" with his interest in imperial relations, developing the tie between the rape of India and the symbolic violation of Rachel Verinder.

As we have seen in chapter 2, Collins's reaction to the Indian Mutiny was more tempered than most. Whereas Dickens told a friend that he would like "to exterminate the Race upon whom the stain of the late cruelties rested . . . and raze it off the face of the Earth,"[14] Collins used his 1858 *Household Words* article, "A Sermon for Sepoys," to temper such responses, providing readers with examples of wisdom and benevolence among the Indians and revealing the common moral ground shared by Western and Eastern religions. "The more gifts you have received, the better use it is expected you will make of them," Collins writes, quoting from the Muslim sage "Abbas": "Spread the example, therefore, of your own benevolence, beyond the circle of those only who are wise and good. Widen the sphere of your usefulness among your fellow-creatures, with every day; and fortify your mind with the blessed conviction that the life you will then lead, will be of all lives the most acceptable in the eyes of the Supreme Being."[15] At a time in which most Englishmen exchanged their hope of civilizing the Indians with the desire to exterminate them, insisting that they were hopelessly immoral and violent (Brantlinger, 200), Collins provides us with an oriental parable of the talents, pointing to "the excellent moral lessons" to be learned from "Oriental literature" (244). Although Collins refers to the rebellious sepoys as "Betrayers and Assassins," he seems to use this rhetoric to pacify Dickens, whose racism was particularly virulent after the Mutiny. Unlike his editor, Collins speaks of educating the rebels rather than exterminating them, and he suggests that they belong to a culture as civilized as Britain's own.

Like "A Sermon for Sepoys," *The Moonstone* questions many of the racist assumptions generated or reinforced by the 1857 uprising. Whereas most Mutiny novels depict the Indians as monstrous figures capable of the most heinous crimes, *The Moonstone* investigates criminality among the English and examines the ways in which the imperialists victimize the Indians while blaming the subject races for their own imperial crimes. Unlike James Grant's *First Love and Last Love: A Tale of the Indian Mutiny* (1868), or Henry Kingsley's *Stretton* (1869), which promote the stereotype of the sexually violent mutineer, *The Moonstone* depicts the British themselves as lustful and murderous, inverting the usual formula of Mutiny novels.[16]

In *Armadale,* Collins addresses contemporary unrest in the West Indies indirectly, in a prologue distanced from his present day by the Emancipation Act and more than 30 years of colonial history. In *The Moonstone,* similarly, Collins represents the Siege of Seringapatam (1799) rather than the Indian Mutiny, in what appears to be an even more distanced approach to contemporary affairs. Yet Collins may well have felt that the Mutiny was too inflammatory a subject to treat directly—that reactions to the uprising were too hostile and too fixed to serve his purposes as a critic of empire. Rather than representing the Mutiny, he directs our attention to what many perceived to be the founding event of British India—the 1799 siege, which gave the British their foothold in the East by defeating Tippoo, an ally of the French.

Collins models his account of the Siege of Seringapatam, in part, on the lawlessness of the British forces in 1857 and 1858. Describing the "deplorable excesses" committed by soldiers and officers alike (36), he reminds his readers of the way in which the British plundered Delhi and murdered its inhabitants after putting down the Mutiny. But his prologue also presents a revisionary and negative portrait of the 1799 siege, a victory of which the British felt proud. As a source for his description of the siege, Collins used Theodore Hook's biography of General David Baird, which contrasts the murderous cruelty of the Muslim ruler with "the gallant conduct" of the British troops, "already chronicled in the annals of fame": "Let it never be forgotten in this great contest, who were, in fact, the oppressors," Hook asserts.[17] But Collins fails to mention Tippoo's cruelty in his account, emphasizing that of John Herncastle instead. Although Hook notes that the British troops pillaged Seringapatam, and that a private in the British Army murdered Tippoo "in cold blood" before plundering the corpse, he "hope[s] the man was a Sepoy" (1:217). Collins offers his readers no such hope in his portrait of pillage and murder. Instead of using the sepoys as scapegoats for the British and their crimes, he exposes that very strategy in his novel. When Godfrey Ablewhite disguises himself as an oriental sailor in his attempt to leave England with the Moonstone, darkening his skin to look "swarthy," Sergeant Cuff catches him in the act. "Washing off his complexion," Cuff reveals, quite literally, the whiteness of the thief (502).

It may seem misleading to identify any one character as the thief in *The Moonstone,* since the diamond changes hands at least six times, and several people are murdered, Ablewhite himself included. Yet Collins clearly suggests that Ablewhite is guilty to an extent that the Hindus are not. Mitigating the crimes committed by the Indians, Collins redefines the nature of their transgressions in his epilogue, explaining their significance in Hindu rather than Christian terms; the three Brahmins have not committed theft and murder, but have forfeited their caste in the service of their god. Although Collins does not justify the means they use to regain possession of the Moonstone, he clearly approves of the end they have achieved, restoring the diamond to its proper place in Central Asia—a sacred gem in a Hindu shrine, not a "marketable commodity" (512) to be sold among the diamond cutters of Amsterdam, as Ablewhite intends. Reminding us that "the Indians . . . originally owned the jewel" (72), and encouraging us to think of them as religious martyrs instead of thieves and murderers, Collins speaks of their need for "purification" rather than punishment: "The god had commanded that their purification should be the purification by pilgrimage. . . . In three separate directions, they were to set forth as pilgrims to the shrines of India" (526).

For the crimes of John Herncastle and Godfrey Ablewhite, however, Collins offers no excuses. Instead, he uses their criminal behavior to unmask the hypocrisy of Britain's imperial mission in the East. Identifying Ablewhite as a philanthropist associated with Exeter Hall (89), the headquarters of the Victorian missionary movement, Collins suggests that the Christian aims of empire building are merely a pretense for satisfying imperial greed. Collins uses the ironically named "Ablewhite" to reveal the ability of whites to make the most of their colonial possessions—in an economic sense. His portrait of John Herncastle serves a similar end. The ostensibly disciplined English officer proves to be more violent and greedy than any other character in the novel, yet Collins treats him as an emblematic figure. He repeatedly refers to Herncastle as "the Honourable John" (63, 65), using the well-known nickname of the East India Company to describe him. In so doing, he associates the criminal deviance of Herncastle, presumably the black sheep of his family, with the established economic practices of the British Empire in the years leading up to the Mutiny. Understood as the action of "the Honourable John," Herncastle's theft of the Moonstone comes to represent the legally sanctioned robbery of India by the British government.

Whereas Collins indicts Herncastle and Ablewhite for their crimes, he appears to exonerate a third Englishman, Franklin Blake. Blake steals the Moonstone from an Indian cabinet in Rachel Verinder's bedroom, but does so unconsciously, under the influence of opium, and with what seem the best of intentions; fearing that "the Indians may be hidden in the house" (510), he attempts to protect the diamond, which Rachel has left unlocked. "Under the stimulating influence" of opium, Ezra Jennings explains to Blake, "any apprehensions about the safety of the Diamond which you might have felt during the day, would be liable to develop themselves from the state of doubt to the state of certainty—would impel you into practical action to preserve the jewel—would direct your steps, with that motive in view, into the room which you entered—and would guide your hand to the drawers of the cabinet, until you had found the drawer which held the stone" (442–43).

Yet the very fact that Blake takes the diamond while under the influence of opium suggests that he, too, plays a role in empire building and bears a portion of imperial guilt. Spurned by Rachel Verinder, Blake leaves England to "wander . . . in the East," "encamp[ing] on the borders of a desert" (339). Collins offers no specific reason for Blake's choice of the East as his destination, yet his presence there seems appropriate. Despite Blake's acquittal at the hands of Ezra Jennings, he acts for "the Honourable John" in delivering the Moonstone to Rachel Verinder, and he reenacts Herncastle's original crime when he steals it from her, with opium providing him with the means of doing so.

As Collins's original readers knew, opium was the most important crop produced in British India. At a time when the British demand for Chinese goods greatly outweighed the Chinese demand for British products, this contraband commodity enabled the British to solve their problem with balance of trade. Shipped from India to China in ships licensed by the East India Company, and providing a substantial portion of the Company's profits, opium was smuggled into China by the British against the laws of the Chinese, in exchange for the goods that were in such great demand at home. When the Chinese began to resist the trade in the late 1830s, the British government intervened. Easily defeated in the Opium War, the Chinese were compelled to cede Hong Kong to the British in 1842, to open additional ports, and to allow the British to carry on their trade unmolested. After a second war in 1860, the British forced the Chinese to sign the Treaty of Tientsin, legalizing the opium trade.

Often compared to the institution of slavery by critics of empire, the opium trade provided them with indisputable evidence of Britain's imperial guilt, evidence provided to readers of Dickens's journals—and hence of Collins's novel—in a host of articles about opium, some addressed to "the Honourable John": "You entice the Chinese to ruin their fortune and health, that you may make money. You condemn the Americans for encouraging and extending slavery; and yet you wink at a traffic quite as iniquitous, for a reason quite as selfish. . . . If you think Christian missions to China good, look around you; for reasonable men among the Chinese laugh with bitter scorn when you bring the Bible in one hand and opium in the other."[18]

It might be objected that Franklin Blake is not an opium merchant but yet another victim of a "foreign" drug,[19] and the ambiguities that surround his theft of the Moonstone and his relation to opium suggest Collins's uneasiness with his role as critic of empire. Yet these ambiguities also enable Collins to purposefully blur the line between protection and violation, collapsing the distinction between them. While attempting to "preserve" the diamond, and keep it "safe" (510), Blake appropriates it, in an act that links his guardianship of Rachel Verinder and the Moonstone with both sexual and imperial conquest. As a number of critics note, Blake's theft from Rachel Verinder suggests her loss of virginity, as does Rachel's sense of shame and outrage after the gem has been stolen, and Cuff's identification of a stained nightgown as crucial evidence in the case.[20] At the same time, Blake's theft also suggests the rape of India by the British: not simply because he takes the diamond from an Indian cabinet, but because Rachel herself resembles the Brahmins—"dark," "lithe," "supple" (190), and animated by an angry desire for independence (87).[21]

In his relation to Rachel, and his dual role of protector and thief, Blake illuminates the paradox of Victorian guardianship, in both its patriarchal and its imperial guises. As Rachel's prospective husband, he promises to protect his future wife, while stripping her of her sexual and legal autonomy and her property rights. As an Englishman with ties to "the Honourable John," he promises to civilize India, while exploiting its people and claiming its wealth for his own.

In *The Moonstone*, as in virtually all of his novels, Collins reinscribes the very ideals he criticizes. He represents Rachel's happy reconciliation with her future husband, despite her "absolute self-dependence" earlier on—"a great virtue in a man," we are told by Mathew Bruff (319); and he parodies the spinster Miss Clack, discrediting the independence of single women. As if to justify imperial rule, he highlights the devotion Blake receives from Jennings, a "half-caste" born in the colonies. The product of an exploitative relationship between an Englishman and a native woman, Jennings is continually subject to prejudice and persecution. But rather than expressing resentment toward the English, Jennings identifies with and serves them. He speaks of "our colonies" (420), champions the use of opium (436), and dedicates himself to vindicating

Blake's innocence: "If I can do you this little service," Jennings tells him, "I shall feel it like a last gleam of sunshine, falling on the evening of a long and clouded day" (446).[22]

Yet Collins questions this idealized colonial relationship at the same time that he invokes it, using Gabriel Betteredge, and the parallel between imperial and class relations, to reveal the pitfalls of identifying with one's masters. In a novel about imperial crime, it proves to be one of Collins's central ironies that Betteredge valorizes Defoe's idyll of empire building, *Robinson Crusoe,* while misapplying its tale of mastery and subservience to his own case. Persistently quoting from Defoe's work, Betteredge identifies with Crusoe, overlooking his ties to Friday. Using Defoe's racist portrait of the cannibals who land on Crusoe's island as a model for the Brahmins who "invade" his own (67), Betteredge fails to see his resemblance to the colonized natives. At one point in the novel, the English servant equates his services with those of Crusoe's slave—when, refusing to assist Sergeant Cuff, he hopes that he has left the detective "without a man Friday to keep him company" (207). But like Jennings, whose "gypsy darkness" he distrusts (371–72), Betteredge prefers to think of himself as a Crusoe figure, overlooking his servitude by comparing his experiences with those of the imperialist and slave master.

Reworking Defoe's novel, Collins develops the connections that Betteredge ignores, reminding us of what imperial myths obscure: that working-class Englishmen may be masters in India but remain servants at home. Betteredge assumes the part of Crusoe in his dealings with Jennings and the Brahmins, but he performs the work of Friday for Lady Verinder and her relations. Denied the privileges of his social superiors, who "have all the luxuries to themselves" (200), he nonetheless accepts his place in the Verinders' social scheme. Although he chooses to pity rather than resent the idle class, and "thank [his] stars" that he has work to do (84–85), a number of working-class figures do not. Unlike Betteredge, Nancy, the kitchen maid, feels things are "wrong" at the Verinder estate: "All the hard work falls on my shoulders in this house. Leave me alone, Mr. Betteredge!" (53).

In *The Moonstone,* Collins leaves it to the working-class women—to Lucy Yolland, particularly—to recognize and express a sense of class injury and to identify Franklin Blake as an enemy. By allowing Nancy and Lucy Yolland to see what Betteredge does not, Collins acknowledges their twofold oppression as women and workers, but he also discredits their discontent by characterizing it as female. "Where's the man you call Franklin Blake?" Lucy Yolland asks Betteredge, "fixing [him] with a fierce look":

> "That's not a respectful way to speak of any gentleman," I answered. "If you wish to inquire for my lady's nephew, you will please to mention him as Mr. Franklin Blake."
> She limped a step nearer to me, and looked as if she could have eaten me alive. "*Mr.* Franklin Blake?" she repeated after me. "Murderer Franklin Blake would be a fitter name for him. . . . Where is he?" cries the girl, lifting her head from the crutch, and flaming out again through her tears. "Where's this gentleman that I mustn't speak of, except with respect? Ha, Mr. Betteredge, the day is not far off when the poor will rise against the rich. I pray Heaven they may begin with *him*." (226–27)

Addressing her remarks to Betteredge in 1848, a year marked by revolutions throughout Europe, Lucy Yolland voices the social discontent that the "respectful" servant does not. At the same time, however, she naturalizes and displaces class oppression and rage. Known as "Limping Lucy" because of her clubfoot, she gives class injury a physical form, transforming it into a birth defect; so, too, does Rosanna Spearman, who suffers from a deformed shoulder. Although Collins uses their handicaps to account for the "temper" of these discontented workers (226), and to justify their marginalized status in the novel, he also suggests that their defects are uniquely female: a sign of the flawed nature common to women of all social classes.

Indeed, the deformities of the working-class women in the novel recall the "one defect" that Betteredge finds in the otherwise perfect Rachel Verinder—that of female independence (87). Despite her call for social revolution, Lucy Yolland's anger, like Rachel's, is that of an independent woman thwarted by men and resentful of male privilege. She turns on Blake not simply because he is a gentleman, but because he is a man. Having wronged Rosanna, and driven her to suicide, he destroys Lucy's hopes for a self-supporting sisterhood. "We might have got our living nicely," Lucy tells Betteredge, describing her education and talents, and those of Rosanna. "I had a plan for our going to London together like sisters, and living by our needles. That man came here, and spoilt it all" (227). Identifying Lucy Yolland as a cannibal of sorts—a woman who "could have eaten [Betteredge] alive"—Collins looks beyond rebellious sepoys and working-class revolutionaries, to angry women who hunger for autonomy. Bringing Betteredge and Blake alike into conflict with Lucy Yolland and Rachel Verinder, he imagines a sexual crisis that can be more easily dismissed (as hysteria) and more easily quelled (through marriage) than that of the Indian Mutiny.

Such displacements play a relatively minor role in *The Moonstone,* but they are central to *The New Magdalen,* a third novel about empire building and resistance to British rule. Representing the threat posed to British hegemony by the rival powers of Germany and France, Collins redefines an imperial crisis as a sexual one. Forming the sisterhood that Lucy Yolland only imagines in *The Moonstone,* the female characters in *The New Magdalen* struggle for self-government and control of their own economic and sexual resources. Yet Collins discredits their sisterhood at the same time that he represents it: as a self-supporting community of prostitutes, who give female autonomy a bad name.

The New Magdalen (1872–1873)

Collins started planning *The New Magdalen* in the spring of 1872, describing it to his Canadian publishers as a story he would write "during the present autumn," and consisting of "not less than four or more than six *monthly* parts."[23] By November he had extended the novel to eight parts, and he was pleased with the "very strong impression" produced by its first two numbers.[24] *The New Magdalen* was serialized in Richard Bentley's *Temple Bar,* from October 1872 to July 1873, in 10 monthly numbers, and published in volume form in May. Adapted for the stage by Collins, it proved a notable dramatic success.

The New Magdalen tells what was, by 1872, a familiar story to Victorian audiences—that of a reformed prostitute struggling to make her way back to "Home and Name."[25] Yet Collins's work differs from others on the same subject by beginning as a novel about European warfare and the political and military hostilities between Germany and France. Whereas *Armadale* is set on the eve of the Emancipation Act, and *The Moonstone* opens with the Siege of Seringapatam, *The New Magdalen* begins in Europe in the present time, as the German army prepares to invade Lagrange during the Franco-Prussian War (1870–1871). Employed as a Red Cross nurse attached to a French ambulance, Mercy Merrick, an Englishwoman, tends the wounded. She also assists a young English lady, Grace Roseberry, stranded on the frontier while returning to England from Italy, where her father has died. Left without money or family ties, Miss Roseberry tells Mercy that she hopes to become the paid companion of Lady Janet Roy, an affluent Englishwoman whom she has never met but to whom she is related by marriage.

During a lull in the fighting, Mercy Merrick tells her own story, at Grace Roseberry's request. The illegitimate daughter of a beautiful but poor actress and a gentleman of rank, Mercy is left a "starving outcast" after her mother's death; she soon joins the ranks of those women "whom Want has driven into Sin" (203). Recounting her reclamation at a refuge for prostitutes, and her gratitude to the minister Julian Gray, Mercy bemoans her fate: despite her repentance, she is tainted by her past and dismissed by her employers whenever they learn of it. "The lost place is not to be regained. I can't get back!" (205), she exclaims. But when Miss Roseberry is struck by a German shell, and left for dead by the French surgeon, Mercy Merrick gets her chance. Assuming Grace Roseberry's identity, and stealing her letter of introduction, she returns to England and becomes the beloved companion of Lady Janet Roy.

Although Mercy is treated as a daughter by Lady Janet, and engaged to marry the affluent gentleman, Horace Holmcroft, she is troubled by secret remorse. Her scheme is further imperiled by the surprising recovery of the real Grace Roseberry, brought back to life from a state of "suspended animation" (243) by a German surgeon who operates on her. Recovering in a German hospital, Grace is mistaken for Mercy Merrick because of the labels on her clothing, borrowed from the nurse. Grace suspects that her identity has been stolen, but her assertions are viewed as symptoms of madness by a number of her doctors and by the English consul called in to hear her case. Nonetheless, the consul writes to his friend Julian Gray to tell him of Grace's claims; the minister whose sermon saved Mercy, we learn, is also the nephew of Lady Janet Roy.

Appointing a meeting with Miss Roseberry at the London home of Lady Janet, Julian Gray tells his aunt and Horace Holmcroft of her claims; both dismiss Grace as an adventuress or madwoman. Although Mercy faints at the sight of Grace, neither lose their faith in her, and she remains safe from exposure. But after discussing the ideas of repentance and forgiveness with Julian Gray, who also believes her to be innocent of the fraud, Mercy chooses to confess. Despite the security of her position, the insulting behavior of Grace Roseberry, and the willingness of Lady Janet to suppress the truth, Mercy tells her story to her companions. Rejected by Horace, who refuses to forgive her, Mercy learns that Julian wishes to marry her. Declining to ruin his prospects by becoming his wife, she rejects his suit and returns to the refuge, although Lady Janet intercedes on her nephew's behalf. But after Julian joins a mission in east London, and falls ill of fever, Mercy nurses him back to health and agrees to marry him. Snubbed by friends and acquaintances, who refuse to introduce their unmarried daughters to Mercy, Julian convinces his wife to emigrate to the New World.

Like *Armadale* and *The Moonstone, The New Magdalen* registers a threat posed to the British Empire—not by native insurrections in the colonies, but by European powers whose imperial ambitions rival Britain's own. Originating in a dispute over the Spanish crown, offered to a nephew of the Prussian king, and exacerbated by the desire of Napoleon III to claim Belgium for France, the Franco-Prussian War reflected the struggle for dominance in Europe, and Germany's unification and rise to power, in the 1870s. Defeated in 1871, the French were forced to give portions of Alsace and Lorraine to Germany, extending its national borders.[26] Yet the conflict between France and Germany extended beyond the boundaries of Europe and anticipated the imperial scramble for Africa, officially recognized in 1878 by the first Berlin Conference. To the dismay of the British, the French had opened the Suez Canal in 1869, demonstrating their influence in Egypt and making India more accessible to Britain's rivals. As the British fought to extend their power in southern and western Africa in the early 1870s, exchanging Sumatra for the coastal territories of the Dutch, the French Parliament approved plans to build a railway across the Sahara to the western Sudan.

In Collins's view, the Franco-Prussian War undermined the moral and religious grounds on which such plans were laid—by demonstrating that the ostensibly civilized powers of Europe were nothing of the kind. Writing to Dr. Emil Lehmann, the brother of his friend Frederick, in August 1870, Collins criticizes the savagery of Europeans, "still ready to slaughter each other" in an age of "progress":

> I am, like the rest of my countrymen, heartily on the German side in the War. But what is to be said of the progress of humanity? Here are the nations still ready to slaughter each other, at the command of one miserable wretch whose interest it is to set them fighting! Is this the nineteenth century? or the ninth? Are we before the time of Christ—or after? I begin to believe in only one civilising influence—the discovery one of these days, of a destructive agent so terrible that War shall mean *annihilation,* and men's fears shall force them to keep the peace.[27]

Recalling his treatment of British savagery in *The Moonstone,* Collins's letter reveals his skepticism about the civilized state—a condition to be achieved not by means of Christian truth but by a "destructive agent" so absolute that any attempt at conquest will be averted. Although the discovery of this "terrible" weapon may end wars altogether, Collins

nonetheless suggests that the state of civilization is merely a technologi-
cally advanced state of primitivism, a point he illustrates in *The New
Magdalen* through the condition of England itself. As France and Germany engage in their primitive warfare, England proves to be "a civilization rotten to its core," one in which social inequities and "political
economy" keep the poor in a state of "savagery" (573). Living in slums
as disease-ridden as Africa (582–83), these English "savages" reveal the
even more savage qualities of the educated classes, whose members
allow such suffering to exist amid the "magnificence" of the empire's
"capital city" (319)—who can "trace back" their imperial lineage "to the
Saxons . . . [and] the Normans" (368), yet prove incapable of Christian
charity and forgiveness.

But while the Franco-Prussian War leads Collins to question the distinction between civilized Europeans and primitive peoples, it also stirs
his antipathy to the French and Napoleon III, the "miserable wretch"
who "set [Europe] fighting." Collins's antipathy is based, in part, on his
sense that French aggression threatens British as well as German interests. Although Collins questions the distinction between the savage and
the civilized in *The New Magdalen,* the novel's treatment of empire suggests that he is also anxious to defend Britain's imperial claims against
those of the French. Deciding on his hero's fate, Collins considers sending Julian Gray to "the West coast of Africa," as a volunteer "to a new
missionary enterprise" (582). Declaring him unfit to survive in the trop-
ical climate, which "would in all probability kill him in three months'
time," Collins sends his hero to "the fertile West of the great American
continent" instead (595–96). In so doing, he both expresses and soothes
his anxieties about French expansionism. He establishes Julian in a
"New World" opened to British settlement and enterprise in the
1870s—by the westward growth of the empire in Canada, and the
defeat of a French Canadian resistance movement in the same year in
which Napoleon III declared war against Germany.

As Collins and his readers were aware, the British confederated their
North American colonies in 1867, forming the Dominion of Canada, a
self-governing possession of the British crown. Two years later, the western regions became part of the confederation as well. Before establishing
the province of Manitoba in 1870, however, the British had to defeat
the separatist movement led by Louis Riel, a member of the Metis people, traders of French descent. Ending French hopes of "block[ing] the
westward advance of the Empire with a French-speaking Catholic

province of their own," they transformed Canada into "an exploitable British whole."[28]

Collins watched these developments with interest, concerned with copyright legislation in North America, but also influenced, perhaps, by the knowledge that his grandfather, Alexander Geddes, had served as an ensign and lieutenant in Canada in the 1780s. In letters written to his Canadian publishers, Hunter and Rose, Collins repeatedly refers to Canada's status as a British possession and "an English colony,"[29] suggests that Canada should, "for all publishing purposes," be considered "a part of England,"[30] and tells them of his "very great interest in visiting 'The Dominion,' "[31] which he did in the winter of 1873, soon after finishing *The New Magdalen*. In this work, Collins represents Canada as a promised land of sorts—a primitive yet idyllic region in which his hero and heroine, and English culture itself, can begin again. "Away from the cities," where society exists "in its infancy," they will reinvent and reinvigorate the empire—in the west rather than the east (595–96, 598). But Canada is also the place from which Grace Roseberry and Mercy Merrick come before the outbreak of the Franco-Prussian War, and Collins's representation of their colonial experience serves as a reminder that the west must be won. While Colonel Roseberry and his family emigrate to Canada from England, after he suffers "pecuniary losses" (222), Mercy Merrick obtains a position there "with an officer's wife," among "gentlefolks who had emigrated." Her employers dismiss her once her sexual past becomes known, but not before she "gain[s] one advantage during [her] stay in Canada," "learn[ing] to speak the French language" from the "French-Canadians" with whom she associates (206).

Allied with French Canadians at the time of confederation and fluent in their language, attached to a French ambulance during the Franco-Prussian War and mistaken for a Frenchwoman (231), Mercy Merrick embodies the threat posed to the British by their imperial rival, while also redefining that threat. Whereas the French compete with the British for new colonial territories, Mercy Merrick competes with men for a place in the public sphere. Characterized as "unconquerable" (360), she declines to recognize the authority of men, or to submit to their control. As a young girl, she refuses to turn to her father for help after the death of her mother, "in resentment of his treatment of [her]" (533): "I never went near my father: child as I was, I would have starved and died rather than go to him" (530). As a young woman, she avoids her future husband as well. As Horace Holmcroft complains, "she persists in pro-

longing [their] engagement. Nothing will persuade her to fix the day
for [their] marriage" (253). Ostensibly, Mercy's reluctance to marry
Horace marks her unwillingness to impose her fraud on the man she
loves. Yet Lady Janet views her behavior as a sign of her independence as
a modern woman: "I don't understand the young women of the present
generation . . . In my time, when we were fond of a man, we were ready
to marry him at a moment's notice. . . . What are the young women of
the present time made of?" (258, 261).

Representing conquest, resistance, and independence in terms of gender relations, Collins makes good on a suggestion he offered to William
Tindell, his literary agent, in 1870, in a letter about the Franco-Prussian
War. Concerned with the war's effect on sales of *Man and Wife*, Collins
humorously recommends that they advertise the novel as a work about
domestic warfare: "If the infamous 'war' is injuring us," he tells Tindell,
"suppose we alter the heading in the advertisements thus": "New
Romance of Domestic War. Man and Wife. or The Mitrailleuse of
Home. . . . This would instantly sell an edition!!!"[32] In *Man and Wife*,
Collins suggests, the savage aggression of Geoffrey Delamayn corre-
sponds to that of Napoleon III, whose troops were armed with the
mitrailleuse. But in *The New Magdalen*, the analogy between the European war and the domestic one is more complex, as Mercy, the seeming
victim, is allied with the French forces, and at times appears more of an
aggressor than the oppressive male characters in the novel.

In *The New Magdalen*, as in *Man and Wife*, Collins represents men as
"objects of horror" (209). He justifies Mercy's antipathy to her father,
who deserted her mother and left them "absolutely penniless" (528);
and he suggests that Mercy's reluctance to marry is also well founded—
based on her knowledge that marriage leaves women without property,
freedom, or autonomy. Before meeting Mercy's father, Mercy's mother
married an abusive man from whom she separated and "gain[ed] her
freedom," but only "on the condition of her sacrificing to [him] . . . the
whole of the little fortune that she possessed in her own right" (528).
Like her mother's husband, Horace Holmcroft demands his prerogatives
as Mercy's future master, anticipating her subordination as his wife: "I
have a right to know what this means. I am engaged to marry you. If
you won't trust other people, you are bound to explain yourself to Me"
(455). Horace concedes that he is "not [her] husband yet," and has "no
right to follow [her]" into her own room (456), but looks forward to the
time when Mercy will no longer be entitled to her independence and
privacy. Thus it hardly seems surprising that Mercy is "in no hurry to be

married" (261) and hopes that "something might happen . . . to prevent it" (276). Rather than become the wife of Horace Holmcroft, Mercy wishes to remain the adopted daughter of Lady Janet, a widow and matriarch who "insist[s] on acting for [her]self" (423).

Yet in *The New Magdalen,* Collins disparages women who act for themselves, associating their desire for self-government with sexual aggression and promiscuity. On the one hand, Mercy's fall illustrates the plight of women subject to male violence and control and offered few respectable ways of earning a living. Working as a starving needle woman in London, and delirious from fever, she is drugged and raped by a man who finds her collapsed on the street, and becomes a prostitute in order to survive. On the other hand, however, Mercy's fall suggests the deviance of the "young women of the present generation," who refuse to marry, seeking to control their own sexual and financial resources instead. As Grace Roseberry tells Mercy, "you haven't been on the streets for nothing. You are a woman with resources" (416). Indeed, Collins's depiction of daily life among the sisterhood of prostitutes high-lights their economic as well as their sexual agency, as they buy one another "little presents" when they have "shillings to spare" (543). While Mercy's profession would seem to set her apart from the respectable women in the novel, it ties her to the independent among them, whose financial freedom and desire for autonomy seem insepara-ble from sexual fallenness. Thus the commanding and opinionated Lady Janet has thousands of pounds at her own disposal, and joins commit-tees on which she exercises the right to vote (291–92), but also secretly imagines what it would be like to have children by men other than her husband (256).[33]

To many Victorians, such "longings" in women (463)—whether satis-fied or not—seemed to pose as great a threat to the empire as native insurrections or imperial rivalries. Drawing an analogy between the red-light districts of London and the embattled cities of India in 1857, Lord Campbell compared the "siege of Holywell street" to "the siege of Delhi," while Ralph Wardlaw, a Congregational minister, attributed "the deterioration of national character" to the prevalence of prostitu-tion.[34]

Although Collins undoubtedly hoped to win sympathy for the prosti-tute in *The New Magdalen,* he reinforces these fears by representing insubordinate women as savages to be civilized by men. When Grace Roseberry resists conversion at the hands of Julian Gray, who hopes "to bring her to a better frame of mind" about Mercy Merrick, the missionary categorizes her as primitive and "tigerish" (413), worse than any savage he might encounter in Africa: "I might as well have pleaded—I won't say with a savage; savages are sometimes accessible to remonstrance, if you know how to reach them—I might as well have pleaded with a hungry animal to abstain from eating while food was within its reach" (470). Unlike Grace, however, Mercy proves "accessible to remonstrance," and Collins puts his fears for the empire to rest by dramatizing her conversion, as she surrenders to Julian's guidance and accepts her subordinate role as the wife of a colonist and missionary. "She felt it, she knew it: her guilty conscience owned and feared its master in Julian Gray!" (277). Characterized by his "manly force" (509) and his missionary zeal, a "Man" with a capital "M" (358), Julian promises to restore virility to an emasculated empire, one that Collins compares with its fallen Roman counterpart (347). He does so by mastering its female savages, and by traveling back in time. Emigrating to "the far and fertile West" with his bride, Julian enters a paradoxically old New World in which women understand their proper place.

Chapter Six
Conclusion:
The Noncanonical Collins

Despite the revival of interest in Collins and his fiction, and the republication, as "World's Classics," of several novels long out of print, a significant body of his work remains unread, except by biographers and the most devoted of literary critics. These works include Collins's melodramas and his late novels, long cited as evidence of his artistic and physical decline. From *The Lighthouse* (1855), performed as an amateur theatrical, to *Rank and Riches* (1882) at the Adelphi, Collins wrote a dozen melodramas, many of them adapted from his novels, but none are readily available, and most have never been printed or revived. After *The Law and the Lady* (1875), Collins published nine more novels, yet these, too, are largely unknown. As interest in Collins develops, it seems appropriate to reevaluate these works and reconsider the reasons for their neglect, particularly since conceptions of literary value have themselves come under scrutiny in recent years, through the influence of feminism, Marxism, and new historicism, among other movements in literary criticism.

The neglect from which Collins's melodramas have suffered is easiest to understand, since twentieth-century audiences have lost their taste for the extravagant emotionalism and the stark moral polarities that characterize the genre. Even in his own day, however, a number of Collins's melodramas were failures—most notably, *The Red Vial* (1858). The story of Hans Grimm, a slow-witted character rescued from an insane asylum, this play contains a scene in which a seemingly dead character comes back to life in a German morgue, the arm of the "corpse" suddenly thrust from behind a curtain and reaching for an alarm bell—a resurrection that Victorian theatergoers found hilarious rather than terrifying, much to Collins's chagrin. He never published the melodrama, although he adapted its plotline years later, in the 1880 novel *Jezebel's Daughter* (*King*, 183). *Rank and Riches* (1882), an excessively convoluted play, proved equally unpopular. Dubbed "Rant and Rubbish" by reviewers, its actors and actresses were forced to endure catcalls on opening night, and Collins abruptly withdrew the play from the Adelphi (*King,* 402–3).

As these failures suggest, Collins's suspenseful and elaborate plot constructions do not work nearly as well in stage productions as they do in novels serialized over a period of months. Nonetheless, a number of his plays met with success on the Victorian stage, despite their unlikely twists and turns, and it is worthwhile to consider why. Although opinions about the literary merit of Collins's melodramas vary, critics generally agree on the ideological work such plays performed, and hence on their value as telling products of their culture. Combining representations of social oppression and expressions of social protest with cathartic triumphs of justice over villainy, Victorian melodramas resolve the plight of their persecuted and disempowered figures through wish-fulfillment fantasies of a sort. They acknowlege and reward the victimized, but do so in sentimental rather than economic or political ways. Registering a host of social anxieties and discontents, these works assuage them as well, by means of the "facile optimism of melodramatic triumph."[1]

For Collins, who so often reinscribes the oppressive social norms he criticizes in his fiction, this mixture of social protest and political escapism must have seemed especially satisfying, and he exploits the tensions of the genre in his own contributions to it. In *The Frozen Deep,* for example, Collins dramatizes a class conflict based, in part, on the ill-fated Franklin expedition to the Arctic.[2] He responds to troubling allegations of cannibalism among the British explorers by developing the political implications of the men's hunger and using cannibalism as a metaphor for a class war in which the privileged feed off their workers, inspiring a "cannibal revolution."[3] Collins's working-class cook, appropriately named "John Want," seems to relish the thought that his officers are dying. Remarking on their hollow coughs as he makes "bone soup," Want asserts that he will be "the last" survivor, a claim that has a particularly ominous and cannibalistic ring under the circumstances.[4] But rather than depicting a cannibal feast among such "mutinous rascal[s],"[5] Collins defuses the threat of class conflict in his final act, staging the heroic self-sacrifice of the starving Richard Wardour, who chooses to save instead of devour his enemy, at the cost of his own life. Rather than indicting the class system, or compensating Wardour for his economic and political wrongs, Collins highlights the moral grandeur of the have nots in the play, granting Wardour the admiration of his privileged superiors, who stand about him "in grief and awe."[6]

Collins's *Black and White* (1869) adheres to a similar pattern, offering a sentimental solution to the hero's political plight. Recalling the abolitionist melodramas of the early 1800s,[7] *Black and White* offers a critique of British imperialism and its legacy of slave trading in the wake of the Jamaica Insurrection, but it ultimately justifies enslavement by recasting it in terms of romantic love.

Written in collaboration with the actor Charles Fechter,[8] the melodrama unfolds in Trinidad in 1830, four years before the emancipation of the slaves in the British West Indies. In its most radical moments, the play identifies the English plantation owners as "barbarians"[9] and represents blackness as a legal construction that serves the economic needs of the empire. The central revelation of *Black and White* forces us to consider racial identity as a construct, since the race of the hero gets redefined. Soon after the French Count, Maurice de Leyrac, arrives in Trinidad from Paris to propose marriage to Emily Milburn, he discovers that he was adopted in infancy by the Count and Countess de Leyrac. Born on the island of Trinidad, he is the illegitimate son of an English plantation owner and a slave, a quadroon named Ruth. Hence, he is himself a slave as long as he remains in Trinidad, and the "old master that bought [him] can claim [him] for his own" (18).

Unwilling to "deny the mother that bore [him]" (31), de Leyrac admits to the authorities that he is Ruth's son and is included in a bill of sale, although he has married Miss Milburn. Purchased by Stephen Westcraft, who "forbid[s de Leyrac's] wife to live on [his] plantation" (32), the slave is freed by the discovery of his dead father's "paper of manumission" (33) and reunited with Emily. While the play treats the resentment of blacks toward "de dam white man" comically, and ridicules their cultural aspirations (13), it uses de Leyrac's experience to criticize the injustices they suffer at the hands of the English. Yet like *The Frozen Deep, Black and White* resolves the hero's political plight in apolitical fashion: through expressions of sentiment rather than calls for social reform. Liberating de Leyrac by means of his father's repentance, not by means of the Emancipation Act, and rewarding him with the love of Emily, not with newly won rights, Collins ultimately evades the issue of racial exploitation raised by the play:

Miss Milburn: "I live again. You are free!" (*takes Leyrac's hand*)
Leyrac: No! (*kisses her hand*) I am your slave! (33)

In these closing lines, Collins represents de Leyrac's enslavement as a metaphoric and a welcome condition, the pleasurable effect of romantic love rather than the unjust consequence of imperial dominion.

Unlike Collins's melodramas, which bring into stark relief the pattern of social critique and reinscription that runs through much of his fiction, his late novels are often criticized on antithetical grounds— because of their explicit and unrelenting social purposes, to which Collins allegedly sacrifices his art. Complaining of the didacticism of the late fiction in an 1889 review, Swinburne coined his now-famous couplet on Collins: "What brought good Wilkie's genius nigh perdition?/ Some demon whispered—'Wilkie! have a mission.' "[10] As Swinburne notes, Collins uses *Man and Wife* to expose the injustice of English marriage law, and *The New Magdalen* to promote the cause of fallen yet reformed women, and virtually all of his late novels champion a specific political cause. In *The Fallen Leaves* (1879), Collins returns to the theme of reformed prostitutes, while he attacks the Jesuits in *The Black Robe* (1880–1881). *Heart and Science* (1882–1883) takes up the antivivisection cause, *The Evil Genius* (1886) examines the plight of women stigmatized by divorce and adultery, and *The Legacy of Cain* (1888) criticizes the tenets of social Darwinism.

Despite his critique of Collins and the novelist's various missions, Swinburne prefaces his remarks by claiming that "nothing can be more fatuous than to brand all didactic or missionary fiction as an illegitimate or inferior form of art" (Page, 262). Yet whether critics defend Collins's late works or consider them illegitimate, their arguments are usually based on a false distinction between novels that have a social purpose and those that do not. As feminist, Marxist, and new historicist critics make clear, the products of artistic genius are shaped by history and politics as well, and serve the ends of their culture, whether they admit to it or not. And because these cultural ends are largely unspoken, the proclaimed mission of a work is often at odds with what these critics term its "political unconscious."[11] Thus, while a number of Collins's late novels can be defended on aesthetic grounds, by virtue of their compelling and innovative representations, they can be usefully discussed as revealing cultural texts as well. They warrant our attention, in part, because of their complex ideological workings, which illuminate the ways in which literature both claims and disclaims its political intentions.

Heart and Science provides a useful example of the insights into Victorian culture and ideology that Collins's late novels frequently offer. In this work, Collins champions the antivivisection movement of the 1870s and 1880s, a cause led by the feminist Frances Power Cobbe, with whom Collins corresponded on the subject. Speaking of the "detestable cruelties of the laboratory" in a letter to her, Collins explains that his novel "trac[es] the moral influence of those cruelties on the nature of the man who practises them, and the result as to his social relations."[12] Set in London in the 1880s, *Heart and Science* represents the cruelties of Doctor Benjulia, who experiments on a host of animals in his quest for medical truth. His cruelty extends to the heroine, Carmina Graywell, an ailing young woman, half Italian and half English, whose fiancé, the doctor Ovid Vere, is abroad. Rather than treat Carmina's potentially fatal illness, Benjulia allows it to progress in order to observe its symptoms. Carmina is only saved from death by the arrival of Ovid Vere, recalled to England by his young sister Zoe. Vere cures Carmina by means of medical discoveries made by one of his own patients—a mulatto doctor and staunch antivivisectionist whom he met in Canada. His ambitions crushed by his medical rival, Benjulia liberates his animals, burns his lab, and commits suicide, while Carmina recovers, marries Ovid Vere, and has a child.

At first glance, Collins's aim in writing his novel seems clear enough. As he explains in his preface, he uses *Heart and Science* to "plead . . . the cause of the harmless and affectionate beings of God's creation,"[13] all too often abused by men—a category that includes women as well as the lower animals. As Frances Power Cobbe's leadership indicates, the antivivisection movement had close ties to the women's movement, and Cobbe herself connects the defense of animal rights with the defense of women's rights in her essays on vivisection and "wife torture."[14] In his novel, Collins makes this connection as well. He compares cruelty to animals and their incarceration in zoos with cruelty toward women and their domestic imprisonment, and he juxtaposes a description of caged animals at the Zoological Gardens with that of Carmina as "Atalanta" (80), the Greek maiden anxious to escape from her male suitors and avoid the confines of marriage. "Right is right all the world over," Carmina's old nurse Teresa exclaims, urging the liberation of the caged monkeys. "If we are to see creatures in prison, let's see creatures who have deserved it" (75–76). Like Teresa, Carmina takes pity on suffering and abused animals, her "fellow-creature[s]" (18), and Collins reinforces their alliance when Benjulia directs his medical attentions to her, giving her a "place . . . in his note-book of experiments" (290).[15]

Yet the nature and origins of Carmina's illness, and the manner in which she is cured by marriage, suggest that Collins pleads a number of different causes in *Heart and Science,* and that the aims he openly acknowledges are at odds with those he does not. While supporting the antivivisection cause and defending the rights of women, Collins represents these issues in a way that subtly ensures their defeat. Like Cobbe, Collins compares victimized women to abused animals, but he does so to their disadvantage. Suggesting that women, like the lower animals, are fixed in a natural state, he undermines the grounds on which women's autonomy and rights are based. In "Wife Torture in England," Cobbe describes the man who abuses his wife as "the only animal in creation which maltreats its mate."[16] Although Collins, too, asserts that "man is an animal" (176) in *Heart and Science,* he reserves his animalistic descriptions for the female characters in his novel. He represents Teresa, Carmina's nurse, as "a wild old creature" (29), a "tigress" who considers Carmina her "cub" (276). When she physically assaults Mrs. Gallilee, Carmina's aunt and legal guardian, for alleging that her niece is illegitimate, Collins compares her "ferocious hands" and "lean brown fingers" to "the claws of a tigress" strangling her prey (250–51). The demure Carmina appears considerably more civilized than Teresa, but she is characterized by her animal physiology as well. She falls victim to hysteria, an illness that afflicts virtually all the women in the novel, and that ties their cerebral diseases and intellectual limitations to their mammalian reproductive systems.[17]

Although the heartlessness of the medical researcher provides Collins with his ostensive theme in *Heart and Science,* he proves more concerned with heartlessness of a different sort—that of the intellectual woman who rejects her role as a creature of emotion and aspires to think and act like a man. With her interest in Geographical Botany (83), electricity and protoplasm (348), and other "scientific pursuits" (299), Mrs. Gallilee neglects her domestic duties, tyrannizes over her husband and children, and rivals Doctor Benjulia as the villain of the novel. She opposes Carmina's marriage to her son Ovid for mercenary reasons, since her brother's estate will come to her and her children if her niece "live[s] and die[s] an unmarried woman" (153). But her desire to prevent Carmina from marrying more subtly expresses and indicts her feminist ideals. Educated and autonomous, Mrs. Gallilee appropriates the powers of her husband, rejects his "conjugal endearments" (167), and finds happiness only after she separates from him, living with another woman as "learned" as herself instead (349).

Presented as a critique of vivisection, *Heart and Science* portrays Doctor Benjulia as the heartless villain who experiments on women as well as laboratory animals and who proves willing to sacrifice Carmina's life in the interests of medical science. Understood as a critique of female emancipation and a defensive response to the second Married Women's Property Act (1882), the novel pits the intellectual and domineering Mrs. Gallilee against the feeling and dependent Carmina, indicting the former for exercizing the rights to which English wives were finally entitled.[18] Although Collins decries the exploitation of animals and women in his novel, he does so in a self-defeating way, and more successfully defends the rights of husbands, fathers, and sons, whom he represents as the emasculated victims of women unwisely liberated from their cages. Reinvigorating the manhood of Mrs. Gallilee's husband and son, Collins returns them to positions of domestic supremacy. Ovid Vere is "unmanned" by "shattered nerves" at the beginning of the novel (79)—and by his mother's domination as well—but he returns to England from Canada in "masterful health and strength," a "remade . . . man" (321) capable of putting his mother where she belongs—under restraint in a private lunatic asylum (317). His stepfather, the "feeble creature" John Gallilee (167), learns to control his own finances as well as his domineering wife. "Assert[ing] his paternal authority" (307), he escapes from her and assumes custody of their children. In so doing, he earns the "respect" of the servants (255) and presumably that of the reader, reassuring us that "father is master" (270).

Promoting *Heart and Science* in his letters to friends and publishers, Collins repeatedly compares its artfulness with that of *The Woman in White,* and a number of critics seem willing to entertain his view. Long disparaged or simply dismissed, it is now considered "one of the best and liveliest of his later novels"—or, less kindly, as the " 'best-of-the-worst.' "[19] Praising the power and artistry of the novel, albeit in qualified terms, critics point out that *Heart and Science* complicates the image of Collins's decline and shows that his inventiveness "flashed on and off like the North Foreland light" (King, 403). But to those interested in the cultural meaning of Victorian fiction and the ideological work it performs, *Heart and Science,* like Collins's other late novels, has significance whether or not it can be defended on high artistic grounds. Variously perceived as highbrow and lowbrow by literary critics, these works of popular fiction operate in much the same way that Collins's most celebrated novels do, and they perform similar ideological labors. Although often judged to be artistic failures, they usefully suggest our need to reexamine our ideas of literary value and to broaden our conceptions of a novel's worth.

Notes and References

Preface

1. Autograph letter signed (ALS) to Harriet Geddes Collins, 18 September 1839. The Pierpont Morgan Library, New York. MA 3150.3.
2. "Reminiscences of a Story-Teller," *Universal Review* 1 (May–August 1888): 182–92, 183.
3. [H. F. Chorley], *Athenaeum* (2 June 1866); and *London Quarterly Review* (October 1866); reprinted by Norman Page, *Wilkie Collins: The Critical Heritage* (London: Routledge and Kegan Paul, 1974), 147, 156.
4. [H. F. Chorley], *Athenaeum* (3 January 1863); and [Margaret Oliphant], *Blackwood's Magazine* (August 1863); reprinted by Page, 131, 143.
5. Charles Dickens to W. H. Wills, 24 September 1858. *The Letters of Charles Dickens,* ed. Walter Dexter, 3 vols. (Bloomsbury: Nonesuch Press, 1938), 3:58; hereafter cited in text as *Letters.*
6. U. C. Knoepflmacher, "The Counterworld of Victorian Fiction and *The Woman in White,*" in *The Worlds of Victorian Fiction,* ed. Jerome H. Buckley, Harvard English Studies 6 (Cambridge: Harvard University Press, 1975), 353.
7. Winifred Hughes, *The Maniac in the Cellar: Sensation Novels of the 1860s* (Princeton: Princeton University Press, 1980), 144.
8. Jerome Meckier, "Wilkie Collins's *The Woman in White:* Providence Against the Evils of Propriety," *Journal of British Studies* 22 (Fall 1982): 104; and Philip O'Neill, *Wilkie Collins: Women, Property and Propriety* (Totowa, N.J.: Barnes and Noble, 1988), 5–7.
9. Richard Barickman, Susan MacDonald, and Myra Stark, *Corrupt Relations: Dickens, Thackeray, Trollope, Collins, and the Victorian Sexual System* (New York: Columbia University Press, 1982), 112. According to Barickman and his collaborators, the themes and structures of Collins's novels are "more radical than the author seems willing to admit." His novels end "by insisting on redemption through marriage, though the novels themselves have undermined that solution" (149).
10. D. A. Miller, "From *roman policier* to *roman-police:* Wilkie Collins's *The Moonstone,*" in *The Novel and the Police* (Berkeley: University of California Press, 1988), 33–57; hereafter cited in text.
11. Miller, "*Cage aux folles:* Sensation and Gender in Wilkie Collins's *The Woman in White,*" in *The Novel and the Police,* 146–91; hereafter cited in text. Miller's argument about sensation and gender is extended and partly contested by Ann Cvetkovich, who devotes one chapter of her study *Mixed Feelings* to "the politics of affect" in *The Woman in White.* Like Miller, Cvetkovich casts doubt on

Collins's reputation as a subversive writer. In her view, the bodily sensations to which Collins's hero is subject seem to render him vulnerable, but they actually serve as a mask for his class ambition and will to power. "The somatic experience of sensation," she argues, "serves as a welcome screen and conduit for Walter Hartright's accession to power" (212, n. 4). See "Ghostlier Determinations: The Economy of Sensation and *The Woman in White*," in *Mixed Feelings: Feminism, Mass Culture, and Victorian Sensationalism* (New Brunswick: Rutgers University Press, 1992), 71–96.

    12.   Tamar Heller, *Dead Secrets: Wilkie Collins and the Female Gothic* (New Haven: Yale University Press, 1992), 93; hereafter cited in text.

    13.   Catherine Peters, *The King of Inventors: A Life of Wilkie Collins* (Princeton: Princeton University Press, 1991), 1; hereafter cited in text as *King.*

    14.   Catherine Peters, " 'Invite No Dangerous Publicity': Some Independent Women and Their Effect on Wilkie Collins's Life and Writing," *Dickens Studies Annual* 20 (1991): 296; hereafter cited in text as " 'Invite.' "

Chapter One

    1.   Wilkie Collins, *Memoirs of the Life of William Collins, Esq., R.A., with Selections from His Journals and Correspondence,* 2 vols. (East Ardsley, England: EP Publishing Limited, 1978), 1:38; hereafter cited in text.

    2.   Wilkie Collins, "A Rogue's Life," *Household Words* 13 (1–29 March 1856): 158.

    3.   ALS to William Winter, 30 July 1887; Morris L. Parrish Collection, Princeton University Library.

    4.   "Our Portrait Gallery: Mr. Wilkie Collins," *Men and Women* (5 February 1887); quoted by Peters, *King,* 31.

    5.   William M. Clarke, *The Secret Life of Wilkie Collins* (Chicago: Ivan R. Dee, 1988), 14, 26; hereafter cited in text.

    6.   Deborah Cherry, *Painting Women: Victorian Women Artists* (London: Routledge, 1993), 137. As Peters notes, Margaret Geddes Carpenter demonstrated "exceptional independence and success in a largely masculine world," and inspired an "unsuccessful movement" to allow women to become members of the Royal Academy (*King,* 8).

    7.   Harriet Geddes Collins, autobiographical manuscript dated 24 April 1853; Harry Ransom Humanities Research Center, The University of Texas at Austin; quoted by Peters, *King,* 10.

    8.   Peters emphasizes this point in her discussion of Collins's relationship with his mother (" 'Invite,' " 297–303), describing Harriet's manuscript and her son's "borrowings" at some length.

    9.   ALS to Harriet Geddes Collins, 2 September 1855. The Pierpont Morgan Library, New York. MA 3150.45.

    10.   See John G. Millais, *Life and Letters of Sir John Everett Millais,* 2 vols. (London: 1899), 1:278–79.

11. The Pierpont Morgan Library, New York. MA 3155. Quoted by Peters, *King,* 416.

12. Wilkie Collins, "A New Mind," *Household Words* 19 (1 January 1859): 112–13.

Chapter Two

1. See, for example, Catherine Peters, who describes the *Memoirs* as an "act of respect to a parent by no means always respectfully treated while he was alive" (*King,* 75).

2. Wilkie Collins, *Rambles Beyond Railways; or Notes in Cornwall Taken A-Foot* (London: Westaway Books, 1948), 40; hereafter cited in text.

3. Alvin Sullivan, ed., *British Literary Magazines: The Victorian and Edwardian Age, 1837–1913* (Westport, Conn.: Greenwood Press, 1984), 185–86.

4. Wilkie Collins, "A Plea for Sunday Reform," *Leader* 2:27 (27 September 1851): 925–26, 925; hereafter cited in text.

5. Alex Owen discusses the subversive power of the clairvoyant in *The Darkened Room: Women, Power and Spiritualism in Late Victorian England* (Philadelphia: University of Pennsylvania Press, 1990). As Owen points out, the seance provided mediums with "a means of circumventing rigid nineteenth-century class and gender norms," but did so "without mounting a direct attack on the status quo" (4).

6. Kirk H. Beetz, "Wilkie Collins and *The Leader,*" *Victorian Periodicals Review* 15 (1982): 25.

7. John Sutherland, *The Stanford Companion to Victorian Fiction* (Stanford: Stanford University Press, 1989), 195, 333.

8. Wilkie Collins, "The Last Stage Coachman," *Illuminated Magazine* (August 1843): 209–11; hereafter cited in text.

9. Peters discusses *Iolani* in "Appendix C," *King,* 441–43.

10. Wilkie Collins, quoted in "Wilkie Collins," *Appleton's Journal of Popular Literature, Science, and Art* (3 September 1870): 278–81, 279.

11. William Ellis, *Polynesian Researches During a Residence of Nearly Eight Years in the Society and Sandwich Islands,* 4 vols. (London: 1831; Henry G. Bohn, 1853), 1:viii; hereafter cited in text.

12. Wilkie Collins, "The Captain's Last Love," in *Mad Monkton and Other Stories,* ed. Norman Page (Oxford: Oxford University Press, 1994), 333–54, 349, 334; hereafter cited in text.

13. Stephen D. Arata, "The Occidental Tourist: *Dracula* and the Anxiety of Reverse Colonization," *Victorian Studies* 33 (Summer 1990): 621–45, 623.

14. Wilkie Collins, *Antonina; or, the Fall of Rome, The Works of Wilkie Collins,* Vol. 17 (New York: AMS Press, 1970), 73; hereafter cited in text.

15. For a discussion of the rape of Indian women by the British, the response to these abuses in Parliament, and the changing representations of

interracial rape in imperial literature, see Nancy L. Paxton, "Mobilizing Chivalry: Rape in British Novels about the Indian Uprising of 1857," *Victorian Studies* 36 (Fall 1992): 5–30.

16.   As Peters notes, "Bentley liked *Basil*," but "took fright at some too-explicit passages." At his urging, the brothel in which Collins's hero originally learned of his wife's betrayal becomes, simply, a "hotel" (*King,* 115).

17.   Wilkie Collins, *Basil,* ed. Dorothy Goldman (Oxford: Oxford University Press, 1990), 82–83; hereafter cited in text.

18.   See Leonore Davidoff and Catherine Hall, *Family Fortunes: Men and Women of the English Middle Class, 1780–1850* (Chicago: University of Chicago Press, 1987), 205–6.

19.   *Dublin University Magazine* (January 1853); and *Westminster Review* (October 1853); reprinted by Page, 50, 52.

20.   *Westminster Review* (October 1853); reprinted by Page, 52.

21.   {D. O. Maddyn], *Athenaeum* (4 December 1852); reprinted by Page, 48.

22.   In *Wilkie Collins: A Biography* (New York: Macmillan; 1952), Kenneth Robinson sees this work as a "successful imitation of the Dickens' model" (68), and Peters notes that John Ruskin found it " 'a gross imitation of Dickens,' " " 'a mere stew of old cooked meats,' " a view she finds too harsh (*King,* 111).

23.   Wilkie Collins, "A Terribly Strange Bed," *Household Words* 5 (24 April 1852); reprinted in *Mad Monkton and Other Stories,* ed. Norman Page, 1–20, 11.

24.   By the middle of September 1856, when Dickens offered Collins a salaried position on the staff of *Household Words,* he had already published 13 of Collins's pieces in his weekly journal. These include "A Terribly Strange Bed" (24 April 1852); "Gabriel's Marriage" (16–23 April 1853); "The Fourth Poor Traveller," a portion of the 1854 Christmas Number entitled "The Seven Poor Travellers" (December 1854); "Sister Rose" (7–28 April 1855); "The Yellow Mask" (7–28 July 1855); "The Cruise of the Tomtit" (22 December 1855); "The Ostler," a portion of the 1855 Christmas Number entitled "The Holly-Tree Inn" (December 1855); "A Rogue's Life" (1–29 March 1856); "Laid Up in Two Lodgings" (7–14 June 1856); "The Diary of Anne Rodway" (19–26 July 1856); "My Spinsters" (23 August 1856); "My Black Mirror" (6 September 1856); and "To Think, or Be Thought For?" (13 September 1856).

25.   These stories include "The Twin Sisters" and "A Pictorial Tour to St. George Bosherville," published in *Bentley's Miscellany* in 1851; and "A Passage in the Life of Perugino Potts" and "Nine O'Clock," published in *Bentley's Miscellany* in 1852.

26.   "The very act of writing for Dickens on the staff of *Household Words* . . . represented a political choice on Collins' part," Tamar Heller argues. Compromising those "elements in his fiction that a predominantly middle-class readership would find subversive," he "affirm[ed] his identity as part of the bourgeoisie" (92–93).

27. Patrick Brantlinger, *Rule of Darkness: British Literature and Imperialism, 1830–1914* (Ithaca: Cornell University Press, 1988), 199; hereafter cited in text. For other discussions of the Mutiny, see Pratul Chandra Gupta, *Nana Sahib and the Rising at Cawnpore* (Oxford: Clarendon Press, 1963); Christopher Hibbert, *The Great Mutiny: India 1857* (New York: Penguin, 1980); and Thomas Metcalf, *The Aftermath of Revolt: India, 1857–1870* (Princeton: Princeton University Press, 1964).

28. Charles Dickens and Wilkie Collins, "The Perils of Certain English Prisoners," *Household Words*, Extra Christmas Number, 1857; reprinted in *The Lazy Tour of Two Idle Apprentices and Other Stories* (London: Chapman and Hall, 1890), 237–327, 260; hereafter cited in text.

Chapter Three

1. See, for example, T. S. Eliot, "Wilkie Collins and Dickens" (1927), in *Selected Essays* (New York: Harcourt, Brace and World, 1964), 409–18, 413.

2. For discussions of Collins's use of the Constance Kent case in *The Moonstone*, see Ian Ousby, *Bloodhounds of Heaven: The Detective in English Fiction from Godwin to Doyle* (Cambridge: Harvard University Press, 1976), 123; and Elisabeth Rose Gruner, "Family Secrets and the Mysteries of *The Moonstone*," *Victorian Literature and Culture* 21 (1993): 127–45. Norman Page discusses Collins's use of *Thelwall v. Yelverton* in his Introduction to *Man and Wife*, and Jenny Bourne Taylor outlines Collins's use of the Scottish case of Madeleine Smith in her Introduction to *The Law and the Lady*.

3. Anthea Trodd emphasizes this point in her analysis of domestic crime in Victorian fiction, and the "triangular opposition of policeman, lady and servant" that characterizes it. She identifies the working-class detective as a "threshold figure" who intrudes upon middle-class privacy, and argues that writers such as Collins use their detective novels to examine the relation between public and private as well as class divisions and ideals of female behavior. See *Domestic Crime in the Victorian Novel* (New York: St. Martin's Press, 1989).

4. ALS to George Bentley, 17 August 1853; Berg Collection, The New York Public Library. Astor, Lenox and Tilden Foundations.

5. Wilkie Collins, *Hide and Seek*, ed. Catherine Peters (Oxford: Oxford University Press, 1993), 25; hereafter cited in text.

6. For one of the best-known discussions of this stereotype, see Sherry B. Ortner, "Is Female to Male as Nature Is to Culture?" in *Women, Culture, and Society*, ed. Michelle Zimbalist Rosaldo and Louise Lamphere (Stanford: Stanford University Press, 1974), 67–87.

7. Alison Milbank misses this point in discussing Madonna's handicap—"a hardly normal condition," in her view—and argues that the female invalids in *Hide and Seek* are not "confined" but rather "contented although

housebound." See *Daughters of the House: Modes of the Gothic in Victorian Fiction* (London: Macmillan, 1992), 56.

    8. Alex Owen discusses this familiar Victorian figure in *The Darkened Room,* and Collins himself wrote about spiritual mediums in a series of articles for the *Leader.*

    9. ALS to Harriet Geddes Collins, 5 April 1856. The Pierpont Morgan Library, New York. MA 3150.50.

    10. Wilkie Collins, *The Dead Secret* (New York: Dover, 1979), 124; hereafter cited in text.

    11. On the association between detection and class leveling, see Trodd; and D. A. Miller, who discusses the ways in which "the Verinder estate is brutally democratized" by Sergeant Cuff in *The Moonstone* (38).

    12. In Heller's view, Collins "contains" the "subversive possibilities" of his novel by making Rosamond a mother—by "channeling . . . Rosamond's energies into maternity and marriage" (9). Yet Rosamond only becomes an amateur detective *after* she becomes a wife and mother, and she treats her baby as yet another object on which to exercise her powers of observation.

    13. Wilkie Collins, *The Law and the Lady,* ed. Jenny Bourne Taylor (Oxford: Oxford University Press, 1992), 117, 121; hereafter cited in text.

    14. ALS to Charles Ward, 22 June 1874; Morris L. Parrish Collection, Princeton University Library.

    15. Taylor, Appendix to *The Law and the Lady,* 415.

    16. Edmund Yates, "Mr. Wilkie Collins and the *Graphic,*" *World* (17 March 1875): 15; Wilkie Collins, " 'The Law and the Lady': To the Editors of the *World,*" *World* (24 March 1875): 21. Taylor reprints these rebuttals in her Appendix, 415–18.

    17. As Taylor explains, the Scottish legal system, unlike the English, allows for a verdict of "Not Proven," which results in an acquittal, while carrying "a stigma" (422–23). Madeleine Smith's trial, like that of Eustace Macallan, ended with a verdict of "Not Proven."

    18. For a discussion of Victorian models of sexual difference, and the relatively new idea that these differences are "incommensurable," see Thomas Lacquer, *Making Sex: Body and Gender from the Greeks to Freud* (Cambridge: Harvard University Press, 1990), particularly chapters 5 and 6.

    19. As Barbara T. Gates notes, acts of self-destruction among Collins's characters are themselves subversive, a point that suggestively illuminates Sara's behavior. See "Wilkie Collins' Suicides: 'Truth As It Is in Nature,' " in *Wilkie Collins to the Forefront: Some Reassessments,* ed. Nelson Smith and R. C. Terry (New York: AMS Press, 1995), 241–56.

    20. Kathleen O'Fallon overlooks the subordinate and conventional side of Valeria's character in her analysis of gender roles in *The Law and the Lady,* arguing that Valeria is Collins's "most forceful" heroine, one who "acts effectively without the supervision of a man" and "never completely gives over control of her self to her husband." O'Fallon bases her argument, in part, on a mis-

reading of the novel's opening scene, in which Valeria signs her married rather than her maiden name in the church register, and her uncle humorously berates her for "forgett[ing] [her] own name" so quickly (8). Reversing these terms, and claiming that Valeria signs her maiden name, O'Fallon goes on to discuss "this symbolic . . . refusal to surrender her own identity and take on her husband's," which she feels "adumbrates Valeria's actions throughout the novel." The reverse, it seems, is true—Valeria is only too willing to become "Mrs. Eustace," Collins ironically suggests. See "Breaking the Laws about Ladies: Wilkie Collins' Questioning of Gender Roles," in *Wilkie Collins to the Forefront,* 227–39, 231–34.

Chapter Four

1. Henry L. Mansel, "Sensation Fiction," *Quarterly Review* 113 (April 1863), quoted by Hughes, p. 18. Like Mansel, Henry James grants Collins "the credit of having introduced into fiction those most mysterious of mysteries, the mysteries which are at our own doors": "This innovation gave a new impetus to the literature of horrors. It was fatal to the authority of Mrs. Radcliffe and her everlasting castle in the Apennines. What are the Apennines to us, or we to the Apennines? Instead of the terrors of *Udolpho,* we were treated to the terrors of the cheerful country-house and the busy London lodgings." See "Miss Braddon," *Nation* (9 November 1865); reprinted by Page, 122–24, 122–23.

2. Unsigned review, *Westminster Review* (October 1866); reprinted by Page, 158–60, 158.

3. Wilkie Collins, *The Woman in White,* ed. Harvey Peter Sucksmith (Oxford: Oxford University Press, 1991), 396; hereafter cited in text.

4. While Winifred Hughes describes the advent of sensation fiction as a reaction against materialism, modern science, and the "prosaic respectability" of middle-class Victorians (36–37), a number of critics attribute its rise to debates over marriage and divorce law in the 1850s and 1860s. For example, Jeanne Fahnestock connects the "bigamy novel," a subcategory of sensation fiction, to the "tangle" of inconsistent marriage laws in mid-Victorian Britain, the "uncertainty" about marriage created by the 1857 Divorce and Matrimonial Causes Act, and the Dublin bigamy trial of *Thelwall v. Yelverton* ("Bigamy: The Rise and Fall of a Convention," *Nineteenth-Century Fiction* 36 [June 1981]: 47–71). Similarly, Patrick Brantlinger situates the novels in the context of "bigamy, adultery, and the problem of divorce law," which "were on the minds of Victorians in the 1860s" ("What is 'Sensational' about the 'Sensation Novel'?" *Nineteenth-Century Fiction* 37 [June 1982]: 1–28), as does John Sutherland, who traces the origins of Collins's sensation fiction to the 1857 Act and the issues of adultery and domestic "spying" ("Wilkie Collins and the Origins of the Sensation Novel," in *Wilkie Collins to the Forefront,* 75–90).

Ronald R. Thomas refers to the 1857 Act as well as to the Married Women's Property Acts of 1870 and 1882 in discussing Collins's sensation fic-

tion, but he is primarily interested in its relation to the problem of social identity among Victorians. In his view, "this fictional form . . . worked directly on
class anxiety and instability," and "offered up the disturbing possibility that the
secret terms in which personal identities and intimate relations had been established within the culture and within the family were themselves fictions, acts of
commerce, forms of trade, commodities to be bought and sold." In Thomas's
view, novels such as *The Woman in White* are sensational because they reveal that
class identities and class boundaries have been "reconfigured," largely at the
hands of middle-class professionals, the "powerful elite" of lawyers and doctors
("Wilkie Collins and the Sensation Novel," in *The Columbia History of the British
Novel,* ed. John Richetti [New York: Columbia University Press, 1994],
479–507). Like Thomas, Jenny Bourne Taylor ties Collins's sensation fiction to
anxieties about cultural transformation and the blurring of class and gender
boundaries, anxieties expressed by means of secrecy and disguise. Focusing on
the "instability of social and psychic identity" in Collins's sensation novels, she
examines his representation of identity as an unstable construct, and his interest
in the relationship between madness and "female transgression." See *In the Secret
Theatre of Home: Wilkie Collins, Sensation Narrative, and Nineteenth-Century Psychology* (London: Routledge, 1988), 1–26.

      Ann Cvetkovich's approach to sensation fiction, by contrast, reveals
the ways in which "sensation" serves to displace rather than register political
issues and problems, and transforms class conflicts and social oppression into
"psychic disturbances." Sensation novels, she argues, "propose individualist
solutions to what are in fact intransigent social problems," reinforce stereotypical conceptions of female hysteria and madness instead of recognizing the
"material deprivation" of women, and work "in a conservative way," "naturaliz-
ing ideology" (9–10, 24–25). See *Mixed Feelings,* 1–25.

      5.   While the 1857 Act clearly registered the sexual double standard of
Victorian England, and the assumption that a wife should forgive her husband's
adultery, since it presumably did her no injury, it also reflected a compromise
between those who felt that divorce should be a male prerogative providing
husbands with a means of punishing wives who might produce spurious heirs,
and those who believed that married women deserved equal legal protection as
married men. For discussions of Victorian marriage and divorce law, and the
issue of married women's property, see Lee Holcombe, *Wives and Property:
Reform of the Married Women's Property Law in Nineteenth-Century England*
(Toronto: University of Toronto Press, 1983); Mary Poovey, "Covered but Not
Bound: Caroline Norton and the 1857 Matrimonial Causes Act," in *Uneven
Developments: The Ideological Work of Gender in Mid-Victorian England* (Chicago:
University of Chicago Press, 1988), 51–88; Mary Lyndon Shanley, *Feminism,
Marriage, and the Law in Victorian England* (Princeton: Princeton University
Press, 1989); and Lawrence Stone, *Road to Divorce: England, 1530–1987*
(Oxford: Oxford University Press, 1990). Hereafter cited in text.

6. Barbara Leigh Smith Bodichon, "A Brief Summary, in Plain Language, of the Most Important Laws of England Concerning Women," in *The Disempowered: Women and the Law,* ed. Marie Mulvey Roberts and Tamae Mizuta (London: Routledge/Thoemmes, 1993), 27.

7. I have taken this phrase from Leonore Davidoff and Catherine Hall, who explain that, under common law, a wife "could not sign Bills of Exchange, make contracts, sue or be sued, collect debts or stand surety . . . since for all practical purposes, on marriage a woman died a kind of civic death." See *Family Fortunes,* 200.

8. Collins provides a strikingly sympathetic portrait of a divorced Englishwoman in his *Household Words* article "A New Mind" (1859), in which he criticizes the "disgraceful" inequities of English divorce law prior to the 1857 Act and dramatizes the plight of "Mrs. Carling," whose second husband refuses to live with her after learning of her prior marriage.

9. Unsigned review, *Sixpenny Magazine* (September 1861); reprinted by Page, 108–9, 109.

10. Unsigned review, *Reader* (3 January 1863); reprinted by Page, 134–36, 134.

11. For Taylor, Walter's uncertainties in this scene are informed by conflicting conceptions of madness in the late 1850s, ambiguities generated, in part, by the lunacy reform movement and debates over "wrongful confinement." See Taylor, 98–130.

12. Janet Oppenheim, *"Shattered Nerves": Doctors, Patients, and Depression in Victorian England* (New York: Oxford University Press, 1991), 141.

13. Both Miller and Cvetkovich focus on the problem of male "nerves" in Collins's novel, and his representation of "gender slippage," and arrive at similar conclusions about his covert and conservative aims. Miller examines "the social significance of nervousness" in *The Woman in White,* arguing that Collins feminizes the presumably male reader by giving him a case of nerves, but only to induce "homosexual panic" in his audience. Having called sexual differences into question among readers and characters alike, he ultimately reinforces them by evoking "heterosexual masculine protest" among readers, by "castrating" Marian and "cretinizing" Laura, and by transforming Walter into a "real man" through his mastery of his wife. See *The Novel and the Police,* 146–91.

Like Miller, Cvetkovich argues that, despite its representation of masculine women and feminine men, Collins's novel serves a conservative function. Examining "the politics of affect" in *The Woman in White,* she argues that Collins displaces social issues with psychic ones, representing "social problems as affective dilemmas." In her view, Walter's feminized and emotional condition is a "ruse" that masks his political ascendancy over Marian and Laura. "Walter's incapacity to control his own body, even as it renders him anxious, permits him to rise to power without appearing to aspire to it" (75). The novel thus dramatizes Walter's acquisition of "patriarchal power" while denying his interest in possessing it. See *Mixed Feelings,* 71–96.

14. W. H. Wills, subeditor of *Household Words,* makes this very point in an article published in Dickens's journal in July 1855, while also suggesting that a wife's legal death may pave the way for her actual murder. When an Englishwoman marries, Wills asserts, "she dies; being handed over to be buried in her husband's arms, or pounded and pummelled into the grave *with* his arms." See "A Legal Fiction," *Household Words* 11 (21 July 1855): 598–99, 598. On the subject of coverture and its relation to the loss of female identity in *The Woman in White,* see Lenora Ledwon, "Veiled Women, the Law of Coverture, and Wilkie Collins's *The Woman in White,*" *Victorian Literature and Culture* 22 (1994): 1–22.

15. Endowed with sexual capital, Mrs. Catherick pays off her debts to men by granting them sexual favors. "How can I pay my debt?" she asks Walter, after he has discovered Sir Percival's secret and unwittingly led to the man's death. "If I was a young woman still, I might say, 'Come! put your arm around my waist, and kiss me, if you like' " (489).

16. Wilkie Collins, *No Name,* ed. Virginia Blain (Oxford: Oxford University Press, 1991), 96; hereafter cited in text.

17. Wilkie Collins, *Man and Wife,* ed. Norman Page (Oxford: Oxford University Press, 1995), 5; hereafter cited in text.

18. Frances Power Cobbe, "Criminals, Idiots, Women, and Minors. Is the Classification Sound?" (Manchester: A. Ireland and Co., 1869), 27 pp; reprinted in *The Disempowered,* 5.

Chapter Five

1. Wilkie Collins, *Armadale,* ed. Catherine Peters (Oxford: Oxford University Press, 1991), 235; hereafter cited in text.

2. For the ideas of "reverse colonization" and imperial guilt, I am indebted to Stephen D. Arata, and his brilliant analysis of Bram Stoker's *Dracula.* As Arata argues, narratives of reverse colonization express "both fear and guilt": fear that "the 'civilized' world is on the point of being colonized by 'primitive' forces," and guilt about Britain's own "imperial practices," "mirrored back in [the] monstrous form" of the invading Other. See "The Occidental Tourist," 623.

3. ALS to Harriet Geddes Collins, 31 July 1861. The Pierpont Morgan Library, New York. MA 3150.61.

4. ALS to Charles Ward, 14 January 1864. The Pierpont Morgan Library, New York. MA 3151.48.

5. One of these articles, on "American Humour," refers explicitly to "the Jamaica troubles," but only to express hatred for "the nigger"—"the cause of the troubles": "our English or 'Anglo-Saxon' breed always hates an inferior race," the writer asserts (*Cornhill* 13 [January 1866]: 28–43, 37). In an equally

racist tone, Gavin S. Jones, a Mutiny survivor, describes the "treachery" of the sepoy "fiends" in "The Story of My Escape from Futtehghur" (*Cornhill* 11 [January 1865]: 109–17). A more sympathetic view of native insurrection is provided in "Maori Sketches" (*Cornhill* 12 [October 1865]: 498–512), which represents the British tricking the natives into signing treaties, and robbing them of their land, actions that should "prick [the] consciences" of the *Cornhill*'s readers (498). During the serialization of *Armadale,* at least two articles about the rise and fall of the Roman Empire appeared alongside those about the British, revealing Victorian anxieties about imperial decline.

      6.   William A. Green, *British Slave Emancipation: The Sugar Colonies and the Great Experiment, 1830–1865* (Oxford: Clarendon Press, 1991), 399. On the subject of the Emancipation Act, the Jamaica Insurrection, and the Eyre controversy, see also Michael Craton, *Testing the Chains: Slavery in the British West Indies* (Ithaca: Cornell University Press, 1982); Bernard Semmel, *Democracy versus Empire: The Jamaica Riots of 1865 and the Governor Eyre Controversy* (Garden City: Doubleday Anchor, 1965); and J. R. Ward, *British West Indian Slavery, 1750–1834* (Oxford: Clarendon Press, 1988).

      7.   See "The Ancient Fenians and Fenian Literature," *Cornhill* 13 (January 1866): 121–28.

      8.   E. J. Hobsbawn, *The Age of Empire, 1875–1914* (New York: Pantheon, 1987), 24.

      9.   For a useful discussion of the imperial role played by motherhood in Victorian systems of belief, see Anna Davin, "Imperialism and Motherhood," *History Workshop* 5 (1978): 9–65.

     10.   As the English physician Thomas Radford argued in 1848, "while we pity the moral depravity of nations degraded by idolatry and superstition, and feel horror at . . . their crimes, especially the sacrifice of human life both before and after birth, we are compelled to acknowledge that the same diabolical acts are, at the present time, perpetrated to a great extent in our own country; . . . the enormity of the crime is much increased by being committed amongst those . . . blessed with the truths of revealed religion, and possessing all the advantages of a high state of civilization." See "On the Value of Embryonic and Foetal Life, Legally, Socially, and Obstetrically Considered," *British Record of Obstetric Medicine and Surgery* (1848): 6–11, 53–56, 77–89, 54.

     11.   ALS to Harriet Geddes Collins, 11 May 1867. The Pierpont Morgan Library, New York. MA 3150.101.

     12.   Wilkie Collins, *The Moonstone,* ed. J. I. M. Stewart (Harmondsworth: Penguin, 1986), 37; hereafter cited in text.

     13.   Patrick Brantlinger, *Rule of Darkness,* 199. Brantlinger discusses these responses at length in his chapter on the Indian Mutiny and Mutiny novels. See *Rule of Darkness,* 199–224.

     14.   Charles Dickens to Angela Burdett-Coutts, 4 October 1857, *Letters from Charles Dickens to Angela Burdett-Coutts, 1841–1865,* ed. Edgar Johnson (London: Jonathan Cape, 1953), 350.

15. Wilkie Collins, "A Sermon for Sepoys," *Household Words* 17 (27 February 1858): 244–47, 247; hereafter cited in text.

16. John R. Reed was the first critic to discuss Collins's critique of imperialism in *The Moonstone* at any length. Basing his argument on Collins's "unconventional" behavior, and on the "appeal" of the unconventional characters in his novel, Reed asserts that "the Indian priests are heroic figures, while the representatives of Western Culture are plunderers" (283). Reed notes that Collins sets his main narrative in 1849, the year in which the British forcefully annexed the Punjab. See "English Imperialism and the Unacknowledged Crime of *The Moonstone*," *Clio* 2 (June 1973): 281–90. Sue Lonoff places Collins's critique of empire in *The Moonstone* in the context of the Eyre controversy (*Wilkie Collins and His Victorian Readers: A Study in the Rhetoric of Authorship* [New York: AMS Press, 1982], 178–79). Brantlinger addresses Collins's attitude toward empire very briefly, and is more tentative in his assessment: "*The Moonstone* . . . distantly reflects the Mutiny, perhaps in an anti-imperialist way" (*Rule of Darkness*, 295, n. 19). Tamar Heller briefly examines "Collins's relation to Orientalism," contrasting his "reservations about imperialism" with Dickens's support of it (190–91, n. 8). For other discussions of empire and imperial crime in *The Moonstone*, see Ashish Roy, "The Fabulous Imperialist Semiotic of Wilkie Collins's *The Moonstone*," *New Literary History* 24 (1993): 657–81; and Ronald R. Thomas, *Dreams of Authority: Freud and the Fictions of the Unconscious* (Ithaca: Cornell University Press, 1990), 203–19.

17. Theodore Hook, *The Life of General, the Right Honourable Sir David Baird, Bart,* 2 vols. (London: Richard Bentley, 1832), 1:102, 217; hereafter cited in text.

18. "Opium. Chapter the Second. China," *Household Words* 16 (22 August 1857): 181–85, 184. For discussions of the opium trade and the Opium Wars, see Michael Greenburg, *British Trade and the Opening of China: 1800–42* (Cambridge: Cambridge University Press, 1951); Christopher Hibbert, *The Dragon Wakes: China and the West, 1793–1911* (New York: Harper and Row, 1970); and Arthur Waley, *The Opium War through Chinese Eyes* (Stanford: Stanford University Press, 1958).

19. Ronald R. Thomas makes this point in "Minding the Body Politic: The Romance of Science and the Revision of History in Victorian Detective Fiction," *Victorian Literature and Culture* 19 (1991): 233–54, 239, 241. In his earlier discussion of *The Moonstone* in *Dreams of Authority,* as well as in this article, Thomas emphasizes Collins's denial of "disagreeable political truth[s]," and ties the strategies of the novel to the dynamics of psychological repression. See *Dreams of Authority,* 203–19, 205.

20. See, for example, Lewis A. Lawson, "Wilkie Collins and *The Moonstone,*"*American Imago* 20 (1963): 61–79; Charles Rycroft, "A Detective Story: Psychoanalytic Observations," *Psychoanalytic Quarterly* 26 (1957): 229–45; and Albert D. Hutter, "Dreams, Transformations, and Literature: The Implications of Detective Fiction," *Victorian Studies* 19 (1975): 181–209. Hutter argues that

"what is stolen from Rachel is both the actual gem and her symbolic virginity" (242), and Sue Lonoff concurs: "Recalling the Victorian maxim that a young girl's virginity is her most precious possession, and the statement in the Prologue that the diamond's luster waxes and wanes on a lunar cycle, I am inclined to agree . . . that the theft is a symbolic defloration" (*Wilkie Collins and His Victorian Readers,* 210).

21. Thomas notes the parallel between Blake's "sexual desire" and "British colonial domination" (*Dreams of Authority,* 205), as does Heller: "By juxtaposing the plots of courtship and colonialism, Collins suggests an analogy between sexual and imperial domination" (145).

22. Both Heller and Thomas discuss Jennings at some length, using him to illustrate Collins's political evasions. Jennings pointedly avoids discussing his past and his family history. For Thomas, Jennings's secrecy reflects that of the novel itself—the imperial crimes repressed by Collins ("Minding the Body Politic," 242). For Heller, similarly, Jennings's "silences" reveal Collins's "great cover-up," and serve as "a synecdoche for the novel's tendency at once to diffuse its social criticism and to draw attention to its own self-censorship" (142, 144).

23. ALS to Hunter, Rose and Co., 21 May 1872; Morris L. Parrish Collection, Princeton University Library.

24. ALS to Hunter, Rose and Co., 2 November 1872; Morris L. Parrish Collection, Princeton University Library.

25. Wilkie Collins, *The New Magdalen, The Works of Wilkie Collins,* Vol. 7 (New York: AMS Press, 1970), 191–602, 248; hereafter cited in text.

26. For discussions of the Franco-Prussian War, see Michael Howard, *The Franco-Prussian War: The German Invasion of France, 1870–71* (New York: Macmillan, 1961); Hermann Oncken, *Napoleon III on the Rhine: The Origin of the War of 1870–1871,* tr. Edwin H. Zeydel (New York: Knopf, 1928); and D. N. Raymond, *British Policy and Opinion during the Franco-Prussian War* (New York. Columbia University Press, 1921).

27. ALS to Dr. [Emil] Lehmann, 7 August 1870; Morris L. Parrish Collection, Princeton University Library.

28. James Morris, *Heaven's Command: An Imperial Progress* (New York: Harcourt Brace Jovanovich, 1973), 351, 341.

29. ALS to Hunter, Rose and Company, 8 April 1871, 12 August 1871, and 21 May 1872; Morris L. Parrish Collection, Princeton University Library.

30. ALS to Hunter, Rose and Company, 10 April 1875; Morris L. Parrish Collection, Princeton University Library.

31. ALS to Hunter, Rose and Company, 11 September 1873; Morris L. Parrish Collection, Princeton University Library.

32. ALS to William Tindell, 23 July 1870; Mitchell Library, Glasgow. Quoted by Peters, *King,* 320.

33. According to Barbara Fass Leavy, who approaches *The New Magdalen* in the context of the European folklore tradition, the power exercised by

Lady Janet ties her to the goddesses of fairy tales, who have "traditionally aroused fear in male-dominated societies" (214). Yet Lady Janet's power, her sexual desire, and her interest in voting tie her to the "women of the present generation" as well—in particular, to the members of the National Society for Woman Suffrage, established in 1868. See "Wilkie Collins' *The New Magdalen* and the Folklore of the Kind and the Unkind Girls," in *Wilkie Collins to the Forefront*, 209–25.

34. *Hansard's Parliamentary Debates,* 7 December 1857, Vol. 148, third series, col. 227; Ralph Wardlaw, *Lectures on Female Prostitution* (Glasgow: 1842), 65; quoted by Lynda Nead, *Myths of Sexuality: Representations of Women in Victorian Britain* (Oxford: Basil Blackwell, 1988), 85, 94.

Chapter Six

1.   James L. Smith, *Melodrama* (London: Methuen, 1973), 54. As Smith argues, Victorian melodrama "shows us what life was really like in the navy, on the farm, out of work or down the mine," yet pairs its social realism and its social protest with a "facile optimism" that "takes the problems of real life, and provides them with model solutions." At one and the same time, Victorian melodrama stages "the fears and threats which oppress us, and reduces them to a comforting emotional pattern" (50, 54). Maurice Willson Disher makes a similar point in his analysis of Victorian melodramas and their providential endings, which ultimately deny the need for social change: "Because the heavens were the sure shield of the virtuous" in these plays, Disher explains, "it were profanity to worry over thousands of little innocents enslaved in factories and turned adrift to perish when labour, even as cheap as theirs, was not wanted." See *Blood and Thunder: Mid-Victorian Melodrama and Its Origins* (1949; New York: Haskell House, 1974), 13.

2.   Sir John Franklin, commanding 128 sailors and officers of the Royal Navy, began his fourth search for the Northwest Passage in 1845. Beginning in 1848, the government dispatched a series of rescue missions to find the missing party, and in 1853, Dr. John Rae discovered what he believed to be evidence of cannibalism among the deceased explorers. His allegations generated much debate in England, and proved particularly distressing to Dickens, who decided to refute the charges by means of the melodrama, recruiting Collins to write a first draft. As his revisions of Collins's manuscript suggest, Dickens did not find his representations of the explorers sufficiently heroic, and toned down the animosity between the sailors and officers, as Collins portrayed it. For discussions of the Franklin expedition, the alleged cannibalism of its members, and the response of Collins and Dickens, see Robert Louis Brannan, ed., *Under the Management of Mr. Charles Dickens: His Production of "The Frozen Deep"* (Ithaca: Cornell University Press, 1966); and Lillian Nayder, "The Cannibal, the Nurse, and the Cook in Dickens's *The Frozen Deep*," *Victorian Literature and Culture* 19 (1991): 1–24.

3. On the subject of cannibalism as a metaphor for social revolution in Victorian literature and culture, see Lee Sterrenburg, "Psychoanalysis and the Iconography of Revolution," *Victorian Studies* 19 (December 1975): 241–64.

4. Wilkie Collins, autograph draft of *The Frozen Deep*. The Pierpont Morgan Library, New York. MA 81, 23–26. This unpublished draft was substantially revised by Dickens in 1856. The fair copy produced by Dickens, his son Charles, and Mark Lemon, and known as the "prompt book," is reprinted by Brannan, but differs substantially from Collins's draft. In quoting from the melodrama, I cite Collins's original text, excluding Dickens's subsequent revisions.

5. Collins, *The Frozen Deep*. The Pierpont Morgan Library, New York. MA 81, 23.

6. Collins, *The Frozen Deep*. The Pierpont Morgan Library, New York. MA 81, 17. Although Wardour serves as an officer on the expedition, and is estranged from Aldersley because the latter plans to marry the woman he loves, Collins allies him with the working-class men in the play. Resentful and violent, Wardour appears as a "starving man . . . clothed in rags," a figure who is not entitled to express interest in a "lady" (MA 81, 56–57). He performs the manual labor assigned to an ailing sailor, acting as "a carpenter instead of a gentleman" (MA 81, 39). In the process, he distinguishes himself from the idle officers and echoes John Want's expressions of class injury.

7. Disher briefly discusses these abolitionist melodramas in *Blood and Thunder,* 106–9.

8. As Collins explains in his essay on Fechter, the actor originally conceived the idea for the melodrama, outlining its plot, while Collins modified and wrote it: "Following Fechter's outline in the first two acts, and suggesting a new method of concluding the story, to which he agreed, I wrote the drama . . . being solely responsible for the conception and development of the characters, and for the dialogue attributed to them." See "Wilkie Collins's Recollections of Charles Fechter," in *Charles Albert Fechter,* ed. Kate Field (1882; New York: Benjamin Blom, 1969), 145–73, 166–67.

9. Wilkie Collins and Charles Fechter, *Black and White: A Drama, in Three Acts* (Chicago: Dramatic Publishing Co., n.d.), 21; hereafter cited in text.

10. A. C. Swinburne, "Wilkie Collins," *Fortnightly Review* (1 November 1889); reprinted by Page, 253–64, 262. Hereafter cited in text.

11. Marxist critic Fredric Jameson develops this concept in *The Political Unconscious: Narrative as a Socially Symbolic Act* (Ithaca: Cornell University Press, 1981). "It is in detecting the traces" of "class struggles," he explains, and "restoring to the surface of the text the repressed and buried reality of this fundamental history, that the doctrine of a political unconscious finds its function and necessity" (20). Examining how Victorian texts *"work,"* feminist critic Mary Poovey extends Jameson's concept in her own formulation of the "hysterical text," which represses and displaces its ideological significance, using gender

issues to "address" and "manage" issues of class. See *Uneven Developments,* 17–19.

12. Frances Power Cobbe, *The Life of Frances Power Cobbe,* 2 vols. (London: 1904), 2:184; quoted by Peters, *King,* 399.

13. Wilkie Collins, *Heart and Science* (Phoenix Mill, England: Alan Sutton, 1994), 2; hereafter cited in text.

14. See Susan Hamilton, ed., *"Criminals, Idiots, Women, and Minors": Nineteenth-Century Writing by Women on Women* (Peterborough, Ontario: Broadview Press, 1995), 171.

15. As Coral Lansbury argues in her discussion of *Heart and Science,* Collins compounds the cruelty of the vivisectionist with sexual sadism and domination, suggesting that "the man who could vivisect a dog would unquestionably find his next victim in his wife or sweetheart." See *The Old Brown Dog: Women, Workers, and Vivisection in Edwardian England* (Madison: University of Wisconsin Press, 1985), 134, 132.

16. Frances Power Cobbe, "Wife Torture in England," *Contemporary Review* (April 1878); reprinted in Susan Hamilton, ed., *"Criminals, Idiots, Women, and Minors,"* 132–70, 133.

17. For an insightful discussion of Collins's treatment of hysteria in *Heart and Science,* and his denigration of women and the maternal, see C. S. Wiesenthal, "From Charcot to Plato: The History of Hysteria in *Heart and Science,"* in *Wilkie Collins to the Forefront,* 257–68.

18. As Mary Lyndon Shanley notes, the 1882 Act "was arguably the single most important change in the legal status of women in the nineteenth century." Undermining the doctrine of coverture, it granted English wives their own legal identities, and enabled them "to act as autonomous economic agents" (103). See *Feminism, Marriage, and the Law in Victorian England,* 103–30.

19. Peters, *King,* 399; C. S. Wiesenthal, 259.

Selected Bibliography

PRIMARY SOURCES
Unpublished Letters and Manuscripts

Because an edition of Collins's letters has not yet been published, Collins scholars rely on various collections of autograph letters. This study draws from the following manuscript sources:

Mitchell Library, Glasgow: 891117
New York Public Library: Berg Collection of English and American Literature
The Pierpont Morgan Library, New York: MA 81; MA 3150; MA 3151; MA 3155
Princeton University Library: Morris L. Parrish Collection
Harry Ransom Humanities Research Center, The University of Texas at Austin: Wilkie Collins Collection

Primary Writings

There is no definitive edition of Collins's works, although *The Works of Wilkie Collins*, in 30 volumes, is often cited by critics and biographers (New York: AMS Press, 1970). This set is itself a reprint of the 1900 edition published in New York by Peter Fenelon Collier. These editions do not include Collins's *Memoirs* of his father, *Mr. Wray's Cash Box*, many of his short stories and essays, or his plays.

NOVELS

With the publication of *The Dead Secret* in 1857, Collins began to serialize his novels in weekly and monthly periodicals and newspapers. The following entries cite these sources, as well as first volume editions, and the best editions currently available.

Iolani; or, Tahiti as it was. Princeton: Princeton University Press, forthcoming. Ed. Ira Nadel. Based on the manuscript originally submitted to Chapman and Hall in 1845, but never before published.
Antonina: or, the Fall of Rome. 3 vols. London: Richard Bentley, 1850. AMS Vol. 17.
Basil: A Story of Modern Life. 3 vols. London: Richard Bentley, 1852. Oxford: Oxford University Press, 1990. Introduction and Notes by Dorothy Goldman.

Hide and Seek. 3 vols. London: Richard Bentley, 1854. Oxford: Oxford University Press, 1993. Introduction and Notes by Catherine Peters.

The Dead Secret. *Household Words* 15 (3 January–13 June 1857). 2 vols. London: Bradbury and Evans, 1857. New York: Dover, 1979.

The Woman in White. *All the Year Round* (26 November 1859–25 August 1860). 3 vols. London: Sampson Low, 1860. Oxford: Oxford University Press, 1991. Introduction and Notes by Harvey Peter Sucksmith.

No Name. *All the Year Round* (15 March 1862–17 January 1863). 3 vols. London: Sampson Low, 1862. Oxford: Oxford University Press, 1991. Introduction and Notes by Virginia Blain.

Armadale. *Cornhill* (November 1864–June 1866). 2 vols. London: Smith, Elder, 1866. Oxford: Oxford University Press, 1991. Introduction and Notes by Catherine Peters.

The Moonstone. *All the Year Round* (4 January–8 August 1868). 3 vols. London: William Tinsley, 1868. Harmondsworth, England: Penguin, 1986. Introduction and Notes by J. I. M. Stewart.

Man and Wife. *Cassell's Magazine* (December 1869–September 1870) and *Harper's Weekly* (20 November 1869–6 August 1870). 3 vols. London: F. S. Ellis, 1870. Oxford: Oxford University Press, 1995. Introduction and Notes by Norman Page.

Poor Miss Finch. *Cassell's Magazine* (October 1871–March 1872). 3 vols. London: Richard Bentley, 1872. Oxford: Oxford University Press, 1995. Introduction and Notes by Catherine Peters.

The New Magdalen. *Temple Bar* (October 1872–July 1873). 2 vols. London: Richard Bentley, 1873. AMS Vol. 7, 191–602.

The Law and the Lady. *Graphic* (26 September 1874–13 March 1875). 3 vols. London: Chatto & Windus, 1875. Oxford: Oxford University Press, 1992. Introduction and Notes by Jenny Bourne Taylor.

The Two Destinies. *Temple Bar* (January–September 1876). 2 vols. London: Chatto & Windus, 1876. AMS Vol. 18.

The Fallen Leaves. *World* (1 January–23 July 1879) and the *Canadian Monthly* (February 1879–March 1880). 3 vols. London: Chatto & Windus, 1879. AMS Vol. 21.

Jezebel's Daughter. Syndicated by Tillotson and Son for serialization in various provincial newspapers (13 September 1879–31 January 1880 in the *Bolton Weekly Journal*). 3 vols. London: Chatto & Windus, 1880. AMS Vol. 27.

The Black Robe. Syndicated by Leader and Sons for serialization in various provincial newspapers (2 October 1880–26 March 1881 in the Cardiff *Weekly Mail*), and serialized in the *Canadian Monthly* (November 1880–June 1881). 3 vols. London: Chatto & Windus, 1881. AMS Vol. 23.

Heart and Science. Syndicated by A. P. Watt for serialization in various weekly newspapers (22 July 1882–13 January 1883 in the *Manchester Weekly*

Times) as well as the monthly *Belgravia* (August 1882–June 1883). 3 vols. London: Chatto & Windus, 1883. Phoenix Mill, England: Alan Sutton, 1990.

"I Say No." Syndicated by A. P. Watt for serialization in various weekly newspapers (15 December 1883–12 July 1884 in the *Glasgow Weekly Herald*) as well as the monthly *London Society* (January–December 1884). 3 vols. London: Chatto & Windus, 1884. AMS Vol. 29.

The Evil Genius. Syndicated by Tillotson and Son for serialization in various provincial newspapers (12 December 1885–24 April 1886 in the *Farnworth Weekly Journal and Observer*). 3 vols. London: Chatto & Windus, 1886. Peterborough, Ontario: Broadview Press, 1994. Introduction and Notes by Graham Law.

The Legacy of Cain. Syndicated by Tillotson and Son for serialization in various provincial newspapers (17 February–29 June 1888 in the *Leigh Journal and Times*). 3 vols. London: Chatto & Windus, 1889. AMS Vol. 26.

Blind Love. *Illustrated London News* (6 July–28 December 1889) and the *Penny Illustrated Magazine* (12 December 1889–5 April 1890). 3 vols. London: Chatto & Windus, 1890. New York: Dover, 1986. Completed by Walter Besant after Collins's death.

NONFICTION BOOKS

Memoirs of the Life of William Collins, Esq., R. A., with Selections from His Journals and Correspondence. 2 vols. London: Longmans, 1848. East Ardsley, England: E. P. Publishing, 1978.

Rambles Beyond Railways; or, Notes in Cornwall Taken A-Foot. London: Richard Bentley, 1851. London: Westaway Books, 1948.

SHORT FICTION

Collins's short stories have recently been collected by Page and by Thompson; their editions are cited below.

"The Last Stage Coachman." *Illuminated Magazine* (August 1843): 209–11. Collins's first published story.

"A Terribly Strange Bed." *Household Words* 5 (24 April 1852): 129–37. Collins's first contribution to Dickens's weekly journal.

Mr. Wray's Cash Box. London: Richard Bentley, 1852.

After Dark. 2 vols. London: Smith, Elder, 1856. AMS Vol. 19. Collection of six interconnected stories, five of which originally appeared in *Household Words*.

A Rogue's Life. *Household Words* 13 (1–29 March 1856). Phoenix Mill, England: Alan Sutton, 1984.

"The Wreck of the Golden Mary." *Household Words.* Extra Christmas Number. 1856. Collaboration with Dickens and other contributors.

"The Lazy Tour of Two Idle Apprentices." *Household Words* 16 (3–31 October
  1857). Reprinted in *The Lazy Tour of Two Idle Apprentices and Other Stories*,
  3–104. London: Chapman and Hall, 1890. Collaboration with Dickens.
"The Perils of Certain English Prisoners." *Household Words*. Extra Christmas
  Number. 1857. Reprinted in *The Lazy Tour of Two Idle Apprentices and
  Other Stories*, 237–327. London: Chapman and Hall, 1890. Collaboration
  with Dickens.
The Queen of Hearts. 3 vols. London: Hurst and Blackett, 1859. AMS Vol. 14,
  7–560. Collection of 10 interconnected stories, 9 of which appeared ear-
  lier in various periodicals.
"A Message from the Sea." *All the Year Round*. Extra Christmas Number. 1860.
  Collaboration with Dickens and other contributors.
"No Thoroughfare." *All the Year Round*. Extra Christmas Number. 1867.
  Reprinted in *The Lazy Tour of Two Idle Apprentices and Other Stories*,
  107–233. London: Chapman and Hall, 1890. Final collaboration with
  Dickens.
"Miss or Mrs?" *Graphic* (13 December 1871). *Miss or Mrs? And Other Stories in
  Outline*. London: Richard Bentley, 1873. AMS Vol. 4, 367–494.
The Frozen Deep. *The Frozen Deep and Other Tales*. 2 vols. London: Richard Bent-
  ley, 1874. AMS Vol. 4, 495–614. A narrative adaptation of the 1857
  melodrama.
"The Captain's Last Love." *Spirit of the Times* (23 December 1876). *Mad Monkton
  and Other Stories*, ed. Norman Page, 333–54. Oxford: Oxford University
  Press, 1994.
The Haunted Hotel. *Belgravia* (June-November 1878). 2 vols. (with *My Lady's
  Money*). London: Chatto & Windus, 1879. New York: Dover, 1982.
My Lady's Money. *Illustrated London News* (December 1878). 2 vols. (with *The
  Haunted Hotel*). London: Chatto & Windus, 1879. Phoenix Mill,
  England: Alan Sutton, 1990.
The Guilty River. *Arrowsmith's Christmas Annual* (December 1886). Phoenix Mill,
  England: Alan Sutton, 1991.
Little Novels. 3 vols. London: Chatto & Windus, 1887. New York: Dover, 1977.
  Collection of 14 short stories reprinted from various periodicals.
Mad Monkton and Other Stories. Ed. Norman Page. Oxford: Oxford University
  Press, 1994. Includes 12 short stories.
Wilkie Collins: The Complete Shorter Fiction. Ed. Julian Thompson. New York:
  Carroll and Graf, 1995. Includes all 48 short stories.

JOURNALISM, DRAMAS, AND MEMOIRS

Few of Collins's melodramas have been published, and neither they nor
his works of journalism have been collected. Nonetheless, his journal
articles remain available in their original periodical sources, and a number are reprinted in *My Miscellanies*.

"A Plea for Sunday Reform." *Leader* 2:27 (27 September 1851): 925–26.

The Frozen Deep. The Pierpont Morgan Library, New York. MA 81. Unpublished autograph manuscript of the melodrama, later revised by Dickens.

"A Sermon for Sepoys." *Household Words* 17 (27 February 1858): 244–47.

"Highly Proper." *Household Words* 18 (2 October 1858): 361–63.

"A New Mind." *Household Words* 19 (1 January 1859): 112–13.

My Miscellanies. 2 vols. London: Sampson Low, 1863. AMS Vol. 20. Collection of articles reprinted from *Household Words* and *All the Year Round*.

Black and White. A Drama, in Three Acts. Chicago: The Dramatic Publishing Company, n.d. Collaboration with Charles Fechter, first performed at the Adelphi Theatre, London, 1869.

" 'The Law and the Lady': To the Editors of *The World*." *World* (24 March 1875): 21. Collins's account of the poor treatment he received at the hands of the *Graphic*.

"Wilkie Collins's Recollections of Charles Fechter." *Charles Albert Fechter*, ed. Kate Field, 145–73. 1882. New York: Benjamin Blom, 1969.

"Reminiscences of a Story-Teller." *Universal Review* 1 (May-August 1888): 182–92.

SECONDARY SOURCES

Biography

Clarke, William M. *The Secret Life of Wilkie Collins: The Intimate Victorian Life of the Father of the Detective Story*. Chicago: Ivan R. Dee, 1988. Written by the husband of Collins's great-granddaughter, provides new information about Collins's relationships to Martha Rudd and their children, drawing on recollections and ephemera of family members.

Davis, Nuel Pharr. *The Life of Wilkie Collins*. Urbana: University of Illinois Press, 1956. Provocative yet somewhat unreliable in its methods, portrays Collins as a man willing to defy conventions and proprieties.

Robinson, Kenneth. *Wilkie Collins: A Biography*. New York: Macmillan, 1952. First scholarly treatment of Collins's life, reinforces the long-standing view of him as a master of plot and suspense, and as a man "indifferent to convention."

Peters, Catherine. *The King of Inventors: A Life of Wilkie Collins*. Princeton: Princeton University Press, 1991. The definitive biography, covers a vast amount of published and unpublished material in representing Collins as a writer preoccupied with problems of identity and "haunted by a second self."

Bibliographical Works

Andrew, R. V. "A Wilkie Collins Check-list." *English Studies in Africa* 3 (1960): 79–98. First substantial bibliography, and still useful, despite some omissions and misattributions.

————. *Wilkie Collins: A Critical Survey of His Prose Fiction, With a Bibliography*. New York: Garland, 1979. Reprints the bibliography cited above.

Ashley, Robert. "Wilkie Collins." *Victorian Fiction: A Second Guide to Research*, ed. George H. Ford, 223–29. New York: MLA, 1978. Provides a useful account of archival resources, although the information on editions and criticism is outdated.

Beetz, Kirk H. *Wilkie Collins: An Annotated Bibliography, 1889–1976*. Metuchen, N.J.: Scarecrow Press, 1978. Lists editions published since Collins's death as well as critical studies, including books, essays, and dissertations.

————. "Wilkie Collins Studies, 1972–1983." *Dickens Studies Annual* 13 (1984): 333–55. A useful, if somewhat outdated, survey of available editions and biographical studies, with detailed descriptions and evaluations of critical approaches to Collins between 1972 and 1983.

Lohrli, Anne, ed. *Household Words: A Weekly Journal, 1850–1859, Conducted by Charles Dickens*. Toronto: University of Toronto Press, 1973. Identifies and briefly annotates Collins's contributions to *Household Words*.

Wolff, Robert L. "Wilkie Collins." *Nineteenth-Century Fiction: A Bibliographical Catalogue*, 254–72. Vol. 1. New York: Garland, 1981. Describes editions and reprints letters in Wolff's private collection and provides comments by Collins on his own works.

Collections of Critical Essays

Smith, Nelson, and R. C. Terry, eds. *Wilkie Collins to the Forefront: Some Reassessments*. New York: AMS Press, 1995. Includes 15 essays, 5 previously published, that approach Collins from various critical perspectives but vary widely in quality.

Books

Heller, Tamar. *Dead Secrets: Wilkie Collins and the Female Gothic*. New Haven: Yale University Press, 1992. Examines Collins's equivocal relation to the female Gothic tradition by considering the motif of buried writing in his novels, and by exploring his tendency to "contain" their subversive elements.

Lonoff, Sue. *Wilkie Collins and His Victorian Readers: A Study in the Rhetoric of Authorship*. New York: AMS Press, 1982. Discusses the bond between Collins and his readers, and the various ways in which Collins's sense of audience, and his desire to both please and shock, inform and shape his fiction.

Marshall, William H. *Wilkie Collins*. New York: Twayne, 1970. Approaches Collins as a novelist caught "between two worlds," and writing for both the ordinary reading public and the intelligentsia.

O'Neill, Philip. *Wilkie Collins: Women, Property and Propriety*. Totowa, N.J.: Barnes and Noble, 1988. Focuses on Collins's treatment of gender as a social construction, his representations of women, and his critique of the proprieties and laws that keep them in a subordinate position.

Page, Norman, ed. *Wilkie Collins: The Critical Heritage*. London: Routledge and Kegan Paul, 1974. Invaluable source of material on the contemporary reception of Collins's novels.

Rance, Nicholas. *Wilkie Collins and Other Sensation Novelists: Walking the Moral Hospital*. Rutherford, N.J.: Fairleigh Dickinson University Press, 1991. Sees Collins's sensation fiction as a subversive response to Victorian moralism and the doctrine of "self-help."

Sayers, Dorothy L. *Wilkie Collins: A Critical and Biographical Study*, ed. E. R. Gregory. Toledo: The Friends of the University of Toledo Libraries, 1977. Based on an incomplete manuscript, combines biographical and literary analyses, but most useful in suggesting Collins's influence on Sayers.

Taylor, Jenny Bourne. *In the Secret Theatre of Home: Wilkie Collins, Sensation Narrative, and Nineteenth-Century Psychology*. London: Routledge, 1988. Approaches Collins's sensation fiction in the context of nineteenth-century psychology and examines the ways in which theories of madness and the mind inform Collins's novels and are challenged and reaffirmed by them.

Thoms, Peter. *The Windings of the Labyrinth: Quest and Structure in the Major Novels of Wilkie Collins*. Athens: Ohio University Press, 1992. Examines the importance of plotting in Collins's novels, and the role of providence and morality in them, contesting those who see Collins as an unorthodox critic of Christianity and patriarchy.

General Studies: Articles and Chapters

Barickman, Richard, Susan MacDonald, and Myra Stark. "Collins." *Corrupt Relations: Dickens, Thackeray, Trollope, Collins, and the Victorian Sexual System*, 111–49. New York: Columbia University Press, 1982. Discusses Collins's qualified radicalism and the "strategies of indirection" he uses to convey his social criticism.

Beetz, Kirk H. "Wilkie Collins and *The Leader*." *Victorian Periodicals Review* 15:1 (Spring 1982): 20–29. Identifies and discusses Collins's contributions to the *Leader* in the 1850s, which reveal his interest in political and social reform.

Gates, Barbara T. "Wilkie Collins' Suicides: 'Truth As It Is in Nature.'" *Dickens Studies Annual* 12 (1983): 303–18. Reprinted in *Wilkie Collins to the Forefront*, 241–56. Examines Collins's fictional treatment of suicide, "taboo as a subject in Victorian England," which appealed to Collins as a subversive act and a test of character.

Hall, Donald E. "From Margin to Center: Agency and Authority in the Novels of Wilkie Collins." *Fixing Patriarchy: Feminism and Mid-Victorian Male Novelists,* 151–74. New York: New York University Press, 1996. Examines the "unfixed nature of gender" and the "transgressive forms of female agency" in *The Woman in White, Armadale,* and *Man and Wife,* disagreeing with those critics who argue for the "patriarchal work" performed by Collins's fiction.

Hughes, Winifred. "Wilkie Collins: The Triumph of the Detective." *The Maniac in the Cellar: Sensation Novels of the 1860s,* 137–65. Princeton: Princeton University Press, 1980. Explains Collins's use of providential plots, triumphant detectives, and narrative frames as ways to impose order on the social chaos that characterizes sensation fiction.

Kent, Christopher. "Probability, Reality and Sensation in the Novels of Wilkie Collins." *Dickens Studies Annual* 20 (1991): 259–80. Reprinted in *Wilkie Collins to the Forefront,* 53–74. Views Collins's sensation fiction as a mode of realism that treats probability and possibility as matters of perception and subjectivity.

Kucich, John. "Competitive Elites in Wilkie Collins: Cultural Intellectuals and Their Professional Others." *The Power of Lies: Transgression in Victorian Fiction,* 75–118. Ithaca: Cornell University Press, 1994. Considers Collins's "deviance" as a self-conscious posture, questions the distinction between "bourgeois and antibourgeois" positions, and argues that the moral transgressions of Collins's heroes reinforce the status and authority of his cultural intellectuals at the expense of established professional men.

Law, Graham. "The Serial Publication in Britain of the Novels of Wilkie Collins." *Humanitas* 33 (1995): 1–29. Presents the most complete information available to date about the serialization of Collins's novels first published in parts and discusses the economic and literary significance of serial publication, in its various formats, for his work.

———. "Wilkie in the Weeklies: The Serialization and Syndication of Collins's Late Novels." *Victorian Periodicals Review* (forthcoming). Follows up on the preceding article, providing additional information on the syndication of the late novels for provincial and metropolitan weeklies.

Lonoff, Sue. "Multiple Narratives and Relative Truths: A Study of *The Ring and the Book, The Woman in White,* and *The Moonstone.*" *Browning Institute Studies* 10 (1982): 143–61. Discusses the innovative structures of Collins's best-known novels, and the solutions that multiple narration provides to epistemological problems.

MacEachen, Dougald. "Wilkie Collins and British Law." *Nineteenth-Century Fiction* 5 (September 1950): 121–36. Pioneering study of Collins's knowledge and fictional use of British law.

Milbank, Alison. "Breaking and Entering: Wilkie Collins's Sensation Fiction." *Daughters of the House: Modes of the Gothic in Victorian Fiction,* 25–53. London: Macmillan, 1992. Questions Collins's feminist sympathies, pointing to the ways in which his novels promote "male erotic pleasure" and female subordination, despite their demystification of the domestic ideal.

———. "Hidden and Sought: Wilkie Collins's Gothic Fiction." *Daughters of the House*, 54–79. Explores the "darker side" of Collins in *Hide and Seek*, *The Woman in White*, and *The Moonstone*, novels which bring him closest to the female Gothic.

Nadel, Ira B. "Wilkie Collins and His Illustrators." *Wilkie Collins to the Forefront*, 149–64. Considers the function of the novels' illustrations and the relation between these images and the texts themselves.

Peters, Catherine. " 'Invite No Dangerous Publicity': Some Independent Women and Their Effect on Wilkie Collins's Life and Writing." *Dickens Studies Annual* 20 (1991): 295–312. Reprinted in *Wilkie Collins to the Forefront*, 11–29. Discusses the independent women in Collins's life, his preference for intelligent women who need male support, his use of his mother's unpublished writing in his own fiction, and the conflicting impulses that inform his representations of independent heroines.

Thomas, Ronald R. "Wilkie Collins and the Sensation Novel." *The Columbia History of the British Novel*, ed. John Richetti, 479–507. New York: Columbia University Press, 1994. Identifies the class anxieties and instabilities of identity informing Collins's sensation fiction.

Vann, J. Don. "William Wilkie Collins (1824–89)." *Victorian Novels in Serial*, 43–60. New York: MLA, 1985. Provides useful information on the publication in parts of Collins's novels.

Studies of Individual Works

THE WOMAN IN WHITE

Balée, Susan. "Wilkie Collins and Surplus Women: The Case of Marian Halcombe." *Victorian Literature and Culture* 20 (1992): 197–215. Approaches the novel in relation to Victorian debates over "surplus women," arguing that Collins represents Marian Halcombe as a "new ideal of womanhood," and pays tribute to the "manly spinster," his "real heroine."

Bernstein, Stephen. "Reading Blackwater Park: Gothicism, Narrative, and Ideology in *The Woman in White*." *Studies in the Novel* 25:3 (Fall 1993): 291–305. Describes Blackwater Park as a type of Gothic "shorthand" and argues that its hidden recesses reveal the desire to expose aristocratic abuses and promote a panoptical social model.

Cvetkovich, Ann. "Ghostlier Determinations: The Economy of Sensation and *The Woman in White*." *Mixed Feelings: Feminism, Mass Culture, and Victorian Sensationalism*, 71–96. New Brunswick, N.J.: Rutgers University Press, 1992. Examines the "politics of affect" in the novel, arguing that Collins uses sensation to displace political issues and transform class conflicts and social oppression into "psychic disturbances."

Elam, Diane. "White Narratology: Gender and Reference in Wilkie Collins's *The Woman in White*." *Virginal Sexuality and Textuality in Victorian Literature*, ed. Lloyd Davis, 49–63. Albany: State University of New York Press, 1993. Describing the woman in white as a "blank page," a "virginal space," and a figure for reference itself, discusses the "problem of referentiality" in the novel, and the various truths, illusions, and uncertainties generated by Anne Catherick and Laura Fairlie.

Kendrick, Walter M. "The Sensationalism of *The Woman in White*." *Nineteenth-Century Fiction* 32 (1977): 18–35. Considers the relation between sensational and realist fiction and argues that Collins combines the two modes in *The Woman in White*.

Knoepflmacher, U. C. "The Counterworld of Victorian Fiction and *The Woman in White*." *The Worlds of Victorian Fiction*, ed. Jerome H. Buckley, 351–69. Harvard English Studies 6. Cambridge: Harvard University Press, 1975. Valorizes the "anarchic and asocial counterworld" of Collins's novel, an antidote to the conventionalities of much Victorian fiction.

Leavy, Barbara Fass. "Wilkie Collins' Cinderella: The History of Psychology and *The Woman in White*." *Dickens Studies Annual* 10 (1982): 91–141. Foregrounds the character of Anne Catherick, the "Cinderella" of the novel, and discusses the topical significance of her alleged lunacy and her persecution at a time in which the laws governing the treatment of the insane were under scrutiny.

Ledwon, Lenora. "Veiled Women, the Law of Coverture, and Wilkie Collins's *The Woman in White*." *Victorian Literature and Culture* 22 (1994): 1–22. Using Lacanian terms, identifies coverture as the "central paradigm" of the novel, the means through which Collins explores women's loss of identity, only to reinforce the legal double standard for husbands and wives.

Meckier, Jerome. "Wilkie Collins's *The Woman in White*: Providence Against the Evils of Propriety." *Journal of British Studies* 22:1 (Fall 1982): 104–26. Represents Collins as a "dissident moralist" who uses providential judgments to undermine Victorian social proprieties.

Miller, D. A. "*Cage aux folles*: Sensation and Gender in Wilkie Collins's *The Woman in White*." *The Novel and the Police*, 146–91. Berkeley: University of California Press, 1988. Examines "the social significance of nervousness" in the novel, arguing that its sensationalism feminizes the male reader and induces "homosexual panic," reinforcing the sexual differences the novel initially seems to question.

Nayder, Lillian. "Agents of Empire in *The Woman in White*." *Victorian Newsletter* 83 (Spring 1993): 1–7. Approaches the novel in the context of the "Italian question," describes the threat of reverse colonization in it, and examines its critique and defense of British imperialism, which Collins compares favorably to Austrian tyranny.

Perkins, Pamela, and Mary Donaghy. "A Man's Resolution: Narrative Strategies in Wilkie Collins' *The Woman in White*." *Studies in the Novel* 22:4 (Winter 1990): 392–402. Representing Hartwright as an unreliable narrator, discounts his growing domination over women in arguing for Collins's genuine wish to expose gender inequities.

Sutherland, John. "Wilkie Collins and the Origins of the Sensation Novel." *Dickens Studies Annual* 20 (1991): 243–58. Reprinted in *Wilkie Collins to the Forefront*, 75–90. Examines the narrative innovations of the novel, its topical interest in detection and circumstantial evidence, and its use of the trial of poisoner William Palmer.

————. "Writing *The Woman in White*." *Victorian Fiction: Writers, Publishers, Readers*, 28–54. New York: St. Martin's Press, 1995. Combines the above article with another previously published (1977), describing two "emergencies" that arose as Collins wrote the novel, which required improvisation and amendation on his part.

NO NAME

David, Deirdre. "Rewriting the Male Plot in Wilkie Collins's *No Name*: Captain Wragge Orders an Omelette and Mrs. Wragge Goes into Custody." *Out of Bounds: Male Writers and Gender(ed) Criticism*, ed. Laura Claridge and Elizabeth Langland, 186–96. Amherst: University of Massachusetts Press, 1990. Examines the relation between form and theme in the novel, connecting its subversion of omniscience to Collins's "liberal sexual politics."

Horne, Lewis. "Magdalen's Peril." *Dickens Studies Annual* 20 (1991): 281–94. Discusses the ambiguities surrounding Magdalen's "moral decline," places her in the ranks of tragic heroines, and considers the relation between tragedy and melodrama in the novel.

Huskey, Melynda. "*No Name*: Embodying the Sensation Heroine." *Victorian Newsletter* 82 (Fall 1992): 5–13. Attributing the effects of sensation fiction to the spectacle of a woman's imminent fall, discusses Magdalen's willful wrongdoing as well as Collins's complex representation of her body, on which he inscribes "her fate."

ARMADALE

Boyle, Thomas. "*Armadale*: 'A Sensation Novel with a Vengeance.' " *Black Swine in the Sewers of Hampstead: Beneath the Surface of Victorian Sensationalism*, 159–73. New York: Viking, 1989. Describes *Armadale* as Collins's most subversive novel, a "proto-modernist experiment" that breaks the pattern of sensation fiction in the extremity of its views and representations.

Peters, Catherine. Introduction and Explanatory Notes. *Armadale*, vii–xxii, 664–74. Oxford: Oxford University Press, 1991. Describes the composition of the novel and its major themes and explains many of its topical references.

THE MOONSTONE

Frick, Patricia Miller. "Wilkie Collins' 'Little Jewel': The Meaning of *The Moonstone*." *Philological Quarterly* 63 (1984): 313–21. Makes a case for the moral superiority of the Brahmins, developing Reed's argument about the critique of empire in the novel.

Gruner, Elisabeth Rose. "Family Secrets and the Mysteries of *The Moonstone*." *Victorian Literature and Culture* 21 (1993): 127–45. Examines Collins's use of the Constance Kent case and argues that the novel explores the Victorian family, exposing its hidden dangers and criticizing domestic ideology.

Hennelly, Mark M., Jr. "Detecting Collins' Diamond: From Serpentstone to Moonstone." *Nineteenth-Century Fiction* 39:1 (June 1984): 25–47. Considers the symbolism of the diamond and Collins's use of gemology, discussing his source material.

Hutter, Albert D. "Dreams, Transformations, and Literature: The Implications of Detective Fiction." *Victorian Studies* 19 (1975): 181–209. Approaching the novel in psychoanalytic terms, calls attention to its sexual subtext, associating the horror of the Shivering Sands with the fear of intercourse, and arguing that Franklin Blake steals Rachel's "symbolic virginity" in stealing the diamond.

Lawson, Lewis A. "Wilkie Collins and *The Moonstone*." *American Imago* 20 (1963): 61–79. Using psychoanalytic theory, discusses the importance of dreams in the novel, examines the sexual implications of the diamond's theft, and claims that the work is based on Collins's own Oedipal desires.

Miller, D. A. "From *roman policier* to *roman-police*: Wilkie Collins's *The Moonstone*." *The Novel and the Police*, 33–57. Berkeley: University of California Press, 1988. Highlighting the novel's dispersal of detection, argues that the work illustrates Foucault's concept of modern discipline, which is given narrative form by the novel's underlying monologism.

Nayder, Lillian. "Robinson Crusoe and Friday in Victorian Britain: 'Discipline,' 'Dialogue,' and Collins's Critique of Empire in *The Moonstone*." *Dickens Studies Annual* 21 (1991): 213–31. Argues for the dialogism of the novel by examining its relation to Defoe's well-known work and considering its critique of British imperialism.

Ousby, Ian. "Wilkie Collins and Other Sensation Novelists." *Bloodhounds of Heaven: The Detective in English Fiction from Godwin to Doyle*, 111–36. Cambridge: Harvard University Press, 1976. Discusses Collins's use of the Constance Kent case, and the relation between detection and problems of perception, which are ultimately resolved by means of providence.

Reed, John R. "English Imperialism and the Unacknowledged Crime of *The Moonstone*." *Clio* 2 (June 1973): 281–90. First critical essay to consider Collins's critique of empire in *The Moonstone* and to develop the contrast between the heroic Brahmins and the plundering Westerners.

Roy, Ashish. "The Fabulous Imperialist Semiotic of Wilkie Collins's *The Moonstone*." *New Literary History* 24 (1993): 657–81. Takes issue with those who read the novel as anti-imperialist, arguing that the dichotomies that inform it produce "a *mythos* entirely consonant with arguments for empire."

Rycroft, Charles. "A Detective Story: Psychoanalytic Observations." *Psychoanalytic Quarterly* 26 (1957): 229–45. Associating Godfrey Ablewhite and Rosanna Spearman with the repressed sexuality of Franklin Blake and Rachel Verinder, describes the diamond's theft as "an unconscious representation of a sexual act."

Thomas, Ronald R. "Minding the Body Politic: The Romance of Science and the Revision of History in Victorian Detective Fiction." *Victorian Literature and Culture* 19 (1991): 233–54. Notes the imperial anxieties informing the novel, and its displacement of imperial crime with "bodily passion," and discusses Collins's use of medical science as a form of social control.

———. "The Missing Dream in *The Moonstone*." *Dreams of Authority: Freud and the Fictions of the Unconscious,* 203–19. Ithaca: Cornell University Press, 1990. Focusing on Blake's "repressed dream," argues that the novel aims to recover the memory of his theft and to reenact it, uncovering the sexual and imperial desires of the community, and displaying the drive to repress and disguise them.

MAN AND WIFE

Page, Norman. Introduction and Explanatory Notes. *Man and Wife,* vii–xxiv, 647–52. Oxford: Oxford University Press, 1995. Discusses the topical issues on which Collins draws in the novel.

THE NEW MAGDALEN

Leavy, Barbara Fass. "Wilkie Collins' *The New Magdalen* and the Folklore of the Kind and the Unkind Girls." *Wilkie Collins to the Forefront,* 209–25. Approaches the novel and its female characterizations in the context of the European folklore tradition.

THE LAW AND THE LADY

O'Fallon, Kathleen. "Breaking the Laws about Ladies: Wilkie Collins' Questioning of Gender Roles." *Wilkie Collins to the Forefront,* 227–39. Highlights the subversive aspects of Collins's treatment of gender norms in the novel.

Taylor, Jenny Bourne. Introduction, Appendix, and Explanatory Notes. *The Law and the Lady,* vii–xxiv, 415–28. Oxford: Oxford University Press, 1992. Discusses the novel's serialization and readership, Collins's publication methods, and his use of the Madeleine Smith case and the female detective, and reprints material pertaining to Collins's difficulties with the *Graphic.*

HEART AND SCIENCE

MacEachen, Dougald B. "Wilkie Collins' *Heart and Science* and the Vivisection Controversy." *Victorian Newsletter* 29 (1966): 22–25. Places the novel in the context of the vivisection controversy and explains the arguments on both sides of the question.

Wiesenthal, C. S. "From Charcot to Plato: The History of Hysteria in *Heart and Science.*" *Wilkie Collins to the Forefront,* 257–68. Examines the construction of hysteria in the novel, which informs Collins's representations of women as "victims of their own ungovernable passions," and of mothers as suffocating and abusive figures.

THE EVIL GENIUS

Law, Graham. Introduction. *The Evil Genius,* 7–30. Peterborough, Ontario: Broadview Press, 1994. Describes Collins's interest in the law and the status of women and discusses his publishing practices.

Articles on Collins and Dickens

Eliot, T. S. "Wilkie Collins and Dickens" (1927). *Selected Essays,* 409–18. New York: Harcourt, Brace and World, 1964. Compares the work of Collins and Dickens, defends Collins as "a master of plot and situation," and praises his talent for the melodramatic.

Lonoff, Sue. "Charles Dickens and Wilkie Collins." *Nineteenth-Century Fiction* 35 (1980): 150–70. Describes the mutual benefits of the Dickens-Collins relationship, while also noting the growing rivalry of the two writers.

Murfin, Ross. "The Art of Representation: Collins' *The Moonstone* and Dickens' Example." *ELH* 49:3 (Fall 1982): 653–72. Examines the influence of *Bleak House* on *The Moonstone,* works concerned with acts of writing and questions of representation.

Index

The Author

Lillian Nayder is associate professor of English at Bates College in Lewiston, Maine, where she teaches courses on Victorian fiction and the English novel. She received her B.A. from Johns Hopkins University and her Ph.D from the University of Virginia. Her research interests center on Wilkie Collins and Charles Dickens, about whom she has published various articles. She is now writing a book about their literary collaborations.

The Editor

Herbert Sussman, professor of English at Northeastern University, is the author of *Victorian Masculinities: Masculinity and Masculine Poetics in Early Victorian Literature and Art; Fact into Figure: Typology in Carlyle, Ruskin, and the Pre-Raphaelite Brotherhood;* and *Victorians and the Machine: The Literary Response to Technology.*